Au jeu/Play Ball

THE 50 GREATEST GAMES IN THE HISTORY OF THE MONTREAL EXPOS

Edited by Norm King

Associate Editors—Greg Erion, Len Levin, Bill Nowlin, Jack Zerby

Society for American Baseball Research, Inc.
Phoenix, AZ

Au jeu/Play Ball:
The 50 Greatest Games in the History of the Montreal Expos
Edited by Norm King
Associate Editors—Greg Erion, Len Levin, Bill Nowlin, Jack Zerby

ISBN 978-1-943816-15-6
Ebook ISBN 978-1-943816-14-9

Cover and book design: Gilly Rosenthol

Photos courtesy of the Canadian Baseball Hall of Fame and Bill Young:
Jim "Mudcat" Grant, Mack Jones, Bill Stoneman, Tim Foli, Chris Speier, Ross Grimsley, Tommy Hutton, Fred Norman,
Bill Gullickson, Jeff Reardon, Jerry White, Pete Rose, Dennis Martinez, Denis Boucher, Joe Siddall, Cliff Floyd, Marquis
Grissom, Pedro Martinez, Mike Lansing, Chris Widger, Vladimir Guerrero.

Photos courtesy of the National Baseball Hall of Fame:
Larry Parrish, Tony Perez, Warren Cromartie, Steve Rogers and Gary Carter celebration, Andre Dawson, Tim Raines,
Rondell White, Henry Rodriguez, Jeff Juden.

Photo courtesy of Russ Hansen:
Gary Carter and Tim Laker.

Cover photo courtesy of the National Baseball Hall of Fame

Society for American Baseball Research
Cronkite School at ASU
555 N. Central Ave. #416
Phoenix, AZ 85004
Phone: (602) 496-1460
Web: www.sabr.org
Facebook: Society for American Baseball Research
Twitter: @SABR

TABLE OF CONTENTS

FOREWORD

By Dave Van Horne

IN MY 32 YEARS AS THE ENGLISH-LANGUAGE broadcaster for the Montreal Expos, I witnessed thousands of great plays, great games, and great moments. Starting with that first game at Shea Stadium, when the team took the field and made Expos baseball a reality, I built a collection of memories that I continue to cherish.

Memories are the backbone of this book, which was written by members of the Society for American Baseball Research and edited by Norm King. *Au jeu/ Play Ball: The 50 Greatest Games in the History of the Montreal Expos* covers all the different eras in the team's history. Fans will immerse themselves in the thrilling games of the team's early days, such as the first Opening Day at Jarry Park, and Ron Fairly's walk-off home run that made Gene Mauch's promise of "70 in '70" come true. They'll also relive how a city rediscovered the thrill of winning and the excitement of a major-league pennant race in 1979 when young, talented players like Gary Carter and Andre Dawson proved just how good they were. And they'll remember the bittersweet teams of the early '90s, when stars like Larry Walker, Marquis Grissom, and Moises Alou grew together and became a force to be reckoned with before the 1994 strike changed everything.

These game summaries remind me of some wonderful times, and refresh the details of some of those games, things I'd forgotten about. I hope this book does the same for you.

EDITOR'S NOTE

By Norm King

AT THE END OF THE LERNER AND LOEWE musical *Camelot*, King Arthur sings of the "one brief wisp of glory" that was Camelot.

The first wisp of glory that the Montreal Expos provided for me happened on May 1, 1969, when I was a 12-year-old kid attending my very first major league game at Jarry Park. My wife will tell you that I can't recall what I had for breakfast, yet I vividly remember the thrill of just being at a ballpark for the very first time, baseball glove in hand, and jumping up and down when Coco Laboy hit a sacrifice fly in the bottom of the ninth to give the Expos a 3-2 victory over the New York Mets. So what if I didn't know what a sacrifice fly was.

My love for the Expos and for the game of baseball only deepened as I grew older, but I think part of that love, then and now, comes from the happy kid at Jarry Park that's still inside me. That kid resurfaced one day in New York, when I dragged my wife to Rusty Staub's restaurant in the hopes of meeting Le Grand Orange. We walked into the restaurant, and when I saw him at the other end of the room, I ran over and interrupted a conversation he was having to tell him what a fan I was. After we left his place, we went to a restaurant we could afford—McDonald's—and I sat there telling my wife repeatedly, "I met Rusty Staub! I met Rusty Staub!" in the exact same level of excitement I would have had if I had met him on that May day many years before.

When I joined SABR in 2010, I didn't know if I could contribute any research to the organization until one day I decided that I was going to do my little bit to keep the memory of the Expos alive by writing biographies of Expos players. I discovered that former Expos great Steve Rogers worked for the Major League Baseball Players Association in New York. My wife and I just happened to be going there again, and Steve graciously agreed to let me interview him. We sat in an MLBPA boardroom for an hour and had a wonderful conversation.

I didn't sit there going "I met Steve Rogers! I met Steve Rogers!" to my wife afterwards, but after completing the Rogers essay, I discovered that I really enjoyed the experience of researching and writing player biographies. I was also encouraged by the feedback I received from other editors whose books I contributed to, and really appreciated the creative freedom that I felt. I try to inject humor into my writing, and whether I'm successful or not, writing for SABR allows me to try and be funny.

This book was a natural progression in my ongoing quest to keep the Expos' memory alive. I started writing game summaries for other books and found that I enjoyed that as much as I liked writing the biographies. One day I discovered on the Internet that some authors had written books about the Mets, Phillies, Twins and Yankees called *162-0*, consisting of 162 game descriptions from each team's history, one for each day of an imaginary baseball season. I thought it would be a great idea to do something like that about the Expos, and began going back in time to find 162 exciting Expos wins to write up. I started getting lazy around game 40, so I decided 50 would be a nice round number, and suggested the idea to Bill Nowlin, who is in charge of team projects for the SABR Biography Project. Bill got the idea approved and this is the result.

Enjoy.

Norm King

ACKNOWLEDGEMENTS

WHEN I FIRST JOINED THE SOCIETY FOR American Baseball Research (SABR), I didn't envision taking on a project as big as editing a book. Now that I've done it, I realize just how complex an endeavour it is, and how many people it takes to make it happen.

I would first like to thank Mark Armour, chairman of the SABR BioProject Committee. Writing biographies and game summaries has become a passion of mine, and Mark's efforts play a big role in allowing me to indulge that passion. Next, I would like to thank Bill Nowlin for steering the idea for this book through the necessary approvals, for guiding me in my maiden voyage as a SABR book editor, and for giving each article a second read.

The authors deserve tremendous thanks for their effort. The success of this book hinges on readers getting more from the game summaries than facts and figures. It works if readers feel as happy that the Expos won as they would if they were cheering the team on at Jarry Park or the Olympic Stadium. The contributors did far more than rehash statistics with their writing; they added liveliness, color and context. I would like to give special thanks to contributors Danny Gallagher and Bill Young. Danny has been a huge cheerleader for the project, and has assisted by publicizing the book through various media outlets. As well, Bill was gracious enough to let me select some pictures from his collection of photographs for the book.

I also want to thank Dave Van Horne and Russ Hansen for their support. It is a great thrill to have a real live Hall of Famer write the foreword for the book, especially when it's someone whose broadcasting of Expos games brought me so much pleasure over the years. Russ had almost unprecedented access to the Expos in their heyday, and he was kind enough to allow me to use some of the photos in his collection.

One of the great surprises and delights for me during this process was the opportunity to interview Sandy Carter about Gary's final at-bat with the Expos. When I spoke to her it felt, for me at least, as if I was talking to an old friend, such was her grace and kindness.

I would also like to thank Greg Erion and Jack Zerby for their contributions as fact-checkers. Fact checking is not an easy task, and they each did their job with precision and good cheer. They also provided some excellent editorial recommendations that enhanced the book's quality. Also, Len Levin did his usual masterful job as copy editor and added the final coat of polish to each piece.

This book would not have been possible without the generous support of the staff and Board of Directors of SABR, SABR Publications Director Cecilia Tan, and designer Gilly Rosenthol who gave the book its fine look.

Many thanks also go to Cassidy Lent and John W. Horne Jr. at the Baseball Hall of Fame for providing me with a huge file of photographs from which I was able to select some pictures for the book.

I could not write a list of acknowledgements without including my wife Lucile. She not only found many of my numerous typos and spelling errors, but has been my biggest cheerleader throughout this process. She is the shining light of my life.

— Norm King

BIENVENUE TO MAJOR LEAGUE BASEBALL

April 8, 1969: Montreal Expos 11, New York Mets 10 At Shea Stadium

By Norm King

WHEN THE INTERNATIONAL OLYMPIC Committee chose Montreal as the host city for the 1976 Summer Olympics, Jean Drapeau, the mayor of Montreal, told the press that the Olympics could no more have a deficit than a man could have a baby. As it turned out, the Olympic debt ballooned into the billions and was not paid off until 2006; the problems associated with the Olympics caused Drapeau to feel sickness not just in the morning, but noon and night as well.

Seven years prior to that debacle, Drapeau was a midwife of sorts for the rebirth of Montreal's great baseball tradition. Montreal had had professional baseball right up until 1960, and the city's Royals were the Triple-A affiliate of the Brooklyn/Los Angeles Dodgers from 1939 until the franchise moved to Syracuse for 1961. Jackie Robinson played his first professional season in a Montreal Royals uniform and many Hall of Famers, including Roy Campenella, Duke Snider, Roberto Clemente, and Don Newcombe, played at Delormier Downs, the Royals' home park, on their way to the majors.

Drapeau didn't sweat the details–everybody involved in any of his ambitious plans did his sweating for him. And when it came to making the Expos a reality, the perspiration flowed right up until the date of their first game, April 8, 1969, as financial and logistical problems–as in where to play–left many wondering if Opening Day would ever come.

But it finally did, at Shea Stadium against the New York Mets. Before the game, Drapeau signed autographs for fans who no doubt wondered who he played for, and he reveled in the attention. He also threw out the ceremonial first pitch to Mets catcher Jerry Grote.

The game wasn't just a big event for Drapeau, as longtime Expos broadcaster Dave Van Horne discovered. As Canadian opera star Maureen Forrester sang Canada's national anthem, Van Horne looked over at his broadcast partner, born-and-bred Montrealer Russ Taylor, and saw tears streaming down his cheeks.

"I thought, 'Wow!,'" remembered Van Horne. "This is much bigger to every Canadian, not just Montrealers and Quebecers, than I had anticipated. I knew even prior to the first pitch that this was a big deal."[1]

The players may not have wept, but they too were caught up in the historical significance of what was happening.

"I think there was a special feeling," said Expos reliever Dan McGinn. "Everybody was excited."[2]

Tom Seaver started for the Mets. Seaver was entering his third campaign after consecutive 16-win seasons. His mound opponent was Jim "Mudcat" Grant, whom the Expos had picked in the expansion draft from the Los Angeles Dodgers, for whom he had gone 6-4 with a 2.08 earned run average in 1968. Conventional wisdom says that pitchers have the advantage over hitters early in the season, but conventional wisdom couldn't get a ticket for this game, which the Expos won 11-10. Seaver and Grant contributed to the festivities by leading a parade of pitchers to and from the mound. The two teams combined to use nine hurlers, and that was back in the days before pitch counts, when starters were expected to throw as many innings as possible.

Mets fans were used to futility; prior to 1969, the Mets had never finished higher than ninth in the 10-team National League and their ineptitude was legendary. It seemed early on that they were in for more of the same, as the Expos took a 2-0 lead in the first inning when former Dodger Bob Bailey drove in two runs with a double.[3] That here-we-go-again feeling continued when the Mets blew a great scoring opportunity in the bottom of the first. Singles by Tommie Agee, Ken Boswell, and Cleon Jones went for naught thanks in part to Rod Gaspar lining into a double play with Agee on first.

It was obvious pretty early that Grant wasn't going to have a long afternoon of work. In the bottom of the second, the first two Mets hitters, Ed Kranepool and Grote, singled. To make things more challenging for himself, Grant walked Bud Harrelson to load the bases with nobody out. He struck out Seaver for the first out, but Agee cleared the bases with a double to give the Mets a 3-2 lead. Grant had to surrender the ball to Expos manager Gene Mauch after Agee's hit.

"He [Grant] had no command of his breaking ball. He was wild in the strike zone," said Mauch. "… He usually hits the corners, but everything came down the middle and they hit him. And hit him good."[4]

Mauch brought in left-hander Dan McGinn, who not only became the first Expos relief pitcher, but the first to pick off a baserunner, when he nailed Agee at second.

"It was a play we had worked on in spring training and [shortstop Maury Wills] put on the sign," recalled McGinn. "I just did what I had been taught to do. We caught him; I don't think he had any idea we would be using a pickoff. He wasn't really paying enough attention."[5]

The Expos tied the game in the third when Rusty Staub drove home Wills, who had doubled. In the fourth, McGinn added to his list of firsts, becoming the first Expo, pitcher or not, to hit a home run, a solo shot that bounced off and over the outfield wall and put the Expos up 4-3. It was McGinn's first major-league hit and only major-league home run.

"He [Seaver] threw a fastball and I just happened to make a good swing and he supplied all the power," said McGinn. "I was rounding first and [first base umpire Stan Landes] gave the home-run signal. In the dugout Rusty and Maury and Gene were all just standing there laughing as I went in. If you're going to hit one you might as well hit it off a Hall of Famer."[6]

McGinn didn't have much time to enjoy the glory as the Mets stormed back in the bottom of the fourth. He walked Grote to lead off the inning, then committed the franchise's first balk (he also threw the franchise's first wild pitch in the second inning), which sent Grote to second base. After striking out shortstop Bud Harrelson and inducing Seaver to ground out, McGinn walked Agee, who was much warier on the basepaths the second time around. Consecutive singles by right fielder Rod Gaspar and second baseman Ken Boswell scored Grote and Agee.

McGinn's day of firsts was over, as Mauch replaced him with Jerry Robertson, who promptly gave up a double to left fielder Cleon Jones. It scored Gaspar, but Expos center fielder Don Hahn (who would later spend four seasons with the Mets) threw to second baseman Gary Sutherland, who relayed the ball home to catcher John Bateman in time to get Boswell at the plate. This play saved at least one run because if Boswell

Jim "Mudcat" Grant

had scored, the Mets would have led 7-4 instead of 6-4, with another runner in scoring position.

After neither team scored in the fifth, Mets manager Gil Hodges made a move he immediately regretted by sending journeyman pitcher Cal Koonce to the mound for the sixth inning. Koonce started the frame by walking the leadoff batter, pinch-hitter Ty Cline. A fielder's choice by Wills erased Cline, but Wills showed he still had some of the base thief in him by stealing second. After Staub walked, Expos left fielder Mack Jones doubled to left, driving in two runs and tying the game, 6-6. The Expos took the lead in the top of the seventh. With two out and nobody on, Koonce committed the unpardonable sin of walking pitcher Don Shaw, a former Met, then compounded his troubles by walking Cline, who had stayed in the game, replacing Hahn in center. Wills drove in Shaw with a single to left. By this time the Mets felt like the boxer who kept thinking he had the fight won only to see his opponent keep getting up off the canvas.

They felt positively punchy after the eighth. Al Jackson took the mound for New York, but maybe he should have given it back because he gave up a solo shot to Staub, then singles to Bailey and Bateman. Hodges replaced Jackson with Canadian Ron Taylor, who surrendered a three-run homer to third baseman Jose "Coco" Laboy, a rookie playing in his first major-league game after spending 10 years in the minors.

Going into the bottom of the ninth, the score was 11-6 Expos. Mets castoff Don Shaw, who had replaced Robertson on the mound in the sixth, was in his fourth inning of relief.

That turned out to be one inning too long, as the Mets made things interesting by scoring four runs, including three on a home run by pinch-hitter Duffy Dyer.

"I left Don Shaw in there too long," admitted Mauch. "He was getting tired, but I wanted him to finish it up if he could."[7]

With two out, Mauch brought in Carroll Sembera to finish the game off. He did, but not before giving up a single to left fielder Amos Otis and a walk to Agee. He finally struck out Rod Gaspar on three pitches, giving the Expos the win and relegating the famous Montreal Canadiens, who went on to win the Stanley Cup in 1969, to the back pages of the sports section.[8]

"Everybody was excited and jumping around [in the Expos' locker room after the game]," said McGinn. "It was a great feeling."

The Expos' first game ever was indeed a wild one. But even if a pitcher hit the franchise's first home run, and the bullpen needed a revolving door because of all the relievers they used, they still won. The front page of the next day's the *Montreal Gazette* said it best: "Look who's in first place!"[9]

NOTES

1   Telephone interview conducted with Dave Van Horne, February 11, 2014.

2   Telephone interview conducted with Dan McGinn, September 4, 2014.

3   After finishing no higher than ninth in their first seven seasons of existence, the Amazin's, as they were fondly called, won the World Series in 1969.

4   Ted Blackman, "Mauch: 'We didn't make a mistake," the *Montreal Gazette*, April 9, 1969.

5   McGinn interview.

6   McGinn interview.

7   Blackman.

8   While the Expos won their first Opening Day game, the Mets, in contrast, had never done so. This game marked their eighth consecutive Opening Day loss. They broke the first-game losing streak on April 7, 1970, when they beat the Pirates 5-3 in Pittsburgh.

9   The *Montreal Gazette*, April 9, 1969.

MACK LAYS CLAIM TO JONESVILLE

April 14, 1969: Montreal Expos 8, St. Louis Cardinals 7 At Jarry Park

By Norm King

HERE'S A HISTORY LESSON. ON APRIL 14, 1969, an American laid claim to Canadian territory for the first time since the War of 1812. The American was Montreal Expos left fielder Mack Jones. The territory was the left-field bleachers at Jarry Park, which was renamed Jonesville after his three-run homer and two-run triple helped the Expos win their first-ever home opener. Jones was happily acclaimed Mayor-for-Life.

Warm and sunny spring weather greeted the Expos and the reigning National League champion St. Louis Cardinals that day for the first regular-season major-league baseball game ever played outside the United States. Preparations for the opener continued right up to game time, including staff—Expos general manager Jim Fanning among them—unfolding 6,000 chairs to serve as temporary seats. More than 29,000 fans (not counting people watching the game standing on snow drifts outside the stadium) and 200 members of the media from the United States and Canada filled the Expos' ballpark to watch the home club take a huge lead, blow it in one atrocious inning, then rebound to win it and send the fans home happy.

"Working under the tireless (team director of operations) Lou Martin, men worked around the clock to finish off the stadium," wrote Ted Blackman. "All that was missing were a few seats in the corners of the ballpark and a perfect playing field, but even the super-critical athletes were willing to abide the discomfort."[1]

Nelson Briles started for the Cardinals, while veteran Larry Jaster took the mound for the Expos. Curt Flood hit a double in an otherwise perfect first inning for Jaster. Briles wasn't so fortunate. Leadoff hitter Don Bosch led off with a single to right. After Maury Wills forced Bosch at second for the first out,

Briles walked Rusty Staub, then gave up Jones's home run to straightaway center field to give the Expos a 3-0 lead. Mayor Jones increased the Expos' lead in the bottom of the second, tripling home Wills and Staub, who had both singled, putting the Expos up 5-0. A hero was born.

"When I got back to the hotel, I had something like 150 phone calls from the hour of 12:00 to 6:00 the next morning," recalled Jones. "And it was all females. I think I got the record for that."[2]

The third inning went better for Briles as he gave up only one run. Coco Laboy walked and advanced to second on a groundout by Gary Sutherland. Jaster singled to score Laboy, giving Montreal a 6-0 lead and causing delirious Expos fans to inquire about World Series tickets.

MACK JONES

Mack Jones

Then came the top of the fourth, an inning in which the Expos committed five errors and saw their 6-0 lead turn into a 7-6 deficit. Expos catcher John Bateman proved a generous host by dropping Mike Shannon's foul popup, keeping his at-bat alive long enough to allow him to reach first when his groundball went through shortstop Wills' legs. Tim McCarver then singled, followed by Julian Javier reaching first when first baseman Bob Bailey booted yet another grounder.

At this juncture, one of the peculiarities of Jarry Park should be pointed out. The songwriting team of Ian and Sylvia may have been thinking of the stadium when they wrote their hit "Four Strong Winds," because all four of the breezes congregated there and blew consistently from left to right. More than one popup to second ended up going over the right-field fence for a home run. That's the only logical explanation for what happened next, when number-eight hitter Dal Maxvill, who had three career home runs in seven major-league seasons, smacked a grand slam to right center.

Jaster got the next two hitters out, and then gave up a single to Curt Flood. After moving to second on a balk, Flood scored on a single by Vada Pinson. Pinson himself arrived at second when his hit got by center fielder Bosch. Jaster's disaster of an inning continued when the next batter, Joe Torre, belted a two-run shot to give the Cardinals a 7-6 lead.

As much out of mercy as anything else, Expos manager Gene Mauch replaced Jaster with Dan McGinn. The Cardinals had batted around, so Shannon came to the plate for the second time in the inning. And for the second time in the inning, he hit a foul popup that an Expos infielder dropped, except this time it was Bailey. Shannon wasn't able to take advantage of his second chance this time, as he popped up to short to end the carnage. Of the seven runs the Cardinals scored, only two were earned.

After playing more like Larry, Curly, and Moe than Tinker, Evers, and Chance in the top of the fourth, the least the Expos could do was make sure that Jaster wouldn't get saddled with a loss, so they scored one in the bottom of the inning to tie the score 7-7. Wills singled, then moved to third on a double by

Rusty Staub. That was enough for Cardinals manager Red Schoendienst, who replaced Briles with Gary Waslewski. Waslewski walked Jones intentionally, then uncorked a wild pitch with Bailey at the plate, allowing Wills to score.

With both starters gone, the next two innings were uneventful. In the bottom of the seventh, Dan McGinn the pitcher became Dangerous Dan the clutch hitter, when he singled home Coco Laboy, who had doubled, for what turned out to be the winning run. McGinn went the rest of the way, giving up no runs on three hits over 5⅓ innings to win the first-ever major-league game outside the US.

"Unfortunately, I gave up one run on two hits and I ended up with the loss," recalled Waslewski. "[The game] is not fair sometimes."[3]

For the visitors, who were used to the manicured field of Busch Stadium, their initial impressions of Jarry Park were not all that positive. "The ground was frozen," said Waslewski, who was traded to Montreal later that season for Jim "Mudcat" Grant. "It was almost like walking on a mattress. You would step in one spot and it would raise in another spot."[4]

"The infield was soft and it was tough to go from first to third," said Flood. "A stolen base is going to be unheard of here until something is done about it. "I've played on some bad diamonds, but this was the worst."[5]

Expos fans didn't care what Flood thought of the field. After a nine-year absence, when the historic Montreal Royals left town in 1960, baseball was back in town. And it was major-league baseball to boot. Lines started forming at the ticket booths as soon as the game was over. A love affair had begun.

SOURCES

In addition to the sources listed in the notes, the author consulted:

Baseball-reference.com.

Daily Capital News (Jefferson City, Missouri).

Les Expos Nos Amours (video).

NOTES

1   Ted Blackman, "Big league ball fever has Expos' fans in a dither," the *Montreal Gazette*, April 15, 1969.

2 Video, *Les Expos Nos Amours*, produced for TV Labatt, copyright 1989.

3 Gary Waslewski, telephone interview, September 10, 2014.

4 Waslewski interview.

5 "Flood Blasts Expos' Park," *Daily Capital News* (Jefferson City, Missouri), April 15, 1969.

STONEY SETS RECORD FOR FASTEST NO-HITTER BY A FRANCHISE

April 17, 1969: Montreal Expos 7, Philadelphia Phillies 0 At Connie Mack Stadium

By Adam J. Ulrey

IT SEEMS THAT THE EXPOS WANTED TO GIVE their fans a lifetime of memories as quickly as possible.

As if the inaugural game at Shea Stadium or the first home win at Jarry Park weren't memorable enough, the Expos quickly adopted a flair for the dramatic in just the franchise's ninth game, on April 17, 1969. That night, Bill Stoneman pitched a no-hitter against the Philadelphia Phillies, allowing *Nos Amours*—a French expression meaning Our Loves—to achieve the feat more quickly than any other team.[1]

Montreal came into the game at Connie Mack Stadium with a 3-5 record and was playing its seventh game on the road after two at Jarry Park. What made this game more improbable was Stoneman's career to date. Drafted in 1966 in the 31st round by the Chicago Cubs, he was called up to the big leagues in 1967 and went 2-5 over the next two years, mostly as a reliever. He earned the nickname Toy Tiger as much for his size (5-feet-10), as for his determination. Chicago manager Leo Durocher gave Stoneman only two starts, while using him in relief 44 times. The Expos selected Stoneman with the 10th pick in the 1968 expansion draft, viewing him as a starter even though he had only two starts in his major-league career. Going into this contest, he had an 0-2 record and a 5.00 ERA.

Stoneman's inexperience showed in his first appearance of the season, when he gave up four earned runs in 1/3 of an inning against the Mets and left the game with a 108.00 ERA. His second outing was slightly better; he pitched 8⅔ innings and gave up all seven runs (but only one earned) in a 7-6 loss to the Cubs. His teammates made three errors behind him.

In this game, though, the defense was excellent from the beginning. Center fielder Don Bosch recovered from a late jump to grab a sinking fly ball by Don Money in the second. In the next inning, Rusty Staub preserved the no-hitter when he snared a liner off the bat of Tony Taylor.

As historic a night as it was for Stoneman, some of his teammates also had noteworthy evenings. In addition to his fielding heroics, Staub put on a batting clinic with four hits, including three doubles and a fourth-inning home run, his third of the season. Staub had 10 total bases in the game and drove in three runs. Le Grand Orange was blossoming.

Also joining the hit parade was rookie Coco Laboy, who rapped out four singles and drove in a run to help the Expos to their fourth win of the year.

Phillies pitchers had forgettable nights. Starter Jerry Johnson went eight innings and gave up four runs (three earned) on 11 hits. The Expos opened the scoring with an unearned run in the third. Laboy singled and went to second when Gary Sutherland reached on an error. After Stoneman struck out, Laboy scored when Tony Taylor made the Phillies' second error of the inning, this time on a Bosch grounder.

Staub homered leading off the fourth inning and with the Expos in front 2-0 in the sixth, run-scoring singles by Ty Cline and Laboy upped the lead to 4-0. In the ninth the Expos put the game away for good with three more runs off Bill Wilson. Staub doubled with the bases loaded, plating Stoneman and Bosch and moving Maury Wills to third. Turk Farrell replaced Wilson and allowed Wills to score on a wild pitch to make the score 7-0.

Stoneman's determination showed in the ninth inning as he finished the game in style, striking out Ron Stone and Johnny Briggs, and then inducing the dangerous Deron Johnson to ground out to Wills. Overall, Stoneman faced 31 batters, struck out eight and walked five. Stoneman later admitted that he wasn't overpowering that night.

"People think that a pitcher who throws a no-hitter totally dominates the game, but that isn't always true," he said. "I had trouble with my control and gave up five walks, which is something that happened a lot in my career."[2]

As sweet as the win was for the players, this game also provided some revenge for Expos manager Gene Mauch, who was fired by the Phillies after 53 games the previous season. Not only did his new team lay a beating on his old one, but he was serenaded by the fans chanting "we want Mauch" from the seventh inning until the end of the game.[3]

The Expos' reaction to the event seems almost quaint by today's standards. Management ripped up Stoneman's contract and gave him a new one with a $2,000 raise. Then, between games of an April 20 doubleheader against the Cubs, public address announcer Claude Mouton asked fans to stay in their seats and then called Stoneman out of the dugout. Team president John McHale pointed to a new Renault car in center field, a gift from the Renault Company. However, the big surprise came when one of the car's doors opened and out stepped Stoneman's mother along with a brother just back from Vietnam.

Nonetheless, Stoneman's first no-hitter was no fluke. He repeated the feat on October 2, 1972, at Montreal's Jarry Park against the Mets, winning by the same 7–0 score. Stoneman struck out nine, but had control problems, walking seven. Ironically, this was the last complete game of his career. He is the only pitcher in major-league history to pitch no-hitters in his first and last career complete games.

Bill Stoneman

SOURCES

In addition to the sources listed in the notes, the author consulted:

Ballparks.com.

Blackman, Ted. "Stoney Staggered by Montreal Huzzahs Over No-Hitter," *The Sporting News*, May 3, 1969.

Baseball-reference.com.

Conniemackstadium.com.

King, Norman. "Expos get first franchise no-hitter right out of the gate," *Baseball Research Journal*, Spring 2012.

Philadelphia Athletics Historical Society.

NOTES

1   In the expansion era, the California Angels held the previous record, when Bo Belinsky pitched a 2-0 no-hitter against Baltimore on May 5, 1962, in the franchise's 181st game.

2   Al Doyle, "Bill Stoneman: The Game I'll Never Forget: Right-Hander Who Tossed Two No-Hitters During His Career Recalls Victory Over Padres in Which He Fanned 14 Batters," *Baseball Digest*, June 2005.

3   Jacques Doucet and Marc Robitaille, *Il était une fois les Expos, Volume I* (Montreal: Éditions Hurtubise Inc.), 82.

MAUCH'S PREDICTION COMES TRUE

September 25, 1970: Montreal Expos 7, St. Louis Cardinals 5 At Jarry Park

By Norm King

70 IN '70!

Most managers get fired for such modest predictions, but for Expos bench boss Gene Mauch, 70 wins represented an 18-game improvement for the second-year Montreal Expos. And when he made that prognostication at a news conference in Montreal in January 1970, he didn't see the number as a final result, but as a benchmark the team would likely surpass.

Fast-forward to September 25, 1970. Thanks in part to the emergence of 1970 Rookie of the Year Carl Morton (18-11), the Expos entered play that night with 69 wins. They got their 70th win that night, and an old pro made sure they won in style.

Their opponents for the game, the St. Louis Cardinals, were finishing a disappointing season. After enjoying a marvelous decade in which they played in three World Series and won two of them, the St. Louis Cardinals weren't much better than the Expos in 1970, with a 74-82 record going into the game.[1] By this point they were just playing out the string.

Two journeymen started the game. Left-hander John O'Donoghue (2-3) took the mound for the Expos. In his ninth season in the majors, he arrived in Montreal on June 15 in a trade with the Milwaukee Brewers for Jose Herrera. Frank Bertaina, the St. Louis starter, was making what would be his last appearance in the major leagues. He had a 1-2 record at game time.

The 20,998 fans at Jarry Park saw the Cardinals start the game with some textbook small ball. Left fielder Lou Brock led off with a single to left and advanced to second on a sacrifice bunt by second baseman Ed Crosby. First baseman Carl Taylor moved Brock to third on a groundout to the right side, and Joe Torre singled him in to make the score 1-0. The Cards weren't finished, as center fielder Jose Cardenal moved Torre to third with a single to left, then showed how dangerous the famous Cardinal speed could be; he attempted to steal second, and in trying to gun him down, Expos catcher John Bateman sent the ball to the outfield, allowing Torre to score easily.

The Cardinals waited until the third inning to reciprocate the gift run. With one out, Don Hahn singled to left. Gary Sutherland followed with a tailor-made double-play grounder to second, but Cardinals second baseman Ed Crosby booted the ball, giving the Expos runners on first and second and the meat of the order coming up. Rusty Staub didn't look that gift RBI in the mouth and put the Expos on the board with a single to right that sent Sutherland racing to third. Cleanup hitter Bob Bailey grounded to short, but shortstop Milt Ramirez played the ball perfectly and chose to take the out at second instead of throwing to the plate. Sutherland scored, tying the game at 2-2.

The score remained that way until the Montreal half of the sixth. Bateman singled to left and advanced on an error by Brock.[2] Bobby Wine showed he was of good vintage that night by singling and sending Bateman to third. Now this is where Bertaina met with some hard luck. Bateman was no speed merchant; he stole 10 bases in a 10-year career, eight of which came in that 1970 season.[3] It would take a hit or a pretty deep fly ball to score him. Ron Fairly, the next batter, hit the requisite fly ball to center field. Somehow it wasn't deep enough to score Bateman, but Wine was able to make it to second. Mauch and St. Louis manager Red Schoendienst then continued their tactical *pas de deux*. Bertaina walked Clyde Mashore intentionally, which loaded the bases with the pitcher coming up. Mauch wanted to keep reliever Mike Marshall in the game—he had come on in the fifth—so up to the plate Marshall went with his .100 batting average and zero RBIs.

If this were fiction, Marshall would have hit a grand slam. The truth is that he didn't get a hit at all, but he did hit a fly ball deep enough to score Bateman. Bertaina didn't allow any more runs the rest of the frame, and ended the sixth, and his career, down by a run.

Marshall breezed through one-two-three innings in the seventh and eighth. His Cardinals counterpart, Canadian Reggie Cleveland, held the Expos scoreless in the two frames, although Montreal threatened in the eighth with one out and runners on first and third. Marshall had a chance to double his RBI total for the season, but his fly to center was not deep enough to score Fairly from third.

Mauch sent a tired Marshall out to start the ninth, even though he had been pitching since the fifth. Back-to-back singles by Luis Melendez and Ted Simmons gave the Cardinals runners on first and second with nobody out. A double by pinch-hitter Joe Hague that scored Melendez and sent Simmons to the hot corner finally convinced Mauch to replace Marshall with Dan McGinn. Julian Javier came on to pinch-hit and he took full advantage of the situation, singling to right to score Simmons and move Hague to third. Brock grounded to the right side, and Fairly was only able to get the out at first while Javier motored to second; with Hague still at third, the Cardinals now had two on with one out.

At this point the managers played the percentages game. With a southpaw on the mound, Schoendienst sent right-handed hitter Jim Beauchamp up to hit for the lefty Crosby. Mauch countered with right-hander Howie Reed to replace McGinn. It seemed that Mauch won the battle of percentages, but Beauchamp came through with a sacrifice fly to score Hague and give the Cardinals a 5-3 lead. Reed got through the rest of the inning without any further damage.

What happened in the bottom of the ninth became the two-year-old Expos' "shot heard 'round Quebec." The two managers used every angle and pulled every string to win this game even though it would not affect the standings. Schoendienst sent righty Frank Linzy to the mound. Mauch countered with left-handed pinch-hitter Mack Jones, and to the delight of his constituents, the Mayor of Jonesville (the left-field bleachers at Jarry Park, so named in honor of the Expos' left fielder) singled to left. Wasting no time, Schoendienst brought in Tom Hilgendorf to get the lefty-versus-lefty matchup with *Le Grand Orange*, Rusty Staub. Hilgendorf won this battle, as Staub flied to right. The next two scheduled hitters were righties, so Schoendienst brought in right-hander Chuck Taylor. Bailey singled, moving Jones to second; Bateman popped out to first.

It was two on, two out, and Mauch's turn in the managerial chess match. Jim Fairey, batting in place of Wine, sank his teeth into a Taylor pitch for a single to center, scoring Jones and bringing up Fairly.

Schoendienst brought in left-hander Al Hrabosky, known as the Mad Hungarian for the way he ranted and raved off the mound between pitches. He became an even madder Hungarian when Fairly smacked a three-run walk-off home run that gave the Expos a 7-5 win, brought "70 in '70" to reality and made Mauch and Expos fans feel as though they won the World Series.

"Mauch displayed a rare show of emotion following the game when he repeatedly raised his arms into the air and received hearty applause from the spectators on the way to the clubhouse," wrote the Canadian Press.[4]

The Expos finished the season with a 73-89 record, better than the three other 1969 expansion teams.[5] The 70th win symbolized a progression that left Expos fans with bright thoughts for the future. Alas, it would be another nine seasons before they would break the .500 mark.

SOURCES

In addition to the sources listed in the notes, the author consulted:

Baseball-reference.com.

NOTES

1 The Cardinals defeated the New York Yankees in 1964 and the Boston Red Sox in 1967, both times in seven games. They lost to the Detroit Tigers in 1968, also in seven games.

2 Brock led the National League in errors by a left fielder nine times in his first 11 seasons, including 1970, when he committed 10 miscues.

3　One of those stolen bases came off future Hall of Famer Johnny Bench on August 18, 1970. Bateman got cocky and tried to swipe second off Bench again the next night. Bench got him.

4　Canadian Press, "Expos Reach 70 Wins," *Ottawa Journal*, September 26, 1970.

5　The Kansas City Royals and Milwaukee Brewers both finished with 65-97 records while the San Diego Padres went 63-99.

STONEY'S SECOND NO-NO

October 2, 1972: Montreal Expos 7, New York Mets 0 At Jarry Park

By Norm King

ON SEPTEMBER 28, 1972, THE ENTIRE COUNTRY of Canada ceased to function. Businesses closed. Kids were let out of school. The occasion was Game Eight of the epic hockey series between a team of Canadian National Hockey League players and the Soviet national team. The series, which Team Canada was expected to win in a skate, had come down to the final game with the series tied at three wins each and one tie. Canucks from coast to coast to coast watched intently as the final minutes ticked away with the score tied 5-5. Finally, Paul Henderson scored with 34 seconds left to play to seal the series victory for Canada and send an entire nation into a state of delirium. Take the Miracle on Ice, multiply by 10, and you will understand the elation Canadians felt after Henderson scored that goal.

Perhaps it was because of the afterglow of that event, or the cool October weather, that only 7,184 hardy souls attended a twi-night doubleheader between the Montreal Expos and the New York Mets at Jarry Park on October 2, 1972. They saw something in the first game that no one had ever seen before–the first major-league no-hitter ever pitched on other than American soil.

"There was only one way, it seems, that we could knock Team Canada from the front page," said Expos president John McHale. "That was for Stoneman to throw a no-hitter — and he did."[1]

The Mets and Expos were winding down disappointing seasons. The Mets had a 79-72 record, good for third place in the National League East Division, 15 games behind the eventual division champion Pittsburgh Pirates. Since coming from nowhere to win the World Series in 1969, they had won 83 games in 1970 and 1971, and would do so again in 1972.

The Expos were 69-82 in their fourth season of existence. Since winning 73 games in 1970 when manager

Gene Mauch predicted "70 in '70" for what was then a second-year franchise, the Expos hadn't improved at all. They went 71-90 in 1971 and were on their way to a 70-86 season in 1972 (the season was shortened by a players' strike at the beginning of the year).[2]

The two starting pitchers had both been slumping. Mets starter Jim McAndrew was in the midst of a losing streak. After defeating the Phillies on September 12 to go 11-5, he had lost his next two starts, including a 4-0 whitewash in St. Louis. Similarly, Stoneman would never sing "Try to Remember That Kind of September" after the month he went through. In seven appearances, he went 1-5 with a 3.86 ERA. Somebody was due to have a good game.

It was clear from the get-go that that somebody was not to be McAndrew. After Stoneman struck out the side in the first (he also walked John Milner), the Expos struck quickly in the bottom of the inning. Leadoff hitter Ron Hunt doubled, moved to third on a Tim McCarver fly ball, and scored on a wild pitch. He would have come home anyway because after Ken Singleton struck out, Ron Fairly gave Montreal a 2-0 lead with a home run.

The Expos put it away in the bottom of the third. McAndrew plunked Hunt to lead off the inning.[3] Hunt moved to third on McCarver's single to center, and scored on Ken Singleton's single; Singleton advanced to second on the throw to the plate. One out later, Jim Fairey was walked intentionally to load the bases for Boots Day. Boots belted the ball to right for a bases-clearing triple to give the Expos a 6-0 lead after three.

The Expos' final run, off Mets reliever Brent Strom in the fourth, was a singular achievement. Singleton singled home Hunt, who had singled and moved to second on McCarver's single. That made the score 7-0.

A big lead after four innings certainly doesn't guarantee a no-hitter. It doesn't even assure victory, at least not in baseball. The Mets came close to scoring in the fifth when Bill Sudakis walked with one out, moved to second when Stoneman flubbed a Don Hahn grounder and to third when Ted Martinez hit into a fielder's choice. With two on and two out, Stoneman fanned pinch-hitter Dave Marshall to end the Mets' only real scoring threat.

Stoneman's performance from the sixth inning on was marked by an oddity in that he didn't have a single three-up-three-down inning. He walked two batters in the sixth and one each in the seventh, eighth, and ninth. He also left one runner on base in each frame (Lute Barnes, who received the first base on balls in the sixth, was erased on a double play).

The Mets' relief corps did a fine job. Strom, who came on with one out in the third, allowed one run. Bob Rauch pitched three scoreless innings and Ray Sadecki gave up one walk in working the eighth.

This was the second no-hitter of Stoneman's career, making him the 16th pitcher in the 20th century to pitch two gems. His first no-hitter was also historic as it came in the ninth game of the Expos' existence on April 17, 1969, and was the first ever thrown in an expansion team's debut season. When he left the major leagues he was the only pitcher to toss no-hitters in his first and last career complete games.

The two games were also similar statistically. In the 1969 game, Stoneman struck out eight and walked five. He struck out nine and walked seven in the 1972 one. Seven walks sounds high, but according to Expos manager Gene Mauch, they were the result of smart pitching rather than of poor control.

"Most of his walks tonight were because he made certain he didn't give the batters anything decent to hit after he fell behind," Mauch explained. "He simply said to hell with this and just gave them nothing to hit."[4]

As with any no-hitter, a pitcher has to rely on his defense to make outstanding plays. Tim Foli made two quality plays to keep the goose egg in the hit column. The first came in the fourth when he went far to his right to snag a blooper off Milner's bat that went behind third baseman Coco Laboy. The second came on the game's last out when Hahn—a former Expo–smacked a grounder that bounced crazily after hitting the edge of the grass. Foli was able to snare it and throw to Fairly at first for the out.

"Both [no-hitters] ended with tough groundballs to shortstop," Stoneman said. "Foli stayed with it. He made the play look easy and it wasn't that easy."[5]

Expos management deserves kudos for arranging to show Stoneman the team's appreciation the very next night between games of another Expos-Mets doubleheader. They gave him a $2,000 bonus check and two Air Canada plane tickets to anywhere the airline flew. His wife, Diane, a former Air Canada stewardess, received a gold watch and his batterymate, McCarver, received a $500 gift certificate.

For his part, Stoneman was happy to have pitched his second no-hitter in the *milieu familier* of Jarry Park for the hometown crowd.[6] "I heard the people yelling. It felt great," he said after the game. "Having pitched one on the road, I know that I'm happier to have pitched it here."[7]

Years later, Stoneman evaluated the two no-hitters not just in terms of what they meant to the fans or the team, but what type of pitcher threw them. "There were a lot of similarities to both games," he said, "but the pitcher who threw the first no-hitter and the pitcher who threw the second were two different pitchers in terms of experience."[8]

SOURCES

In addition to the sources listed in the notes, the author consulted:

Baseball-reference.com.

SI.com.

NOTES

1 Ian MacDonald, "Stoneman repeats his no-hit gem," the *Montreal Gazette*, October 3, 1972.

2 This was the first players' strike in major-league baseball history.

3 Hunt led the National League in HBP seven straight years, from 1968 to 1974. He set the 20th-century single-season major-league record of 50 in 1971. Hughie Jennings set the all-time record when he was hit 51 times in 1896.

4 MacDonald.

5 Video, *Les Expos, Nos Amours*, Volume I, produced by TV Labatt, 1989.

6 *Milieu familier* is the French translation of *friendly confines*.

7 MacDonald.

8 *Les Expos, Nos Amours*.

STEVE ROGERS TOSSES ONE-HIT SHUTOUT TO WIN FIRST BIG-LEAGUE GAME

July 26, 1973: Montreal Expos 4, Philadelphia Phillies 0 At Veterans Stadium

By Gregory H. Wolf

"HE CAN PITCH," SAID MONTREAL EXPOS skipper Gene Mauch about rookie right-hander Steve Rogers, who tossed a brilliant one-hit shutout over the Philadelphia Phillies to earn his first big-league win in his second start. "Rarely does a man with such experience have the confidence in his control of so many pitches."[1] Described by Pat Jordan in *Sports Illustrated* as a "cowboy-lean, smooth-cheeked young man," the 23-year-old Rogers commanded a repertoire of pitches that included sinkers, fastball, sliders, curves, and changeups.[2] The New York Mets' Tom Seaver, widely regarded as the best righty in the NL, considered Rogers' slider "one of the most devastating" in the major leagues.[3]

The Expos were reeling when they arrived to play a doubleheader at Veterans Stadium in Philadelphia on Thursday, July 26, 1973. They had lost eight of their last 10 games during a season-long 17-game road swing, to fall to 44-51 and fifth place in the National League East. Less than three weeks earlier, on July 7, the club had evened its record at 40-40, marking the latest date in the season that the Expos had possessed a .500 record in their history. Philadelphia's first-year manager, Danny Ozark, had inherited a club that was coming off two consecutive last-place finishes in the NL East, including a miserable 59-97 record in 1972. The Phillies had not enjoyed a winning campaign since 1967, when Mauch guided them to what was then a franchise record sixth consecutive winning season.

Philadelphia sent ace Steve Carlton to the mound. The 28-year-old southpaw was the best hurler on the planet the previous season, leading the majors with 27 wins, 346⅓ innings, 310 strikeouts, and an NL-best 1.97 ERA for the NL's worst club; however he was struggling in 1973. His record stood at 9-10 and his ERA had more than doubled to 4.22 in 183⅓ innings. In desperate need of a starting pitcher, the Expos had called up Rogers on July 16. After beginning the 1973 season with the Quebec Carnavals of the Double-A Eastern League, Rogers was transferred to the Peninsula (Hampton, Virginia) Whips in the Triple-A International League, where he proved his big-league readiness by tossing four consecutive complete games. Rogers' "career with the Expos got off to a rocky start," wrote SABR member Norm King, when Canadian customs agents did not initially permit the pitcher into the country without his signed contract, forcing the rookie to spend an extra night in the US.[4] The next day, contract in hand, he legally entered Canada to realize his dream. In his first big-league start, on July 18, Rogers yielded two runs on four-hit ball over eight innings in a no-decision against the Houston Astros in the Astrodome, which the Expos eventually won 3-2 in 10 innings.

A good crowd of 34,459 spectators turned out for the first game of the Expos-Phillies three-game series, and was treated to a classic scoreless pitchers' duel through six innings. Carlton yielded only three hits (one in each of the first three innings), and permitted as many as two baserunners in an innng only once when he issued consecutive two-out walks in the fifth inning. Not to be outdone by his veteran counterpart, the Missouri native Rogers retired 13 of the first 14 batters he faced. His only blemish was a walk to Del Unser, whom catcher John Boccabella cut down at second in a steal attempt. The Phillies nicked Rogers for their only hit in the game in the fifth inning. Light-hitting third baseman Jose Pagan, in his 15th and final season, "topped a ball down the third base line," reported the AP. Third sacker Bob Bailey "tried to pick it up bare-handed but couldn't hold" and Pagan was safe without a throw.[5]

The pitchers' personalities stood in stark contrast to each other. Carlton, a nine-year veteran with 113 big-league wins, was enigmatic, had a reputation as a recluse who refused to speak with reporters, and seemed unemotional while pitching, tuning out distractions. Rogers was the exact opposite. "On the mound, he talks to himself," said Pat Jordan. "He curses an inadequate pitch, exhorting himself to a superior effort. If he is particularly displeased, he remains in his follow-through for a moment, his feet firmly planted, and then executes a tiny leap into the air."[6] Rogers recognized that his emotions and intensity got him into trouble early in his professional baseball career and had worked hard to keep them in check. "I'm not exactly a stoic pitcher," he said. "I've always been an emotional person. In the minor leagues it used to destroy my concentration."[7]

The Expos scored the game's first run in the seventh inning. Boccabella singled and moved to second on shortstop Pepe Frias' sacrifice. Rogers recorded his first big-league hit on a hard-hit ball that drew first baseman Willie Montanez away from the bag. Rogers was safe when Carlton "failed to cover first on [the] infield grounder," reported the AP.[8] Boccabella had raced to third, and later scored on second baseman Ron Hunt's single to center. The Expos tacked on three more runs in a wild eighth inning that included two hits, three walks (two intentional), an error, a double play, a sacrifice bunt, and two men left on base. Right fielder Ken Singleton smashed a double to center to drive in pinch-runner Mike Jorgensen for the first run of the rally; Frias' bases-loaded single to left plated Bailey and Singleton to give the Expos a 4-0 lead.

Carlton tossed a complete game, but was not at his best in the loss, yielding eight hits and seven walks. In the ninth inning he picked off Jorgensen at first; however, in the ensuing rundown he committed the Phillies' third and final error when he threw wildly,

allowing Jorgensen to scamper to third. But the story of the game was Rogers, who closed out the game in impressive fashion. He set down 12 of the final 13 batters he faced, walking one, to pick up his first of 158 victories and 37 shutouts in a 13-year career. "I'm not disappointed," said Rogers of settling for a one-hitter. "[The hit] came too early in the game to be thinking of a no-hitter.[9]

"I've done everything I'm capable of doing in these last two games," added Rogers matter-of-factly.[10]

But Rogers had more in store for Montreal. Four days later he tossed his second consecutive shutout, a seven-hitter, against the New York Mets at Shea Stadium. Rogers has the "most super concentration I've ever seen," said Expos pitching coach Cal McLish when asked to explain Rogers' immediate success.[11] In a magical debut season, Rogers dazzled baseball by going 10-5 with a sparkling 1.54 ERA in 134 innings, and finished second in NL Rookie of the Year voting behind Gary Matthews of the San Francisco Giants.

In the second game of the doubleheader, Expos starter Steve Renko (6⅓ innings) and reliever Mike Marshall (2⅔ innings in relief) held the Phillies to six hits in a 5-1 victory.

SOURCES

In addition to the sources listed in the notes, the author consulted:

Baseball-Reference.com.

Retrosheet.org.

SABR.org.

NOTES

1 Ian MacDonald, "Expos Experimenting Waging Torrid Romance With Rookie Rogers," *The Sporting News*, August 16, 1973, 32.

2 Pat Jordan, "Mr. Intensity of the Expos," *Sports Illustrated*, April 29, 1974.

3 Tom Seaver, quoted in Bill James and Rob Neyer, *Neyer/James Guide to Pitchers An Historical Compendium of Pitching, Pitchers, and Pitches.* (New York: Touchstone, 2004), 363.

4 Norm King, "Steve Rogers," *SABR BioProject*.

5 Associated Press, "Phillies Lose Pair to Expos, 4-0, 5-1," *Standard-Speaker* (Hazleton, Pennsylvania), July 27, 1973, 20.

6 Jordan.

7   Ibid.

8   Associated Press, "Phillies Lose Pair to Expos, 4-0, 5-1."

9   Herschel Nissenson, Associated Press, "Rogers' 1-Hitter Leads Expos By Phils Twice; Cards Sweep," *Monroe* (Louisiana) *News-Star*, July 27, 1973, 14.

10   Nissenson.

11   Jordan.

MONTREAL'S FIRST LEAD IN A PENNANT RACE

September 17, 1973: Expos 5, St. Louis Cardinals 4 At Jarry Park
(First Game Of A Twi-night Doubleheader)

By Rory Costello

DURING THEIR FIRST FOUR SEASONS, THE Montreal Expos were never in first place after April.[1] In 1973, however, Montreal got its first case of pennant fever amid a five-team dogfight for the National League East Division title. On the evening of Monday, September 17, the Expos climbed into a virtual tie for first place after winning the opening game of a doubleheader at Jarry Park. The stirring 5-4 victory came on a two-run rally in the bottom of the ninth. Its strange ending was a communication lapse that let an infield popup fall.

That taste of life at the top was fleeting, because Montreal lost the nightcap, a 12-inning crusher. In a turnabout, a win slipped away from the Expos in the ninth inning. They did not hold the lead again in a September pennant race until 1979.

The *Montreal Gazette* columnist Michael Farber later wrote, "The Expos stumbled onto a pennant race by default" in 1973.[2] The division was dubbed the "National League Least" because all teams were struggling to get to or stay above the .500 mark.

Montreal reached .500 on September 15, when Jarry Park's single-game attendance record of 34,331 was set.[3] The Expos won their fifth straight on September 16 and drew within half a game of the first-place Pittsburgh Pirates, who lost to St. Louis. That set the stage for the twin bill against the Cardinals. A crowd of 20,160 arrived that cool, cloudy evening.

The first game began at 6:05 P.M. The starters were Rick Wise for St. Louis and hot rookie Steve Rogers for Montreal. Neither was especially sharp, but they still kept their teams in the game. Rogers allowed 10 hits and three earned runs in seven innings before giving way to iron-man reliever Mike Marshall, making his 83rd appearance of the season. Wise gave up three earned runs through eight innings.

In the second inning, the Expos loaded the bases with nobody out but got just one run as Tim Foli grounded into a 6-4-3 double play. Rogers (a .138 lifetime hitter) then struck out. St. Louis scored twice in the third, but Montreal's Ron Fairly tied it in the sixth with a leadoff home run.

The Cardinals went ahead in the seventh. Brock led off witth a walk, stole second (his second theft of the game), reached third on catcher Bob "Scrap Iron" Stinson's wild throw, then scored on Ted Sizemore's shallow sacrifice fly.

In the bottom of the seventh, however, Stinson tied it again with another leadoff homer. He said, "God, that felt good. I want to win so badly. I know I have trouble back there [behind the plate], but I can't be in the right place for every pitch."[4]

A remarkable subplot then unfolded. The brothers Felipe and Matty Alou had played most of the year for the New York Yankees, but the Yankees dealt them both away on September 6. St. Louis picked up Matty; Montreal acquired Felipe, the club's future skipper, on waivers for $50,000.

At the batting cage before the first game, Matty told Felipe, "We're going to finish this pennant talk about the Expos tonight. We're going to win the doubleheader."[5] Afterward, Felipe said with a laugh, "He was just kidding me. But after what he did, I think maybe he was serious."[6]

Indeed, Matty's pinch-hit RBI single off Marshall in the eighth gave St. Louis a 4-3 lead, which Wise took into the bottom of the ninth inning. However, after a leadoff single by Jim Lyttle, Cardinals manager

Red Schoendienst brought in reliever Al Hrabosky. Recalled again from the minors that June, "The Mad Hungarian" had not yet become the Cardinals' bullpen ace. But he did strike out over a batter an inning for St. Louis in 1973, something that was much less common then.

Rookie Tony Scott ran for Lyttle. He went to second when Hrabosky's first pitch to pinch-hitter Clyde Mashore sailed over the head of catcher Ted Simmons. Mashore then tried to bunt but managed only a weak little popup. First baseman Joe Torre grabbed it with a slide that took him almost to home plate.

Hrabosky then struck out Foli. The Expos were down to their last out when Felipe Alou pinch-hit for Marshall. He later said, "I had it in my mind that I'm going to show Matty."[7] On a 2-and-2 pitch, high and outside—he called it "a very bad pitch"—Alou hit a sharp grounder between first and second.[8] It looked like a sure base hit. But Sizemore, the Cardinals' second baseman, stopped it with a headlong dive to his left. Sizemore rose to his knees but had trouble getting the ball out of his glove. He tried to get Alou at first anyway, but Felipe, who still ran well for a 38-year-old, was safe by a step.

Meanwhile, Scott was steaming around third base, waved on by coach Dave Bristol. Torre's rushed throw home was high and wide, and Scott—sliding into Simmons and colliding heavily—scored the tying run. Alou still got credit for an RBI, but Torre was charged with an error because Alou took second on the play.

Mauch then sent up his third pinch-hitter of the inning, Ron Woods, to bat for rookie second baseman Larry Lintz. The crowd was "ready to come apart at the seams," as the *Montreal Gazette* sportswriter Tim Burke put it, but the suspense only intensified. The count went full, and then Woods fouled off seven pitches.

Finally, Woods hit a towering popup just short of the mound. Hrabosky, Torre, shortstop Mick Kelleher, third baseman Terry Hughes, and Simmons all called for the ball. No one took charge. The ball dropped for a base hit and Alou—running hard all the way because he'd seen such plays many times in his career—came around to score the winning run. After the game,

Mauch praised the veteran for his presence of mind, saying that a less experienced player might have conceded the out and headed for the dugout.[9]

Red Schoendienst said, "It was a foolish mistake. My team fell asleep on that play. At the last second, Hrabosky yelled at Hughes to catch it, he made a lunge and missed. The pitcher should have called the man much earlier."[10] Hughes also took his eye off the ball, distracted by Torre's late charge.[11] Mauch observed how unusual that was for Torre, who had been in control of hundreds of such popups during his career.[12]

"It was the nicest hit of my career," said Woods. "It was probably the shortest too."[13] Expos president John McHale, a religious man, said that "something spiritual" guided the comeback.[14]

The win lifted Montreal's record to 75-73. The Pirates went into their 8:05 P.M. game against the New York Mets at 74-72. The winning-percentage calculation needed five digits—.50676 to .50684—to show how slightly Pittsburgh was ahead.

Awareness of the standings was high. Ron Fairly said, "In 1970, we had a slogan, 'Win 70 in '70'—since when is that a goal to be proud of? That was always tough for me, coming through the Dodgers' system, where we expected to win a hundred games. Expansion teams are going to take a beating until the minor-league system produces, and it's not a lot of fun.

"But this was a different area for a lot of the guys. They got excited, and I remember the fans talking about it too."[15]

The opener in Montreal ended a little before 9 P.M. At Pittsburgh, the Pirates drubbed the Mets, 10-3. That game included a 75-minute rain delay. Thus, it was pushing midnight when the final score was posted at Jarry during the second game. The Expos had been watching the scoreboard—as Fairly said, "You always do that. Anybody who tells you they're not isn't telling the truth. At the same time, you have to win your game."[16]

Rain also delayed the nightcap for 72 minutes in the top of the 12th. It didn't end until nearly 2:00 A.M., past press time for many newspapers—some September 18 headlines still showed Montreal tied for first.[17]

The team then faded out of the race but was not mathematically eliminated until it lost its final game on Sunday, September 30. "We had a shot at it," said Fairly, "and it would have been a great story."[18] For his efforts, Gene Mauch was named NL Manager of the Year for the third time.[19]

Expectations, however, had leaped. Veteran Montreal sportswriter Dink Carroll stated, "The task … won't be entirely completed until the Expos win the pennant, which could happen as early as next year because the club has become a solid contender."[20] The smell of success ended the innocent phase of the romance between city and ballclub. As Carroll's colleague Ian MacDonald later wrote, "The fans weren't about to accept only hustle and effort now. They wanted results."[21]

SOURCES

In addition to the sources listed in the notes, the author consulted:

Bangor (Maine) *Daily News.*

NOTES

1   The Expos were leading the NL East as late as April 30, 1972, and April 29, 1971.

2   Michael Farber, "Rogers an Expo in good, bad times," the *Montreal Gazette*, June 25, 1983.

3   Jarry's listed capacity was just 28,456. September 15 was a beautiful weekend afternoon, and there was also a wool-hat promotion—though desire to see the Expos win was what drew the record crowd. Ted Blackman, "Expos, Jarry Park paying off for team owners and Montreal," the *Montreal Gazette*, September 25, 1973.

4   Tim Burke, "Expos use gremlins to win again," the *Montreal Gazette*, September 18, 1973.

5   Ibid.

6   Ibid.

7   Ibid.

8   Ted Blackman, "Felipe Alou was great buy for the Expos in September," the *Montreal Gazette*, September 18, 1973.

9   E-mail from Dave Van Horne, then the Expos' English-language broadcaster, to Rory Costello, July 6, 2015.

10 Vito Stellino, "Cards Let Montreal Sweep Get Away," *Beaver County* (Pennsylvania) *Times*, September 18, 1973: C-1.

11 Photo, "Pop goes the ball game!," the *Montreal Gazette*, September 18, 1973: 1.

12 E-mail from Dave Van Horne to Rory Costello, July 6, 2015.

13 "Red Birds, Expos split twinbill," *Southeast Missourian* (Cape Girardeau, Missouri), September 18, 1973.

14 Burke.

15 Telephone interview, Ron Fairly with Rory Costello, July 27, 2015 (hereafter Fairly interview). In 1973 just three men on the Montreal roster remained from the 1968 expansion draft: Bill Stoneman, Bob Bailey, and John Boccabella. Fairly joined partway through the first season, 1969.

16 Fairly interview.

17 The headline in the *Sarasota Herald-Tribune* September 18, 1973 declared, "Expos Win Opener, Gain Tie for Top," while the *Palm Beach Post* headline said, "Expos Tie for 1st on Woods' Hit." If the rain had not abated and the second game had been called, Montreal would have been just one-half game behind Pittsburgh and would have played a doubleheader against St. Louis on the afternoon of September 18.

18 Fairly interview.

19 Mauch also received this award in 1962 and 1964 for his work with the Philadelphia Phillies.

20 Dink Carroll, "It was Expos' critical year, but McHale's now optimistic," the *Montreal Gazette*, October 2, 1973.

21 Ian MacDonald, "Eight-year Jarry love affair ends on desperate note," the *Montreal Gazette*, September 28, 1976.

EXPOS BLOW UP BIG RED MACHINE

June 11, 1974: Montreal Expos 16, Cincinnati Reds 6 At Jarry Park

By Gregory H. Wolf

"THE EXPOS EXPLODED IN STARTLING FASHION," wrote Ian MacDonald in the *Montreal Gazette*.[1] Trailing 5-1, the Montreal Expos put together the greatest two-inning outburst in team history, scoring 15 runs and sending 21 batters to the plate in the seventh and eighth innings to crush the Cincinnati Reds, 16-6. "I've never been in a game where a team scored 15 runs in two innings," said 18-year veteran first baseman Ron Fairly.[2] Expos offseason acquisition Willie Davis led the charge with two homers, including a grand slam, and a career-high seven RBIs. "That's the biggest thrill since I've been playing and I've had a lot of thrills," said Davis of the ninth and final game with two round-trippers in his 18-year career.[3]

On June 11, 1974, the Expos arrived at *Parc Jarry* to play the second game of a three-game set with the reigning National League West champion Reds on a positive note. The night before, they had defeated the Big Red Machine, 3-1, in a game interrupted twice by rain and ultimately called with one out in the top of the ninth inning. More importantly, the victory gave skipper Gene Mauch's squad a psychological boost, evening its record at 25-25, good for third place in the NL East. The Reds, after a horrible start (13-14), were on a roll, having won 19 of their last 28 games. Skipper Sparky Anderson's slugging club was aiming for its fourth division crown in five years, but faced an uphill struggle. Despite the hot streak and the second best winning percentage in baseball, they trailed the Los Angeles Dodgers by eight games.

In the previous offseason, the Expos made a startling trade, sending disgruntled fireman Mike Marshall to the Los Angeles Dodgers in exchange for 34-year-old Willie Davis. The 30-year old, right-handed Marshall, arguably baseball's best reliever at the time, was coming off two superb years. He posted ERAs of 1.78 and 2.66,

set a big-league record with 92 appearances in 1973, and finished third and second respectively in Cy Young Award voting. But the outspoken pitcher clashed with Mauch and management. Davis, who had thus far amassed in excess of 2,000 hits in his 14-year career, had held down center field for the Dodgers since 1961; he was named to his second All-Star team in 1973 and also earned his third consecutive Gold Glove Award.

The trade benefited both teams. Davis gave the aspiring Expos some much-needed "star power," and led the club in '74 in practically every offensive category, including hits (180), runs (86), doubles (27), triples (9), RBIs (89), batting average (.295), and stolen bases (25); while Marshall set a standard for relievers that as of 2014 was still unmatched, with 106 appearances and 206⅓ innings pitched to become the first reliever to win a Cy Young Award.

A sparse crowd of 12,450 spectators showed up at Jarry Park on a cool, windy Tuesday evening. The Expos struck first when their leadoff hitter, left fielder Mike Jorgensen, connected for his eighth hit in his last 15 at-bats, a solo shot in the bottom of the first off Reds starter Roger Nelson. A 30-year-old righty with a 28-32 record in parts of eight big-league seasons, Nelson retired 17 of the next 20 batters, yielding just three hits. "[He] had the Expos eating out of his hand through six," wrote MacDonald.[4]

Cincinnati took a 2-1 lead on Johnny Bench's two-run double in the third inning off Dennis Blair, Montreal's 20-year-old rookie making just his fourth career start. The Reds chased the ineffective Blair (three earned runs, five hits and four walks in 3⅔ innings) in the fourth with Nelson's run-scoring single, and tacked on single runs in the fifth and seventh innings to increase their lead to 5-1.

The game's momentum changed in the bottom of the seventh. Nelson "couldn't get ... his breaking stuff (over)," said shortstop Tim Foli.[5] With runners on first and second, catcher Barry Foote slapped a two-out single, driving in third baseman Bob Bailey and opening the floodgates, as the next four batters reached base. After pinch-hitter Ron Woods drew a walk from reliever Tom Hall to load the bases, Jorgensen rapped an RBI single. Foli greeted the normally reliable Pedro Borbon by sinking his teeth into a fastball for another bases-loaded single, driving in two runs to tie the score, 5-5. Willie Davis, who had hit at a .366 clip (41-for-112) in his last 28 games, broke the contest open by sending Borbon's inside offering careening like a missile over George Foster's head in right field for a three-run homer and an 8-5 Expos' lead. "The pitch looked like it might hit him," said Bench after the game. "That guy must use a matchstick for a bat. He got around so quickly."[6]

The Expos, an average club on offense that finished seventh in batting average and runs scored in 1974, continued their unexpected offensive outburst by scoring a franchise-record eight runs in the eighth inning. Following run-scoring singles by Foote and reliever Chuck Taylor off Reds reliever Dick Baney, skipper Sparky Anderson brought in southpaw Mike McQueen to face the left-handed-hitting Davis with two out and the bases loaded. The plan backfired as Davis connected for the fourth and final grand slam of his career, extending Montreal's lead to 14-5. Two batters later, first sacker Ron Fairly, who had played with Davis on the Dodgers' three pennant-winning teams of the 1960s, smashed Montreal's fourth homer of the evening, tying a team record, to make it 16-5. All of the clouts went to right field, aided by a swirling wind.[7]

Chuck Taylor, who replaced Marshall as the Expos' closer in 1974 and turned in a career season (61 appearances and a 2.17 ERA in 107⅔ innings), pitched the final two innings, yielding two hits and a run in the final frame. He ended the 2-hour 55-minute contest by punching out Foster and Cesar Geronimo. Expos hurler Tom Walker, who gave up three hits and a run in two innings of relief, was the beneficiary of the Expos' offensive surge and got the win. Tom Hall was charged with the loss.

"I can never recall a team putting innings back to back like that," said an incredulous Mauch after the game.[8] The Expos scored 15 runs in the seventh and eighth innings on 10 hits and 5 walks, and finished the game with 14 safeties. "To be so far behind and come on to win — that's fantastic," added an excited Davis, whose 7 RBIs tied a team record held by Bob Bailey and John Bateman. "To keep on scoring when you're ahead, that's great."[9]

SOURCES

In addition to the sources listed in the notes, the author consulted:

Baseball-Reference.com.

Retrosheet.org.

SABR.org.

NOTES

1 Ian MacDonald, "Willie D's right — he is 'fantastic' (7 RBIs)," the *Montreal Gazette*, June 12, 1974, 29.

2 Ibid.

3 Stu Camen, "Expos Rip Cincinnati," *Naugatuck* (Connecticut) *Daily News*, June 12, 1974, 10.

4 MacDonald.

5 Ibid.

6 "Expos Club Cincy," *The Press-Gazette* (Hillsboro, Ohio), June 12, 1974, 12.

7 Ibid.

8 MacDonald.

9 Ibid.

TIM FOLI GETS ON HIS CYCLE

April 21-22, 1976: Expos 12, Chicago Cubs 6 At Wrigley Field

By Norm King

THE MONTREAL EXPOS' 1976 SEASON WAS A soap opera. Clubhouse dissension, along with the second-worst record in franchise history (55-107), made for a long, frustrating year, so it only seemed appropriate that fans had to "tune in tomorrow" to find out if Tim Foli became the first Expo to ever hit for the cycle (spoiler alert: He did).[1] His cycle was a natural one—he hit a single, double, triple, and home run in that order in a 12-6 Expos victory over the Cubs. As if that wasn't enough to make the game unusual, the umpires accused both clubs of pulling off stunts when the skies threatened to bring the game to an early end.

The Expos had a reasonable 3-5 record when they faced the Cubs in the second of a three-game series. Steve Rogers had gone 8⅓ innings on April 19 in a 4-3 Montreal win over Chicago's Bill Bonham. After an offday on April 20, Geoff Zahn of the Cubs took the mound against old pro Woodie Fryman. Zahn was the author of his own misfortune in the first inning. He walked the first two Expos hitters, Pepe Mangual and Nate Colbert. A groundball fielder's choice by Mike Jorgensen forced Colbert at second but allowed Mangual to reach third. Zahn then muffed a comebacker to the mound by right fielder Gary Carter, which scored Mangual to give the Expos a 1-0 lead. The Cubs took a short-lived 2-1 lead in the bottom of the first when Jose Cardenal homered with leadoff hitter Rick Monday, who had singled, on base.

The Expos rallied in the top of the second. Barry Foote led off with a single and reached third on Foli's first hit of the game, a line-drive single to left. Pete Mackanin got the Expos' third consecutive single, which drove in Foote and sent Foli to second. Fryman moved the runners up with a sacrifice bunt. Both Foli and Mackanin scored on a single by Mangual. The Expos led 4-2 and were on their way to a rout.

Foli got his double in the third. With one out and new Cubs pitcher Tom Dettore on the mound, Larry Parrish singled to left and moved to third on a double by Foote. Foli's two-bagger drove home Parrish and Foote, giving the Expos a 6-2 lead. The clubs traded solo shots in the fourth, with Mike Jorgensen going yard for Montreal and Cubs catcher Steve Swisher responding in the bottom of the inning. Then came the fun-filled fifth.

Wrigley Field didn't have lights back in 1976, so games in those days could still be called because of darkness. This particular game had already started 15 minutes late because of the weather, and had endured rain delays of 30, 31, 20, and 27 minutes. When the rain began falling in the top of the fifth, the Expos wanted to get through the inning quickly so the game would be official.

"The game became almost a comedy in the fifth when rain was threatening," wrote the *Des Plaines Herald*. "The Expos were trying to get the inning over to make the game official while the Cubs were doing everything they could to prevent it."[2]

The last thing the Expos needed was baserunners. Leadoff hitter Foote followed the script by grounding out to first. Foli was up next and swung at the first pitch from new Cubs pitcher Paul Reuschel, even though it was in another area code. He swung again and hit a screamer down the left-field line. He started running, touching first, then, second, then third—the triple was in the books—but kept on running and was an easy out at the plate.

"I wanted to get five innings finished," admitted Foli. "That's why I kept running. We needed the outs."[3]

Mackanin was the next batter. When he let the first two pitches go by, players in the Expos' dugout started jumping and screaming to get his attention and remind him that speed was of the essence. He swung at the next pitch and smacked it to right-center for another triple. Unlike Foli, Mackanin held up at third. Fryman was the next batter and he hit a single to drive Mackanin home. But instead of holding up at first, Fryman tried to stretch the hit into a double. Now, Fryman was 36 years old at the time and could never be confused with Lou Brock or Maury Wills—he was out by 10 feet, ending the inning. Umpiring crew chief Billy Williams was not happy with the Expos' actions, and told the two managers between innings to stop the shenanigans.

"Montreal made a farce of the game," Williams said later. "I'm referring to the baserunning of Woodie Fryman and Tim Foli. There was no way I was going to let that go further. Fans pay to see teams and the players do their best."[4]

The Cubs, for their part, wanted to pour molasses on the proceedings to prevent the game from becoming official. Leadoff hitter Rick Monday kept stepping out of the batter's box to clean his spikes, and when they weren't clean enough, he walked over to the on-deck circle to go over them with a towel. These delaying tactics didn't work and the game continued after the Cubs went down in order.

In the top of the sixth, Reuschel stymied the Expos' plans for a quick inning by letting them score at will. Mangual led the inning off with a single. New center fielder Jerry White homered. (In the bottom of the fifth, Mangual had replaced Colbert in left and White took Colbert's spot in the lineup.) Jorgensen and Carter both walked, and Jorgensen scored on a single by third baseman Larry Parrish. The score now was 11-3.

Don Carrithers replaced Fryman in the bottom of the sixth, and came through the inning unscathed. The umpiring crew suspended the game at that point not because of the weather, but because of darkness, which meant that the game had to resume the next day. The hot-tempered Foli went ballistic, charging at Williams and arguing that the game should be called on account of rain. That would have meant the game was official and didn't need to continue the next day. To his credit, Foli was more concerned about the win than the personal milestone of hitting for the cycle.

Tim Foli

"It is ironic that Foli was furious when that game was suspended because of darkness with the Expos ahead 7-3[*sic*]," wrote Ian MacDonald. "He was the most volatile of the Expos who wanted the game called because of rain."[5]

Before play resumed the next day, Foli brought the lineup card out for Expos manager Karl Kuehl so he could apologize for his behavior the previous day. When the action started again in the seventh, Buddy Schultz was on the hill for the Cubs, while Carrithers was still in there for Montreal. In the bottom of the inning, the Cubs made a minor dent in the Expos' lead when Monday drove home shortstop Dave Rosello to make the score 11-4. Foli got that run back with his history-making home run in the top of the eighth. The Cubs scored too little too late in the bottom of the ninth. Third baseman Bill Madlock drove home two runs to end the scoring. The Cubs got some revenge and ended a five-game losing streak at the same time when they beat Montreal 5-4 in the regularly scheduled game.

Foli's cycle was one of the few bright spots in an otherwise forgettable year for Montreal. Kuehl was fired on September 3 after compiling a 43-85 record. Expos management eventually got tired of Foli's tantrums and traded him to the San Francisco Giants on April 27, 1977, in an even-up deal for shortstop Chris Speier, who, ironically, became the second Expo to hit for the cycle.

SOURCES

In addition to the sources listed in the notes, the author consulted:

Baseball-reference.com.

Sarasota Herald-Tribune.

Webster, Gary. *When in Doubt, Fire the Skipper: Midseason Managerial Changes in Major League Baseball* (Jefferson, North Carolina: McFarland & Company, 2014).

NOTES

1   The team had its worst record ever in 1969, the franchise's first season, when it went 52-110.

2   "Cubs' stall tactics backfire," *Daily Herald,* Arlington Heights, Illinois, April 22, 1976.

3   Ian MacDonald, "Umps holler foul at delay tactics," the *Montreal Gazette,* April 22, 1976.

4   Ibid.

5   Ian MacDonald, "Top Expo Foli lets a hot bat do the talking," the *Montreal Gazette,* May 4, 1976.

PARRISH GOES 5-FOR-5, HITS THREE CONSECUTIVE HOMERS

May 29, 1977: Montreal Expos 14, St. Louis Cardinals 4 At Busch Stadium

By Alan Cohen

IN 1976, LARRY PARRISH HAD BATTED ONLY .232 in 154 games, and his prospects in 1977 appeared cloudy. However, he had a torrid spring and was named the starting third baseman by Expos manager Dick Williams. Unfortunately the hopes of spring soon faded as Parrish slumped both at the plate and in the field, and he was benched in favor of left-hand-hitting Wayne Garrett three times in May, as the Expos suffered 15 losses in 17 games, including an 11-game losing streak.

The Expos had not had a winning season during their first eight years and were coming off a 106-loss season in 1976. Manager Williams hardly seemed bound for the Hall of Fame. The Expos had lost 25 of their first 40 games despite the presence of three future Hall of Famers (Tony Perez, Gary Carter, and Andre Dawson) with potent bats. This was offset by an incredibly unreliable pitching staff when Steve Rogers was not on the mound. On May 29 Dan Warthen got the start as the Expos faced the St. Louis Cardinals at Busch Stadium before 15,219 spectators. Pitching for the Cardinals was Bob Forsch, who came into the game with a 7-1 record.

Those who dawdled on their way to the ballpark essentially missed the turning point of the game. The outcome was decided in the top half of the first inning as the Expos exploded for eight runs. The output tied for the Expos' second highest single-inning run total since they first took the field in 1969.

With one out, Chris Speier walked and was moved to second base by an Ellis Valentine single. A double off the bat of Gary Carter scored Speier. A single to right field by Warren Cromartie scored Valentine and walks to Del Unser and Andre Dawson brought

Gary Carter home with the third run of the inning. Larry Parrish, who as the game progressed became his own one-man wrecking crew, contributed to the first-inning onslaught with an opposite-field single to right field that scored his team's fourth and fifth runs. His hit convinced Cardinals manager Vern Rapp that it was not Forsch's day, and he was replaced by Buddy Schultz. A single by Dave Cash plated Dawson with the sixth run. Parrish came around to score the seventh run of the inning when Cardinals right fielder Jerry Mumphrey overthrew third base as Parrish advanced on Cash's single. Speier's single brought Cash home with run number eight.

Wild Dan Warthen, who averaged more than 10 walks per nine innings in 1977 (43 in 38⅔ innings), was staked to an eight-run lead. Would it be enough? With his parents and brother in the stands, having traveled to St. Louis from Omaha, Warthen went to work.

The Cardinals wasted no time chipping away at the Expos' big lead as Mumphrey led off the first inning with a double and came around on a one-out double by Tony Scott. The second inning was quiet as both squads went down in order.

Parrish had his second at-bat in the top of the third and banged out his second single of the afternoon with one out. He advanced to second on a bunt by Warthen and scored when right fielder Mumphrey was unable to handle a fly ball off the bat of Dave Cash for his second error of the game. In two trips, Parrish had come around to score on Mumphrey errors. In his next three trips, such help would not be needed. The Cardinals' Scott homered in the bottom of the inning, but the score through three innings was 9-2 for the Expos. In the top of the fifth, the Cardinals brought in their third pitcher of the game, John Urrea, and with one out Parrish came to the plate for the third time and homered to left-center field to extend the Expos' lead to 10-2. At the time, Parrish was perfectly content with his 3-for-3 performance. "Well, you know, after you get three hits you kinda say, 'Hey, this is a good day.' You get placid," he said after the game.[1] In the bottom of the inning, the Cardinals, aided by two Warthen walks, manufactured a run to cut the deficit to seven runs. Mumphrey walked and advanced to second base on a single by Garry Templeton. A walk to Scott loaded the bases and prompted manager Williams to consider removing his starter. Warthen indeed was one pitch from a trip to the showers when he got Ted Simmons to hit into a double play that scored Mumphrey. Warthen said, "I just took a little off the fastball. He (Simmons) hit the ball pretty good, but was out front."[2] Warthen got the third out on a grounder by Roger Freed, and there was no further damage.

Cardinals manager Rapp was not about to use any more pitchers than necessary and Urrea was still pitching in the seventh inning when two of his pitches were rerouted to the seats by the Expos. Del Unser's two-run homer scored Warren Cromartie, who had singled to lead off the inning. Parrish then came to the plate. Tony Perez, who was sitting the game out after appearing in each of his team's first 40 games, caught Parrish's ear. "C'mon man, what you did today? Three hits. Now that's nuthin'. Now you gotta get four."[3] Parrish took Urrea deep for his second homer and the Expos had a 13-3 lead.

But Parrish's day, and Perez's needling, were not yet complete. As he prepared to leave the dugout for his fifth at-bat, with two out in the ninth, he heard Perez exclaim, "What's four hits, man? That's all you got today. Go get another one."[4] There have been more dramatic situations but nonetheless Parrish, urged on by Perez, came to the plate for the fifth time in the game and slugged his third consecutive homer, this time off Butch Metzger, giving the Expos a 14-3 lead.

Meanwhile, Warthen was cruising along like a ship in the Bermuda Triangle. He walked six batters, and had he looked over his shoulder, he would have seen Billy Atkinson getting ready to enter the game at a moment's notice. Warthen allowed his second homer and fourth extra-base hit of the game as Mike Anderson lifted one out leading off the bottom of the ninth. That finished the scoring, and three outs later Warthen had his second win and his first (and only) complete game of 1977.

The victory was Warthen's 12th and his last in the major leagues. Later that season he was sent to the Phillies and his major-league career ended in 1978 in Houston. He pitched in the minors until 1982.

Gary Carter was the first Expo to hit three consecutive homers, doing so on April 20, 1977, against Pittsburgh. He said, "It's a great thrill. I know because it happened to me."[5]

Parrish, with his 5-for-5 performance, raised his batting average from .237 to .264. The next day, in the first game of a Memorial Day doubleheader against the New York Mets, manager Williams moved Parrish up from eighth in the batting order to sixth, and Larry singled in each of his first two visits to the plate to extend his consecutive hit streak to seven hits in seven at-bats. But his bat cooled off later in the season and his batting average dropped from a high of .271 on May 30 to a final .246.

In the early history of the Expos, Parrish became the third player to have five hits in a game and was the first Expo to score five runs in a game. The 23-year-old Parrish would go on to play for 15 major-league seasons and hit 256 career homers, and would again hit three homers in a game the following season against Atlanta. He played with the Expos through 1981 and was traded to the Texas Rangers in 1982 for Al Oliver. With the Rangers, he had two more three-homer games.

SOURCES

In addition to the sources listed in the notes, the author consulted:

Baseball-Reference.com.

MacDonald, Ian. "Parrish Bashes in Three Homers, Leads Expos, Warthen to Victory," the *Montreal Gazette*, May 30, 1977.

MacDonald, Ian, "Heavier Bat, Light Banter Made Parrish Powderkeg," *The Sporting News*, June 18, 1977.

NewspaperArchive.com.

NOTES

1   Ian MacDonald, the *Montreal Gazette*, May 30, 1977.

2   "Expos Rout Cards, 14-4." *Joplin* (Missouri) *Globe*, May 30, 1977, 4B.

3   MacDonald.

4   MacDonald.

5   "Expos Rout Cards, 14-4." *Joplin* (Missouri) *Globe*, May 30, 1977, 4B.

LARRY PARRISH'S BAT, ELLIS VALENTINE'S ARM HIGHLIGHT EXPOS' COME-FROM-BEHIND VICTORY

June 9, 1978: Montreal Expos 10, Los Angeles Dodgers 9 At Olympic Stadium

By Gregory H. Wolf

WHEN THE MONTREAL EXPOS AND THE LOS Angeles Dodgers headed to *Stade Olympique* to play the second game of a four-game series on June 9, 1978, they were going in seemingly opposite directions. Skipper Dick Williams, in his second year at the Expos' helm, had his club playing its best ball of the year. They were riding a four-game winning streak, had won 11 of their last 15, and trailed the upstart Chicago Cubs by just 1½ games in the National League East (30-24). Tommy Lasorda had guided the tradition-clad Dodgers to the NL pennant the previous year, his first full season as manager, but his club was struggling of late. They had won just four of their last 15 games, transforming a share of the NL West lead into a five-game deficit behind the rival Cincinnati Reds.

The Dodgers were determined to right the ship. They had managed only one hit (Reggie Smith's home run) in a 4-1 loss to Expos ace Steve Rogers the night before. But on this autumn-like evening in Montreal they came out swinging in the first inning against 33-year-old southpaw Rudy May, acquired in the offseason after a career year with the Baltimore Orioles (18-14). Following Bill Russell's one-out single, Smith launched a round-tripper to give Los Angeles a 2-0 lead.

The Dodgers tacked on three more runs on only one hit in the third inning to make it 5-0, as the Expos committed three errors, issued four walks, and had a wild pitch and passed ball. The 33-year-old Smith, en route to the sixth of his seven All-Star berths, led off the inning with a walk and moved to second on a wild pitch. He then stole third and scampered home for the Dodgers' third run on catcher Gary Carter's errant throw to third. But it was a costly run as Smith injured his shoulder, which had undergone an operation two years earlier. (He was sidelined the next 2½ weeks.) Steve Garvey (who had reached on May's error) later scored on reliever Bill Atkinson's throwing error to first, and Dusty Baker (who had singled) sped home on Carter's passed ball to complete the scoring.

Dodgers starter Tommy John, who had recovered from revolutionary elbow surgery in 1974 to win 20 games in 1977, was shaky from the outset. Chris Speier led off the third inning with the Expos' fifth hit of the game, and scored on Tony Perez's one-out double. Four of the next five Montreal hitters collected singles; two of those singles (by Andre Dawson and pinch-hitter Stan Papi) drove in two more runs. Dawson later pulled the Expos to within a run, 5-4, when he raced home on John's bases-loaded wild pitch. "Anyone slower than Dawson wouldn't have scored," wrote Bob Morrissey of the *Montreal Gazette*.[1]

John's struggles continued in the fourth inning. After the 35-year-old hurler hit Warren Cromartie with a pitch, Perez belted another double to tie the game. Carter's single drove in Perez, giving the Expos a 6-5 lead and sending John to the showers. "Many hits against John were squibblers that hardly had the momentum to roll 25 feet," wrote Morrissey about the tough-luck hurler who surrendered 12 hits and was charged with eight runs, all earned.[2] Bobby Castillo relieved John with one out. The 23-year-old righty, in his first full season, intentionally walked Dawson to fill the bases and play for an inning-ending twin killing with slow-footed Larry Parrish the next batter.

Described by Expos beat writer Ian MacDonald as "oft harangued," Parrish had exasperated managers and fans by making an NL-high 93 errors since taking over as Montreal's starting third baseman in 1975, including 12 already in 1978.[3] After batting just .232 and .246 in the previous two seasons, Parrish had gotten off to a promising start at the plate in 1978, but had cooled down and was hitting just .225 (18-for-80) in his last 24 games. "When I'm going bad, I'm my own worst enemy," said the affable Floridian, whose trademark was a powerful swing that sent his cap flying off his head. "I think of my hands and my feet. I don't concentrate on the ball."[4]

The 6-foot-3, 200-pound Parrish belted Castillo's initial offering for a grand slam, the first of five bases-clearing blasts among his 256 career homers. "I knew I hit it good," he said.[5] The crowd of 21,719 cheered wildly as Parrish rounded the bases to put an exclamation point on the six-run inning that gave the Expos a 10-5 lead. The yelling did not die down until Parrish came out of the dugout to don his cap in the first of three standing ovations. "It's a lot easier to play when you're getting ovations like that," he said. "They might even be more of a thrill that hitting the ball."[6]

Castillo's reaction was understandably different. "The first thing I wanted to do when I let it go was call time," said the LA native. "I wanted to put it low and away and maybe get him to hit into a double play."[7] Tommy Lasorda, whose humor and one-liners endeared him to sportswriters throughout his long tenure as Dodgers pilot (1976-1996), quipped, "The first pitch he throws is a hanging slider. I could have hit that."[8]

The Dodgers trimmed the Expos' lead to 10-6 in the sixth inning when Smith's replacement, Lee Lacy, doubled to left field to drive in Bill Russell, who had singled. It was the only run given up by Dan Schatzeder, who took the mound in the fourth and held the Dodgers to three hits in four innings. Two Dodgers relievers, Castillo and knuckleballer Charlie Hough, held the Expos scoreless from the sixth through the eighth inning to set up an exciting conclusion to the game.

Right-handed reliever Mike Garman, who took over in the eighth inning for Montreal, retired Baker for the first out of the ninth before coming undone. He issued consecutive walks to Billy North and pinch-hitter Vic Davalillo and gave up an RBI double to Rick Monday. Rubber-armed southpaw Darold Knowles replaced Garman and walked the first man he faced, Davey Lopes, to fill the bases. Representing the tying run, Russell hit a liner to right field to drive in Davalillo and Monday and bring the Dodgers within one. The speedy Lopes, meanwhile, was determined to make it to third base, thereby challenging right fielder Ellis Valentine.

Since becoming the Expos regular right fielder in 1975, the 23-year-old Valentine had established a reputation as having one of the strongest arms in baseball. He shut down the opponents' running game from first to third, dared hitters to stretch singles into doubles, and forced batters to run out singles instead of jogging to first base. Valentine fielded Russell's liner cleanly and fired a missile to third baseman Parrish that cut Lopes down in a potential game-saving play. "On an average man's arm, [Lopes is] going to make it," reported the *Ottawa Journal*. "[Valentine's] not only got the best arm in baseball, but he's as accurate as any."[9]

"None of the Expos pitchers was effective on this miserably cold night," wrote MacDonald.[10] But Knowles had enough gas to retire Lacy on a grounder to third. Parrish scooped up the ball and fired to Del Unser, who had replaced Perez at first, to preserve the Expos' 10-9 victory. Schatzeder picked up his first win of the season; Knowles earned his third save, while John fell to 7-4.

"That's the sign of a good ballclub, a club that won't give up," said skipper Dick Williams resolutely after the game.[11] The 48-year-old manager missed Valentine's electric throw, one of his league-leading 25 assists on the season. Third-base umpire John Kibler had ejected the feisty pilot earlier in the inning. "I still don't know why he threw me out," said Williams. "He said I should sit down, but I don't have to sit down in my own dugout."[12] The Expos victory marked the first time in franchise history that the club was seven games above .500 (31-24),

SOURCES

In addition to the sources listed in the notes, the author consulted:

Baseball-Reference.com

Retrosheet.org

SABR.org

NOTES

1   Bob Morrissey, "Knew I'd made a mistake—Castillo," the *Montreal Gazette*, June 10, 1978, 40.

2   Ibid.

3   Ian MacDonald, "Big O becomes happy parish for Larry," the *Montreal Gazette*, June 10, 1978, 39.

4   Ibid.

5   Ibid.

6   "Yes, Montreal, Les Expos are for real," *Ottawa* (Ontario) *Journal,* June 10, 1978, 19.

7   Morrissey.

8   Ibid.

9   "Yes, Montreal, Les Expos are for real."

10   MacDonald.

11   "Yes, Montreal, Les Expos are for real."

12   Ibid. The game summary on Retrosheet.org does not indicate that Williams was ejected.

CHRIS SPEIER HITS FOR THE CYCLE

July 20, 1978: Montreal Expos 7, Atlanta Braves 3 At Olympic Stadium

By Norm King

CONSPIRACY THEORISTS LOVE COINCIDENCES. They point out that John F. Kennedy's secretary's name was Lincoln and Lincoln's secretary's name was Kennedy and somehow see that as connecting two presidential assassinations that occurred almost 100 years apart.

What, then, to make of the fact that Tim Foli, the first Expo to hit for the cycle, was traded to the San Francisco Giants in 1977 for Chris Speier, the second Expo to perform the same feat? Foli did it the year before Elvis supposedly died, Speier the year after. Hmmm.

Speier's cycle came after a clubhouse dispute with Expos general manager Charlie Fox, who–here's another coincidence–was his manager in San Francisco and who had engineered the trade that brought him to Montreal. Fox was angry with Speier over his recent prolonged spell of poor hitting that saw his batting average drop from .277 on June 20 to .243 at game time. Expos player representative Steve Rogers got involved because he didn't like the way Fox was talking to Speier. The exchange between Fox and Rogers escalated from a discussion to a profanity-filled argument to an exchange of blows. Fox got Rogers with a good one on the chin.

"I thought that at a certain point the conversation [between Fox and Speier] was becoming very heated," said Rogers. "I think that type of thing is detrimental to a clubhouse atmosphere."[1]

"He had no business interfering when I'm talking with one of my players," said Fox.[2]

Maybe Fox should have berated Speier before every game because the tongue-lashing led to a 4-for-4 night with six RBIs and a run scored.

Old reliable Woodie Fryman, whom the Expos had reacquired from the Chicago Cubs on June 9, started for the Expos against journeyman Braves pitcher Jamie Easterly.[3] After a scoreless first, Fryman faced left fielder Jeff Burroughs, third baseman Bob Horner, and first baseman Dale Murphy, the meat of the Braves lineup, in the second. The three sluggers would tie for the team lead in home runs at the end of the season with 23 apiece, but they had very little to do with the only Braves rally of this game. Burroughs struck out to start the inning and Horner followed that with a groundout to short. Murphy did a little better than his fellow sluggers, getting on base with a single, then moving to second on another single by second baseman Glenn Hubbard. Fryman walked catcher Joe Nolan to load the bases with Easterly coming up. That tactic didn't work—he walked the opposing pitcher with the bases loaded to bring Murphy in from third.

Chris Speier

Shortstop Jerry Royster drove in two more runs with the third single of the frame. The Braves led 3-0.

Speier brought the Expos within a run in the bottom of the second. With one out, Warren Cromartie walked and advanced to second on a single by Gary Carter. Speier followed with a triple–perhaps the most difficult of the hits needed for a cycle–that drove in two runs. The score stood 3-2 Atlanta after two.

The next few innings were scoreless, but Speier hit a single in the fourth to continue his perfect night at the plate. He put the Expos ahead to stay in the sixth, belting a three-run homer off after third baseman Larry Parrish singled and Easterly hit Cromartie with a pitch.

When you give up a triple and a home run to a player who had only three triples and five homers all season, the evidence indicates that you're having a bad night on the mound, which Easterly clearly was. With the score Speier 5, Atlanta 3 after six frames, Braves manager Bobby Cox decided that Easterly would not be prevailing, so he brought left-hander Mickey Mahler in to pitch the seventh. Expos center fielder Andre Dawson was tired of Speier having all the fun, so he took things into his own hands–and feet. He walked, stole second, reached third on a wild pitch by Mahler, and scored on a balk to make the score 6-3 Expos.

Speier, though, wasn't finished. Carter led off the eighth with a walk and raced home on the double that completed Speier's cycle. In the ninth, the Braves' Hubbard led off with a single and moved to second on a walk to pinch-hitter Bob Beale. Fryman gave way to Mike Garman, who earned the save. Final score Expos 7, Braves 3.

In the clubhouse after the game, Speier's locker was the magnet for the media, who not only wanted to ask about the cycle, but about the spat with Fox as well.

He didn't want to talk about the ruckus, and he didn't seem overly impressed with his achievement, either.[4]

"I had no idea what I had done, not even after I did it," he said. "It was only when I went back out to the infield when I thought about my at-bat."[5]

Years later Speier provided more details on the confrontation with Fox to journalist Alain Usereau:

There was probably a lot of frustration. I remember Charlie coming in. You have to know Charlie Fox, very old-school guy, he talks, screams and raves. That's how Charlie was and he came down. At that time I wasn't doing very well, and he came down to the clubhouse, telling me to step it up a little bit. I got a little upset about it. That was Charlie.[6]

Fox's fight with Rogers seemed to have a detrimental effect on the team. The Expos embarked on a seven-game losing streak, and what was supposed to be a promising season proved to be a disappointment. Fox was fired after the season ended.

SOURCES

In addition to the sources listed in the notes, the author also consulted:

Baseball-reference.com.

Pittsburgh Press.

NOTES

1   Ian MacDonald, "Expos' spat over, but still unresolved," The *Montreal Gazette*, Montreal, July 22, 1978.

2   Ibid.

3   Fryman had his first stint with Montreal in 1975-76. After his return, he was with the Expos until his career ended in 1983.

4   Speier hit for the cycle again on July 9, 1988, as the San Francisco Giants pounded the St. Louis Cardinals 21-2.

5   Canadian Press, "Expo Bickering Fires Up Speier," *Ottawa Journal*, July 21, 1978.

6   Alain Usereau, *The Expos in Their Prime* (Jefferson, North Carolina: McFarland & Company, 2013).

EXPOS VISIT THE LAUNCHING PAD

July 30, 1978: Montreal Expos 19, Atlanta Braves 0 At Fulton County Stadium

By Alan Cohen

THE 1978 MONTREAL EXPOS WERE HOPING TO finish above .500 and had assembled a cast of hitters that included future Hall of Famers Andre Dawson, Gary Carter, and Tony Perez. Ross Grimsley and Steve Rogers headed their pitching staff, and manager Dick Williams was in his second year at the helm. As late as May 17 they were in first place and then somebody pressed the down button on the elevator. As July came to a close, the Expos were in fourth place in the six-team East Division of the National League. After a 9-6 loss at Atlanta on July 29, their record stood at 48-57 and they were 9½ games out of first place. The Braves, at 48-54, were in fifth place in the NL West, 12½ games out of first.

When the sun came up on Sunday, July 30, the Expos hadn't a clue as to how this day would eclipse anything that had come before, or since. Williams handed the ball to Woodie Fryman. The 38-year-old brought a 5-7 record into the contest and his mound opponent was the Braves' Tommy Boggs. During his three years in the big leagues, Boggs had amassed a record of 3-15 with an ERA of 4.44. However, in his most recent start, on July 25, he had recorded the first shutout of his career, blanking the Philadelphia Phillies 4-0, striking out seven batters.

Fryman, who had come over from the Chicago Cubs in June for his second stint with the Expos, was staked to a one-run lead in the top of the second inning. Larry Parrish, en route to a 4-for-6 performance, opened the frame with a double and scored on a single by Gary Carter. The bleeding was stopped momentarily when right fielder Gary Matthews gunned down Warren Cromartie at the plate later in the inning.

In the top of the third, the Expos removed any doubt about the game's outcome with four homers as they took a 9-0 lead. Andre Dawson started the barrage with a leadoff homer and after the Expos had put Ellis Valentine on third and Tony Perez on first, Parrish came up for the second time in as many innings and clouted a three-run shot to knock out Boggs. On came Craig Skok and by the time he had escaped the minefield, Dave Cash had also banged a three-run homer and Andre Dawson had hit his second solo shot of the inning.

Meanwhile, Fryman was sailing along. Through three innings, he had kept the Braves scoreless on two hits. Parrish was the leadoff hitter for the Expos in inning four and he banged his second homer of the game to stretch the lead to 10-0. Skok escaped further damage in the inning. With the Braves hopelessly behind, manager Bobby Cox decided to send Skok out for another inning in the fifth. Skok did not exactly justify his manager's faith in his ability to avoid further damage. After two quick outs he allowed a single to Ellis Valentine and up stepped 37-year-old Tony Perez. The former Reds slugger, who was in his second year with the Expos, belted a Skok pitch out of the park to extend the Expos' lead to 12-0. Up stepped Parrish. In his fourth trip to the plate in as many innings, he belted his third consecutive homer and the Expos were up 13-0. Around the time the ball landed, Skok had a visitor. Bobby Cox had seen enough and handed the ball to Mickey Mahler. Few of the announced 10,834 fans in attendance were still around at that point, and Skok's line was horrific: 2⅔ innings, nine hits, eight runs, and five homers. His ERA had ballooned from 2.45 to 4.29.

Once the Expos had completed their turn at bat, Williams decided to give some of his players a rest and Perez, Cash, Cromartie, and Valentine were replaced by Tom Hutton, Stan Papi, Del Unser, and Sam Mejias.

Larry Parrish

The Braves continued to come up empty against Fryman, and the Expos, showing no mercy, victimized Mahler as they had done his predecessors. Chris Speier homered with Carter on board and Dawson contributed an RBI single as the Expos tallied three in the sixth inning to go up 16-0. Speier, who went 2-for-3 in the game, was given the rest of the afternoon off. With two outs, Parrish stepped up to the plate. Could he join the exclusive group of players who had hit four homers in a game? "Yes, I was going for number four," he said after the game. "When you're that far ahead, you can start thinking about personal records. And I was trying real hard for number four. I was trying so hard, I struck out twice on breaking balls."[1] He struck out in the sixth and eighth innings, and both time was the last out in the inning.

Pepe Frias replaced Speier and he was not about to miss out on the fun––never mind the score. In the top of the seventh inning, Gary Carter doubled for his third hit of the game and Frias drove him home with a single.

Cox was not about to use any more pitchers than necessary, and Mahler was in for the duration. Miracle of miracles, the Expos did not score in the eighth inning. Mahler recorded the third out when he struck out Parrish for the second time, but Larry had already had a great game with a double and three homers.

Were there any hits left in those Expos bats? They had scored 17 runs on 24 hits through eight innings, but not everyone had been able to make a contribution. Also, as Parrish noted, "We were aware that we had tied the major-league record when we got the eighth home run, and we all were trying for the record."[2] So it was that Del Unser, who entered the game in the sixth inning, led off the top of the ninth with a single. Gary Carter followed with his second double, and fourth hit of the game.

After a fly ball by Frias scored Unser, Fryman, who was no slouch with the bat, stepped to the plate. In his first 12 seasons, he batted .142 with four doubles and two homers. He had a single and a sacrifice bunt in his first five plate appearances in this game. Chances were he would not be bunting this time around. Swinging away, he just missed a homer, doubling off Mahler for the Expos' team record 28th hit and sending Carter home with Montreal's 19th and last run. After the game, manager Williams noted, "I thought the one Woodie Fryman hit was out."[3]

Fryman's mound work was not quite finished. He allowed his seventh and final hit after two groundouts, and when Hutton fielded a grounder by the Braves' Joe Nolan and stepped on first base for the final out, the Expos had the most lopsided victory in their history. Williams spoke highly of Fryman's effort: "You don't figure in that kind of heat and humidity for anybody to go too long, and then to throw the shutout besides and go the full distance, it's truly amazing."[4]

In addition to tying the major-league record with eight homers, the Expos' 58 total bases set a National League record. Their four home runs in the third inning set a team record.

Andre Dawson, who was the 20th major leaguer to hit two homers in the same inning, was inducted into the Hall of Fame in 2010. Tony Perez, whose fifth-inning homer was the 305th of his career, went on to play a total of 23 seasons, was named to seven All-Star teams, batted in over 100 runs seven times, and was elected to the Hall of Fame in 2000.

On May 29, 1977, Larry Parrish had become the second Expos player to have three homers in a game, the third to have five hits in a game, and the first to score five runs in a game. In his second three-homer game with the Expos, on July 30, 1978, he set a team record with 14 total bases in four consecutive at-bats. The 24-year-old Parrish would go on to play for 15 major-league seasons and hit 256 homers. He would hit three homers in a game twice more during his career.

SOURCES

In addition to the sources listed in the notes, the author consulted:

Baseball-Reference.com.

NOTES

1   "Eight Homers Cap Expos' 19-0 Win," *San Bernardino County Sun-Telegram,* July 31, 1978.

2   Ibid.

3   "Expos Blast off at Launching Pad," *Ottawa Journal,* July 31, 1978.

4   *Kingsport* (Tennessee) *Times,* July 31, 1978.

TWENTY WINS FOR ROSS THE BOSS

Oct 1, 1978: Montreal Expos 5, St. Louis Cardinals 1 At Busch Stadium

By Gregory H. Wolf

SOUTHPAW ROSS GRIMSLEY WAITED UNTIL THE last inning of the last game of the 1978 season to become the Montreal Expos' first and only 20-game winner. With one out and two men on in the final frame of a tie game against the St. Louis Cardinals on October 1, Grimsley strolled to the plate. "He was going to go all the way," said Expos manager Dick Williams. "I debated whether to have him bunt, but after he faked one he had the defense guessing and everything worked out perfectly."[1] Grimsley singled to load the bases, and the Expos went on to score four runs and win 5-1 in the Gateway City.

Grimsley was one of baseball's most colorful characters during the 1970s. He was superstitious, carried around charms on game days, and even consulted a witch to help him end a slump during his rookie season with the Cincinnati Reds in 1971. After three productive years with the Reds, who were known for their conservative and staid approach to the game, the short-haired, cleancut Grimsley was traded to the Baltimore Orioles. A "consummate free spirit," Grimsley began sporting his trademark long, shaggy, curly hair, which bulged from underneath his cap, along with a bushy mustache.[2] Nicknamed "Scuzzy" for his unkempt look, Grimsley could also pitch, winning 18 games and tossing a career-best 295⅔ innings for the AL East champs in 1974. He had large, penetrating green eyes, which he often accentuated with colored contact lenses, which gave rise to another moniker, "Crazy Eyes."

The Expos signed Grimsley as a free agent after finishing fifth (75-87) in the NL East in 1977, Williams' first season as the club's pilot.[3] A proven winner and workhorse, Grimsley sported a career record of 87-68 and had averaged more than 200 innings pitched per season over his seven-year career. With Grimsley and Steve Rogers (17-16, 301⅔ innings in 1977) at the front

of the rotation, the best young catcher in the league (Gary Carter), and one of the best outfield trios in baseball (Warren Cromartie, Andre Dawson, and Ellis Valentine) the Expos were expected to challenge for the division crown in 1978.

The script did not go as planned despite a remarkably healthy team. After flirting with first place through June 9, Montreal slumped, winning just 30 of its next 79 games, and finishing in fourth place. The players taking the field on that Sunday afternoon had little to play for other than pride and personal records.

A sparse St. Louis crowd of just 6,182 showed up to watch the season finale. The three-game series drew fewer than 15,000 people, as many Redbird fans apparently wished to forget the tradition-laden club's worst season since 1924. The Cardinals went through three

Ross Grimsley

managers that season and finished fifth (69-93) in the NL East, ahead of only the moribund Chicago Cubs.[4]

The Expos came out swinging; they loaded the bases on two singles and a walk against Cardinals starter Pete Vuckovich, but did not score. One of the Redbirds' few bright spots that season, the 25-year-old right-hander, whose Fu Manchu rivaled Grimsley's walrus 'stache, had been acquired from the Toronto Blue Jays in the offseason. He worked his way into the starting rotation in '78 after primarily relieving in his first three years in the big leagues, and finished with a 12-12 record and an impressive 2.54 ERA.

The Expos scored the game's first run in the fourth inning. First baseman Tony Perez led off with a single and moved to second on Gary Carter's one-out walk. Chris Speier then singled to drive in Perez. Vuckovich got out of the jam by inducing third baseman Stan Papi to hit into an inning-ending double play, one of the Cardinals' three twin killings that day.

Earlier in his career, Grimsley had relied on his fastball to overpower hitters, but after his trade to the Orioles he developed into one of the best slowball hurlers in baseball. "Changing speeds," responded Grimsley when asked about his success. "That's the secret. The way you can throw it right down the pipe and the hitter is off balance. They have no power. They can only hit with their hands."[5] Blessed with good control, Grimsley had an arsenal including a slider, curveball, sinker, and changeup, all of which he threw at varying speeds. "When you have both the location and you are changing speeds, you have the hitter really confused," he said. "That's real fun."[6]

Grimsley baffled Cardinals hitters all afternoon with "his tantalizing assortment of throwing speeds," wrote Expos beat reporter Ian MacDonald.[7] The Cardinals tied the game in the fifth inning when catcher Steve Swisher led off with a triple and scored on second baseman Mike Tyson's sacrifice fly.

The Expos' bats woke up in the ninth inning against rookie right-hander, Dan O'Brien, the Cardinals' second reliever of the game. With one out, Speier walked, Papi reached on an error, and Grimsley singled. Second baseman Dave Cash belted a two-run double

to give the Expos a 3-1 lead. Three batters later, Perez singled with two outs to drive in two more. It was the "Big Dog's" fifth hit of the game, matching a career high. Cromartie popped up to end the inning. He needed two hits in the game to finish the season with a .300 batting average, but went 0-for-4.

Grimsley, no doubt energized by the chance to reach a milestone all pitchers dream about, pitched a 1-2-3 ninth. First baseman Roger Freed "took a mighty swing and missed one of Grimsely's slower-than-slow deliveries to end the game," wrote Ian MacDonald.[8] Grimsley's teammates "charged the mound in ecstasy," celebrating as if they had just clinched a division crown instead of a 5-1 victory.[9] Stockily built backstop Gary Carter "crushed Grimsley as he clamped on a bear hug and waved the pitcher up and down like a rag doll," reported the *Montreal Gazette*.[10]

"This is the best I've pitched through an entire season, said Grimsley after completing the game in just 1 hour and 59 minutes.[11] In his career year, "Crazy Eyes" finished with a 20-11 record, etched out a 3.05 ERA in 263 innings, and completed 19 of 36 starts; he was also named to his first and only All-Star team in July. One day after the season ended, he was unanimously chosen as the team's player of the year.

Grimsley's personal accomplishment was tempered by the Expos' poor season, which prompted him to voice his frustration with the selfishness of some of his teammates. "Some players will have to change attitudes," he said sternly after the game.[12] Despite his quirkiness, Grimsley was a team player and knew the kind of commitment needed to win. He had pitched for division winners with the Reds (1972 and 1973) and the Orioles (1974).

"They must sacrifice personal interests and put the team first," he said. "I have played for winners. I know what I am talking about."[13] Hard-nosed skipper Williams, who had guided the Boston Red Sox to the "Impossible Dream" American League pennant in 1967 and the Oakland A's to two World Series titles (1972 and 1973) echoed Grimsley's sentiments. "[It was a] sour season but for a few individuals."[14]

SOURCES

In addition to the sources listed in the notes, the author consulted:

Baseball-Reference.com.

Retrosheet.org.

SABR.org.

NOTES

1 Ian MacDonald, "Cro's .300 Gamble Misses," the *Montreal Gazette*, October 2, 1978, 51.

2 Bruce Markusen, "Cooperstown Confidential: Ross Grimsley and the swingin' 70s," *The Hardball Times*, May 21, 2010. hardballtimes.com/cooperstown-confidential-ross-grimsley-and-the-swingin-70s/.

3 Coincidentally, Grimsley's father, Ross Sr., who spent 16 years hurling in the minor leagues, was a reliever for the Triple-A Montreal Royals of the International League in 1951. He also had a cup of coffee with the Chicago White Sox that year, his only season in the big leagues.

4 The three mangers were Vern Rapp (6-11), Jack Krol (1-1), and Ken Boyer (62-81).

5 *The Sporting News*, April 29, 1978, 13.

6 Ibid.

7 Ian MacDonald, "Cro's .300 Gamble Misses."

8 Ian MacDonald, "Grimsley Unanimous Pick for Expos' Player of the Year," the *Montreal Gazette*, October 3, 1978, 40.

9 Ibid.

10 Ibid.

11 Ian MacDonald, "Cro's .300 Gamble Misses."

12 Ian MacDonald, "Grimsley Unanimous Pick for Expos' Player of the Year."

13 Ibid.

14 Ian MacDonald, "Cro's .300 Gamble Misses."

HOW 'BOUT THEM EXPOS

May 29-31, 1979: Montreal Expos 9, Philadelphia Phillies 0
Montreal Expos 2, Philadelphia Phillies 0
Montreal Expos 1, Philadelphia Phillies 0
At Olympic Stadium

By Norm King

IN FOOTBALL THEY TALK ABOUT "STATEMENT" games, when Team A thrashes Team B, thus sending a message to the opponent and the world that Team A is damn good and don't you forget it.

There are too many games in a baseball season to pinpoint one match as a "statement" game. But the Montreal Expos had a statement series when they swept the Philadelphia Phillies May 29-31, 1979, with three complete-game, error-free shutouts that told the rest of the National League that the mediocre teams of the Expos' early years were no more.

The Expos had never played above .500 prior to the 1979 season. They won 79 games in 1973 and 1974, but had never had a truly successful season. During those years, however, they had developed terrific young talent, including Gary Carter, Andre Dawson (both future Hall of Famers), Larry Parrish, and Steve Rogers. The team was starting to jell in 1979 and was off to its best start ever with a 25-15 record when Philadelphia came to town.

The Phillies were no slouches; they won the National League East Division title three consecutive seasons and had future Hall of Famers Mike Schmidt and Steve Carlton on their roster. They came into Olympic Stadium sporting a 27-17 record, a half-game behind Montreal. They also wanted a measure of revenge because the Expos had swept them rather convincingly at Veterans Stadium May 18-20 by scores of 5-3, 10-5, and 10-6.

Game One saw Rogers matched up against veteran Dick Ruthven. Ruthven was in his second stint with the Phillies; he broke in with them in 1973, then pitched

for the Atlanta Braves before returning to the Phils during the 1978 season.[1]

After a scoreless first inning, the Expos took the lead in the second. Tony Perez led off with a double, but could not advance when Gary Carter reached first on an error by third baseman Mike Schmidt. Larry Parrish singled, but Carter overslid second and was out 9-3-4. With runners on first and third, Chris Speier doubled, scoring Perez and Parrish, to give the Expos a 2-0 lead.

Perhaps this game could be called the "Ellis Valentine's Day Massacre" because if there was another star in the game besides Rogers, it was the Expos' right fielder, who hit a three-run homer in the fifth as part of a five-run rally that put to rest any thoughts of a Phillies comeback.

Rogers started the fifth with a single, and was sacrificed to second by leadoff hitter Andre Dawson. Rodney Scott singled, and with runners on first and third, Warren Cromartie doubled to drive both runners home. Ruthven walked Tony Perez intentionally with first base open, and after Carter moved the runners up with a groundout to third, Valentine launched a bomb that put the Expos up 7-0 and brought Ruthven's evening to an end. Rawly Eastwick relieved him.

Scott led off the seventh with a walk, but was forced at second on a fielder's choice by Cromartie. Cromartie then scored on a double to right by Tony Perez. One out later, Valentine got his fourth RBI of the night when he drove home Tommy Hutton (who was pinch-running for Perez) with a double.

Rogers, meanwhile, pitched as if he were teaching an Arthur Murray dance class. After giving up a single to Bob Boone to start the second inning, it was 1-2-3, 1-2-3, as Rogers retired 20 of the next 21 batters he faced. He gave up two two-out hits in the eighth and a single to Greg Luzinski in the ninth, but was never in serious trouble. The fans acknowledged Rogers' effort with a two-minute standing ovation when he came to bat in the bottom of the seventh inning.

The players were excited after the victory, but veteran Speier warned his teammates that one victory does not a pennant make: "We've got to keep an even keel," he said after the game. "Even if we sweep the Phillies we can't stop there because we have other teams to play. We have to go out there with the same attitude."[2]

Attitude was practically the middle name of Bill Lee, the Expos' starter for Game Two. "Spaceman" came to the Expos from the Red Sox after the 1978 season in an even-up deal for utility infielder Stan Papi because Lee did not get along with Red Sox manager Don Zimmer—he once called Zimmer a gerbil—or the team's front office. Lee's opponent was Nino Espinosa, who had a 5-4 record going into the game.

This one was over early, literally, as the Expos triumphed 2-0 in a game that whizzed by in only one hour and 53 minutes. Carter provided the offense in the second inning when he followed a Perez single with his ninth home run of the season. (He finished with 22 homers and 75 RBIs.)

Lee pitched well, but didn't dominate. In going all the way, he gave up six hits, struck out five, and walked two. He also pitched from the seventh inning on without his fastball, according to Expos manager Dick Williams.

"He told me he only had three fastballs left in the sixth inning," said Williams. "He used two of them up on Luzinski's ground out [to end] that inning."[3]

Lee was aided by the Phillies' inability to drive in runners from second base. They had runners at the keystone sack in five of the game's nine innings, yet were unable to score. None of these runners even reached third.

"We haven't had a key hit in five days," lamented Phillies manager Danny Ozark.[4]

Espinosa, for his part, deserved a better fate. On most nights a pitching line of two runs on four hits with zero walks and one strikeout over six innings would garner a victory, but that's baseball. Ozark pinch-hit Jose Cardenal for Espinosa in the sixth, and put Tug McGraw on the mound for the seventh and eighth. McGraw gave up no runs on one hit, with one walk and one strikeout.

Anyone who had a manicure prior to going to Olympic Stadium for Game Three regretted that decision because they saw a nail-biter. Scott Sanderson, 3-3 going into the game, had the unenviable task of keeping the Expos' shutout streak alive against Larry Christenson, who was 0-1.

Ty Cobb would have loved this game, as the Expos scored the only run on good old-fashioned small ball in the bottom of the first inning. Dawson led off with a double, was sacrificed to third by second baseman Rodney Scott, and scored on a Cromartie sacrifice fly. The rest of the game was pitching and defense. The Phillies got only one runner as far as third base (Luzinski singled in the fourth with one out and moved to third on a single by Del Unser). That threat ended when Boone grounded into a 6-4-3 double play.

Poor Christenson. After giving up the run in the first, he allowed only one other baserunner—Scott singled in the fourth and was erased on a double play—until he was lifted for a pinch-hitter in the top of the eighth.

Sanderson finished with a flourish against the meat of the Phillies order. He started the ninth inning by striking out Bake McBride, got Schmidt on a popup to short, then struck Luzinski out to complete the win.

After that series, the two teams' fortunes went in opposite directions. The Phillies finished fourth with an 84-78 record after winning three straight division titles. The Expos won 95 games, but lost the pennant race on the last day of the season to the Pittsburgh Pirates. If you ask the Expos players, that series went a long way toward instilling the confidence they needed to win.

"That series, I think, helped everyone on the team feel we did have a championship-calibre [club]," said Sanderson.[5]

"It was a real sign we had arrived," agreed Rogers. "We were legitimate."[6]

SOURCES

In addition to the sources listed in the notes, the author consulted:

Baseball-reference.com.

Galveston Daily News.

NOTES

1   Philadelphia traded Ruthven to the White Sox on December 10, 1975, along with Alan Bannister and Roy Thomas for Mike Buskey and Jim Kaat. The White Sox traded Ruthven to Atlanta two days later with Ken Henderson and Ozzie Osborn for Larvell Blanks and Ralph Garr.

2   Terry Scott, "Expos must 'keep an even keel'—Speier," *Ottawa Journal*, May 30, 1979.

3   Glenn Cole, "Carter's HR wins it," the *Montreal Gazette*, May 31, 1979.

4   Ibid.

5   Alain Usereau, *The Expos in Their Prime,* (Jefferson, North Carolina: McFarland & Company, 2013), 53.

6   Ibid.

BACK-TO-BACK-TO-BACK JACKS

June 17, 1979: Montreal Expos 19, Houston Astros 3 At Olympic Stadium

By Norm King

WE ALL REMEMBER OUR FIRST TIME. WE FELT anxious, excited, nervous, hoping that we wouldn't get hurt or screw it up. Ultimately we hoped for a happy ending.

There's only one first time when your team goes from being an expansion punching bag to a kick-ass pennant contender (what were you thinking about?). For Montreal Expos fans, that year was 1979, when an 11-year-old franchise that had never played above .500 was finally sniffing the rarefied air of first place deep into the season.

"For fans inured to the perennial success of the National Hockey League's Canadiens, Montreal's sports is proving anything but blasé in its support of the baseball Expos," wrote a Canadian Press reporter. "The 11th year National League club is making its most credible run yet at the East Division title, and fans are flocking to Olympic Stadium in what can be projected as record numbers."[1]

The team's young talent had finally matured and was beating opponents with pitching, speed, defense, and hitting. On some nights they would use all of these elements. On other nights only one was required. On June 17, 1979, the Expos chose to use hitting against Joe Niekro and the Houston Astros. Boy, did they use it! Astros pitchers left the game with cricks in their necks from whipping their heads around to watch baseball after baseball travel deep into the Olympic Stadium seats. The Expos tied a team record for runs in a game, banged out 24 hits, including five home runs, and hit back to back-to-back home runs for the first time in franchise history as they pounded Houston 19-3 before 30,245 fans in a battle of National League division leaders.

No National League pitcher was hotter than Niekro was going into the game. He had a 10-2 record with a 2.43 ERA, and had won nine consecutive decisions,

including eight starts in a row. The knuckleballer was in a groove. Expos starter Dan Schatzeder had a 1-1 record as he was used primarily out of the bullpen. This game marked his 13th appearance, but only his fourth start.

Niekro may have known pretty early that this wasn't his night. He walked Expos leadoff hitter Warren Cromartie, who came home two outs later on Tony Perez's first homer of the game. Niekro got through the bottom of the second inning unscathed, although he walked both number-eight hitter Chris Speier and Schatzeder with two out.

Niekro got the first two outs of the third inning easily enough when he struck out Rodney Scott and Andre Dawson. Then the floodgates opened. Perez singled, then Niekro hit Carter with a pitch; they both scored on a Valentine double. Parrish followed that up with a two-run shot to make the score 6-0. Speier singled, and in a case of adding insult to injury, Schatzeder doubled to drive in the Montreal shortstop. That was enough for Astros manager Bill Virdon, who replaced Niekro with George Throop. Cromartie greeted Throop with a single to bring home Schatzeder, making the score 8-0 and completing the line on Niekro, whose ERA for the year ballooned from 2.43 to 3.00.

Art Howe hit a two-out solo shot in the top of the fourth to make the score 8-1, but that dinger only served to rile Expos batters in the bottom of the inning. Dawson led off with a single, then fans heard the thwap, thwap, thwap of Perez, Carter, and Valentine going yard one after the other, forcing Virdon to visit the mound again with a towel and a bar of soap. Bert Roberge was the next victim, er, pitcher, and the Montreal supporters were thrilled with what their team did to the hurler with the French-sounding name. Parrish greeted Monsieur Roberge with a single. Speier doubled to drive Parrish home and Schatzeder got his second RBI of the game with another base hit — the team's seventh consecutive safety, which tied another club record. Schatzeder then showed his inexperience as a baserunner when he went too far up the line on a Cromartie fly ball and was doubled off first. Scott, the only regular who didn't get a hit in the game, grounded out to Roberge to end the inning with the Expos ahead 14-1.

At this point Expos manager Dick Williams decided to rest the regulars and turn things over to the bench, otherwise known as the BUS Squad. "BUS" stood for Broke Underrated Superstars, and was the brainchild of Expos sub Tommy Hutton during spring training in Daytona Beach, Florida.

"Daytona Beach is a long way away from most of the other spring training sites," said Hutton. "The Carters and the Valentines, the star players, didn't make a lot of those trips, if you know what I mean. I just thought they ought to call us the BUS squad, 'cause we're always on this bus. [M]ost of us weren't high-paid players, we were all underrated and none of us were superstars, so [we] were the Broke Underrated Superstars."[2]

Besides having a name that was good for team spirit, the BUS squad also provided the bench strength that every contending club needs. Williams gave them an opportunity to strut their stuff in this game and they took full advantage of it, but not before Houston got its last two runs of the game in the top of the sixth. Pinch-hitter Jimmy Sexton started the inning off with a single. One out later, he moved to second on a single by Jeffrey Leonard and scored on yet another single, this time by Enos Cabell. Howe walked to load the bases, then Julio Gonzalez, pinch-hitting for pitcher Tom Dixon (he pitched the fifth), hit a groundball to Tony Solaita, who had replaced Perez at first. Solaita threw to second for the force on Howe, during which Leonard scored from third. Cabell also tried to score on the play, but was thrown out at the plate. The score was now 14-3 Expos.

Williams made an unusual move in the bottom of the sixth, probably because the substitutions he had made thinned out his bench. With one on and one

Tony Perez

out and the Astros' Randy Niemann on the mound, Williams used another pitcher, David Palmer, to pinch-hit for Schatzeder, who had gone 2-for-2 with two RBIs. The move backfired as Palmer ended up hitting into a double play.[3] Palmer then came on to pitch perfect seventh and eighth innings.

The BUS squad got into the scoring fun in the bottom of the seventh. Cromartie, the only regular to play the whole game, led off and said "Hello Niemann" with a double. Dave Cash, playing second in place of Scott, singled to drive home Cromartie and moved to second on the throw to the plate. One out later, he scored on a single by Solaita. Solaita himself moved to third on a double by backup catcher Duffy Dyer, and they both scored on a triple by Hutton, who was spelling Valentine in right field. Hutton came home on Ken Macha's single (Macha was playing third base for Parrish). That made the score 19-3.

There was no more scoring after that. Frank Riccelli gave up one harmless Expos single in the bottom of the eighth, and Rudy May got out of a bases-loaded jam in the ninth to end it.

The blowout was ironic because Williams decided to give the players a break from batting practice before the game. It was Father's Day and with the players' families there, Williams told his charges to report at 12:30 P.M., one hour before game time. Who's to say if that had anything to do with it, but Cromartie's analysis probably summed it up best:

"It was one of those days," he said.[4]

NOTES

1   "Habs not only game in town," *Ottawa Journal*, June 18, 1979.

2   Alain Usereau, *The Expos in Their Prime: The Short-Lived Glory of Montreal's Team, 1977–84* (Jefferson, North Carolina: McFarland & Company, 2013), 49.

3   Schatzeder had a pretty good season with the bat by a pitcher's standards. He batted .216 with one home run and 8 RBIs.

4   "Expos Thrash Astros," *Ottawa Journal*, June 18, 1979.

EXPOS REGAIN FIRST PLACE
FROM PIRATES

September 24, 1979: Montreal Expos 7, Pittsburgh Pirates 6 At Three Rivers Stadium

By Rod Mickleburgh

IN 10 YEARS OF MOSTLY FUTILE BASEBALL, THE Montreal Expos had fluttered few Canadian hearts outside Quebec. Despite some solid players and occasional individual brilliance, they had yet to finish a single season with a winning record. All that changed in the late summer of 1979. Buoyed by a roster of emerging young stars that included future Hall of Famers Gary Carter and Andre Dawson, augmented by a good mix of dependable veterans, the Expos went on a tear that had them battling for the team's first pennant throughout September with the powerful Pittsburgh Pirates. Awakening from their long baseball slumber, Canadians from coast to coast were caught up in a frenzy of Expo fever. They hung on every game. They bombarded the Canadian Broadcasting Corporation with complaints whenever the hapless Toronto Blue Jays were on TV instead of the Expos. Media accreditations tripled, as newspapers from across Canada sent reporters to cover the team.[1]

From late August to mid-September, the Expos won 17 out of 18 games. They couldn't seem to lose. Sportswriters began calling them "the miraculous Expos" for all their comebacks and late-inning heroics. They stole one game against the Cubs with two out in the bottom of the ninth when Rusty Staub's harmless bouncer hit an infield seam zipper that caused the ball to carom high off the first baseman's glove and allowed the tying and winning runs to score. Adding to the stretch saga was an incredible spate of doubleheaders. Forced into a rain-induced horror show of Ernie Banks' cheery mantra "Let's play two!" they had to endure six doubleheaders in 10 days, including two back-to-back twin bills.

Yet crusty field boss Dick Williams managed his overtaxed pitching staff brilliantly, while deploying to perfection pinch-runners, pinch-hitters, and fill-ins from Tommy Hutton's celebrated BUS (Broke Under-rated Superstars) squad, when regulars needed a rest. "Dick Williams was a genius," recalled Expos hurler Bill Lee. "He had switch-hitters, left- and right-handed relievers. He could make moves other teams couldn't."[2]

Despite their win streak, the Expos couldn't shake the Pirates, led by 39-year-old Willie Stargell, who were on a magical run of their own. The Expos did not nose in front until September 13, by all of 3 percentage points. Thereafter, the lead changed hands like a greasy pigskin.

Finally, with one week left in the season, it was showdown time. Clinging nervously to a half-game lead, the Expos headed to Pittsburgh for a four-game, head-to-head match-up against the Pirates.

In Montreal, the tension was almost unbearable. The *Montreal Gazette* newspaper cartoonist Aislin captured the city's mood with a cartoon of a priest counseling a young man on his knees: "Yes, my son, it would be sinful to pray for Dave Parker to break a leg. On the other hand, just a slight sprain might add up to nothing more than a few Hail Mary's...."[3] The rest of the nation held its breath, too. For the first time, a Canadian team had a whiff of baseball's storied postseason. Expomania was off the charts.

Naturally, the series started with yet another doubleheader, this one a twi-nighter. The Pirates were a confident bunch. The Expos always had trouble beating them. Just a week earlier, on September 16-17,

Tommy Hutton

the Bucs had walked into the Big O and taken two straight from the home team.

Game One followed the script. Overawed by the moment and the raucous Pittsburgh crowd, the young Expos went down meekly 5-2, committing three errors. The Pirates were back on top.

Game Two started out even worse. After five innings, Pittsburgh had raced to a 6-2 lead against Montreal starter Rudy May, helped by three more Expos errors, all by second baseman Dave Cash. The Pirates even managed to get four starting innings out of aging retread and recent pickup Dock Ellis. The Expos also lost Carter for the season with a jammed thumb from a play at the plate in the fourth inning. They seemed as dead as the proverbial doornail. Then, against all expectations, it became a night of the improbable. As the clock ticked toward midnight, Dick Williams worked his magic.

Bench warmer Duffy Dyer, a lifetime .221 hitter who replaced Carter, promptly knocked in Dawson

with a base hit to right in the sixth. As the Expos came to bat in the eighth, however, it was still 6-3. Pittsburgh fans who remained to watch the mopping-up of the doubleheader sweep were roaring "Deee-fense!"

Six outs left. Dawson flied out, but Staub worked reliever Joe Coleman for his third walk of the game. Dyer also received a free pass. Pittsburgh manager Chuck Tanner had seen enough. He called for the Rubber Band Man.

In strode Kent Tekulve to douse the rally, as he had so many times against Montreal. The pencil-thin 6-foot-4 right-hander with outsized fog glasses and an unorthodox submarine delivery was like no other relief pitcher in the majors. Instead of a one-inning closer, Tekulve was a workhorse, summoned whenever Tanner needed him. He appeared in 94 regular-season games that year, pitching 134⅓ innings. He particularly befuddled the Expos. "If I had a team that I owned, it was that team," said Tekulve years later. "Warren Cromartie was the only left-handed hitter in the lineup. The rest of the guys hit right. The way I pitched, that was to my advantage."[4] Lee said Tekulve kept it simple: "Down and in. Down and in."[5]

Although Tekulve had already pitched three scoreless innings in the twin-bill opener, Tanner didn't hesitate to bring him in to close out the nightcap. Ellis Valentine quickly grounded into a fielder's choice, erasing Dyer at second. Two out. But Larry Parrish kept the Expos' faint hopes alive with an infield single, scoring Staub. Valentine advanced to second. 6-4.

Once more, Dick Williams reached into his bag of tricks. He put in rookie speedster Tim Raines, just up from the minors, to run for the slower Parrish. He also pinch-hit for light-hitting Rodney Scott.

At the end of the bench, Williams spied little-known John Tamargo, a journeyman third-string catcher obtained in June from San Francisco, where he had hit .a measly .200. Since then he had had only 10 plate appearances with the Expos. Now, with two out, runners on first and second, and the season likely riding in the balance, this was the mighty Casey Williams chose to face Tekulve. But Williams knew two things about John Tamargo. He was a switch-hitter, so he could bat left against the Pirate right-hander. And he had a smidgen of power. Five of his dozen hits for the Giants were for extra bases. Yet, really! Tekulve against Tamargo? Duck soup!

Tekulve went into his delivery. Tamargo jumped on the first pitch, lashing a screaming double down the first-base line. Valentine scored easily, as did Raines. The game was tied. For only the sixth time in 91 appearances, Tekulve had blown a save.

Williams's legerdemain continued. To pitch the eighth, he bypassed his fleet of worn-out relievers for starting pitcher Ross Grimsley and his bulging 5.38 ERA. Eight days earlier, Grimsley had been booed off the mound at home, after being shelled for six hits and three runs in just two innings. This night, he was Warren Spahn. He retired the Bucs in order, striking out dangerous Dave Parker for the third out.

In the fateful ninth, the Expos faced Grant Jackson. Cash singled, then was thrown out trying to steal. Dawson fanned. Two out, nobody on. Up came Staub. Brought back to the team in July for a last hurrah, *Le Grand Orange* was a shadow of his former Expo self, but he still knew the plate. He strolled to first with his fourth walk. Despite Staub's glacial speed, Williams disdained a pinch-runner. The red-hot Dyer followed with yet another unlikely clutch single, moving Staub to second. Valentine was next, 0 for the doubleheader. But the struggling outfielder finally prevailed, smacking a single to right. Staub lumbered around third and chugged for home, beating the rifle-armed Parker's

throw. As he slid in, the Expo dugout erupted. "It was like cheering for a train going backward," Williams said later with a grin.[6] The Expos were on top, 7-6.

The Expos manager left Grimsley in for the ninth, even after he began the inning by walking Rennie Stennett with the ever-dangerous Willie Stargell advancing to the plate. Williams played the percentages: southpaw Grimsley against the left-handed slugger. It worked. Stargell grounded into a double play. Closer Elias Sosa secured the final out. The jubilant Expos rushed the field to celebrate their miracle, come-from-behind victory, as if they'd won the World Series. With five games to go, they were back in first place.

SOURCES

In addition to the sources listed in the notes, the author consulted:

Hurte, Bob, *SABR Baseball Biography Project: Kent Tekulve*.

Proudfoot, Jim. "Those miracle Expos refuse to recognize any kind of defeat," *Toronto Star*, September 25, 1979.

NOTES

1   Brodie Snyder, *The Year the Expos Almost Won the Pennant!* (Toronto: Virgo Press, 1989), 176-178.

2   Bill Lee, telephone interview, April 2015.

3   Reprinted in Snyder, 191.

4   Kent Tekulve, telephone interview, March 2015.

5   Lee telephone interview.

6   Snyder, 190.

TRIPLE (PLAY) YOUR PLEASURE

August 12, 1980: Montreal Expos 4, St. Louis Cardinals 0 At Busch Stadium

By Norm King

THE BASEBALL SEASON IS LONG ENOUGH THAT on any given day, a team like the 1962 New York Mets can channel the power of the 1927 Yankees. And when the lousy team lays it on the good one, the sweetest revenge is a shutout win the next night, with a triple play thrown in for good measure. Such was the scenario on August 12, 1980, at Busch Stadium in St. Louis.

The Expos were in a dogfight with the Pittsburgh Pirates for the National League East Division lead with a 63-49 record, while the Cardinals were mired in fifth place with a 49-60 mark. The Expos could be forgiven if they thought they had played the St. Louis Cardinals football team the previous night because they lost by more than two touchdowns, 16-0. They were embarrassed and they wanted revenge. Besides, the loss left them one game behind the Pirates; every victory was essential and they could ill afford to lose to bad teams.

The opposing pitchers in the August 12 game were Fred Norman for the Expos and John Fulgham for the Cardinals. Both were winding down their major-league careers; the difference was that Norman had pitched for 16 years and had two World Series rings, while Fulgham was in the second year of his two-year stay in the majors.[1] This was a rare start for Norman (he appeared in 48 games during the season but started only eight), who had signed with the Expos as a free agent after the 1979 season. He had a 2-2 record going into the game.

The first three innings were scoreless, as both pitchers started well. The first hit didn't come until the bottom of the third inning, when Cardinals second baseman Ken Oberkfell singled. He was sacrificed to second by Fulgham but was thrown out trying to steal third, completing an inning-ending strikeout-throw-out double play that started when Norman struck out center fielder Tony Scott.

National League catchers didn't sleep well when they had to face Montreal during the 1980 season, as the Expos had two of the top four basestealers in the league at the top of the lineup. Leadoff hitter Ron LeFlore led the league with 97 stolen bases, while number-two hitter Rodney Scott was second with 63. Not surprisingly, thievery figured in the Expos' first run, but this time right fielder Ellis Valentine was the villain. He led off the fourth inning with a single, stole second, and scored on a double to left by catcher Gary Carter. (The Expos stole four bases in the game; Leflore had two and Valentine and Scott one each.)

The Cardinals tried to get that run back and more in the bottom of the inning and had the makings of a rally when the first two batters, first baseman Keith Hernandez and catcher Ted Simmons, singled to left. Right fielder George Hendrick was the next batter and he hit a line shot right at Expos third baseman Larry Parrish. Parrish snagged the liner to get Hendrick, then threw to Scott to double off Hernandez. Scott relayed to first baseman Warren Cromartie to triple off Simmons. It was the first triple play in the National League that season and the first committed against the Cardinals since June 25, 1969. The Expos had turned that one as well—the first in franchise history (this triple play was the fifth).

The triple play took the steam out of the Cardinals, even though they were down by only one. They went down in order in the fifth and sixth. In the seventh, Norman hit Hernandez with a pitch and gave up a single to Simmons to start the inning, but again the Cardinals couldn't do anything with the opportunity as Expos pitchers Elias Sosa and Woody Fryman retired the next three batters in order.

For a pitcher with a brief major-league career, Fulgham acquitted himself well in this game. He pitched eight innings, giving up only four hits and the one run. Cardinals manager Whitey Herzog sent Tom Herr to pinch-hit for Fulgham in the eighth—Herr popped out to first—and so was forced to go to his bullpen in the ninth. The Expos took full advantage.

Veteran Jim Kaat took the mound and gave up a double to Cromartie. Herzog didn't like what he saw and yanked Kaat for John Littlefield. Carter then singled to third, and both runners scored on a Parrish double to left-center. After Parrish moved to third on a single by shortstop Chris Speier, Herzog brought in his third pitcher of the inning, John Urrea, who was in a heap of trouble with two on and nobody out. Urrea may have hastened the trade that sent him to the San Diego Padres by giving up an RBI single to Fryman, a hit that doubled Woodie's hit and RBI totals for the season. Urrea got the next three batters out to end the inning. The Cardinals went down 1-2-3 in the bottom of the ninth to give the Expos their win.

The victory brought the Expos back into a first-place tie with the Pirates, but it didn't give them the momentum they needed to pull away down the stretch. They lost their next four in a row, including three straight to Pittsburgh. They stayed in the race until the end of the season, but the Bucs faded after that. After winning their third straight against the Expos (a 5-1 win in which Norman was the losing pitcher), Pittsburgh plummeted, going 16-29 the rest of the way. The Phillies, meanwhile, got scorching hot and came back to take the division crown over Montreal on an 11th-inning home run by Mike Schmidt in the second-to-last game of the season.

Fred Norman

SOURCES

In addition to the sources listed in the notes, the author consulted:

Baseball-almanac.com.

Baseball-reference.com.

Ottawa Journal.

Toronto Sun.

NOTES

1   Fulgham pitched in his last major-league game August 27, then spent two more years in the minors. He compiled a respectable 14-12 lifetime record with the St. Louis Cardinals.

"THIS IS A DUMB MAN'S GAME"

August 24, 1980: Montreal Expos 12, San Diego Padres 9 At Olympic Stadium

By Norm King

THIS GAME FEATURED FIVE FUTURE HALL OF Famers, yet Montreal Expos manager Dick Williams likened it to one of his son's Little League games.[1]

"(The) last time I was at a Little League game (to watch one of his sons) the Commissioner threw me out for going on the field," said Williams. "I haven't been close to a Little League game since—not until today."[2]

Williams' assessment came after witnessing a 3½-hour marathon in which the teams combined for 21 runs, 27 hits, 3 errors, 16 walks, 94 plate appearances, 10 pitchers, and a seven-run lead blown in one inning. One can only imagine what Williams' take on the game would have been if the Expos had lost. As it was, it completed a sweep of the Padres. Nonetheless, Montreal remained two games behind the National League East Division-leading Pittsburgh Pirates, who had taken their brooms with them on the road to Cincinnati.

It's possible that the game's starting pitchers, Charlie Lea for the Expos and Bob Shirley of the Padres, had premonitions that the game was going to be a slugfest and wanted to minimize their role in the carnage. Lea had made his major-league debut just two months earlier, going eight innings in a 9-1 victory over San Diego on June 12 at Olympic Stadium. The Padres players wanted revenge because they pounded Lea for four earned on three hits in just 1⅔ innings.

Lea gave up only one run in the first, although how it was scored indicated to Williams that it was going to be a long day. After getting the first two batters out easily, Lea gave up a double to right fielder Dave Winfield, then walked the next three batters in succession, first baseman Willie Montanez, center fielder Jerry Mumphrey, and third baseman Luis Salazar, to give the Padres a 1-0 lead.

Lea zipped through the first two batters again in the second but, as in the first, gave up a double to the third hitter, left fielder Gene Richards. Ozzie Smith singled, scoring Richards, and advanced to third on a two-base error by Expos right fielder Jerry White. Winfield singled, scoring Smith, at which point Lea surrendered and was replaced by Stan Bahnsen. Bahnsen provided Montanez with his second free pass, then gave up run-scoring singles to Mumphrey and Salazar before striking out catcher Gene Tenace to end the frame.

Shirley (it's okay to call him that) meanwhile breezed through the first two innings but couldn't make it through the third, even with a 5-0 lead. He started off by giving up a single to Bobby Ramos, who was pinch-hitting for Bahnsen. Then the track team that was the top of the Expos order went to work. Left fielder Ron Leflore, who led the National League in stolen bases that season with 97, singled, as did second baseman Rodney Scott, who stole 63 on the year. With the basesloaded, Shirley walked center fielder Andre Dawson to drive in Ramos for the Expos' first run of the game. Third baseman Larry Parrish drove Leflore home with a sacrifice fly to make the score 5-2 San Diego after three innings.

The fourth and fifth innings were uneventful, but all hell broke loose in the sixth as the Padres built up a seemingly insurmountable lead and the Expos proved why Yogi Berra was right when he said it ain't over 'til it's over. Hal Dues, on the mound since the fourth, started off by walking Winfield. After Montanez popped up to second, Mumphrey singled, allowing Winfield to reach third. Mumphrey then showed the Expos that they weren't the only team with good basestealers when he swiped second.[3] Salazar singled to score Winfield. Mr. Fiore Gino Tennaci, better known

— 53 —

as Gene Tenace, was the next batter and he cleared the bases with his 11th home run of the season to drive in three more. The inning ended with the Padres up 9-2.

Now it was time for the Expos to have some fun. John Curtis was on the mound, having retired seven straight batters since replacing Shirley (we don't know what Padres manager Jerry Coleman was calling him after his performance) with two gone in the bottom of the third. Carter was the first batter up and he ended Curtis's streak quickly by singling to left. White walked, then first baseman Ken Macha reached on an error by Smith to load the bases. Shortstop Chris Speier followed that with a bases-clearing double to bring the Expos back into the game at 9-5. But *Nos Amours* weren't finished. Curtis struck out the next two batters, but Scott came up and singled to left, driving in Speier. After a rattled Curtis hit Dawson with a pitch, Eric Rasmussen replaced him, and promptly allowed Scott to steal third. Scott scored on Parrish's single. Carter came up for the second time in the inning and doubled to left, scoring Dawson and Parrish and tying the game at 9-9. Rollie Fingers replaced Rasmussen, who had failed to record an out.

"This is a dumb man's game," is how Speier analyzed his at-bat in that inning. "You're not supposed to think too much. Guys get in a slump and worry about moving their foot or dropping their arm. They think too much. You just go up there and try to meet the ball solidly."[4]

The Expos gave another clinic on the effectiveness of small ball in the seventh. Macha led off with a single. Speier went up and met the ball solidly again for another single that sent Macha to third. Pinch-hitter Warren Cromartie hit yet another one-bagger to give the Expos their first lead of the game. Fingers walked Leflore to load the bases, at which point Coleman had seen enough and brought in Gary Lucas.

It's usually a good idea to emulate a future Hall of Famer, but not when he has just walked a batter, and especially not when that free pass drives in another run. Nonetheless that's exactly what Lucas did, giving up a bases-loaded base on balls to Scott, scoring Speier. After Dawson moved the runners up on a fielder's choice, Parrish drove in the third run of the inning on a sacrifice fly, making the score 12-9 Expos. That's how the game ended.

Baseball is similar to figure skating in that it can be graceful and elegant when played well. Fortunately for the Expos that day, they didn't have to worry about style points or what score the French judge would give them. In a game where they displayed more klutz than lutz, the Expos got a win they needed to stay in the 1980 pennant race.

SOURCES

In addition to the sources listed in the notes, the author consulted:

Baseball-Reference.com.

SI.com.

NOTES

1 The Hall of Famers were Ozzie Smith, Dave Winfield, and Rollie Fingers for the Padres, and Gary Carter and Andre Dawson for the Expos.

2 Ian MacDonald, "Expos down Padres again but fail to gain on Pirates," the *Montreal Gazette*, August 25, 1980.

3 The Padres were the only team to steal more bases than the Expos in 1980 (239 to 237). Mumphrey stole 52.

4 MacDonald.

EXPOS ROOKIE GULLICKSON WHIFFS 18

September 10, 1980: Montreal Expos 4, Chicago Cubs 2 At Olympic Stadium

By Gregory H. Wolf

"I'M NOT A STRIKEOUT PITCHER," SAID ROOKIE right-hander Bill Gullickson of the Montreal Expos after he whiffed 18 Chicago Cubs in a dominant complete-game victory, 4-2, to establish a new record for most strikeouts by a rookie (since broken by the Cubs' Kerry Wood in 1998).[1] "He was just awesome," said his batterymate, Gary Carter, who did not mince words. "With that performance, he's up there with the Koufaxes and the Drysdales and any other strikeout pitcher."[2]

As the Expos headed to *Stade Olympique* on September 10, 1980, to play the first game of a two-game series with the Cubs, skipper Dick Williams was determined to avoid another late-season meltdown. The previous September, the Expos were in first place, a half-game in front of the Pittsburgh Pirates, on September 24, only to lose four of their last five games and finish in second place in the NL East despite a team-record 95 wins. After a slow start in 1980 (21-20), the Expos worked their way into the pennant race. Winners of six of their past eight games, they were in first place (75-63), a half-game in front of the Philadelphia Phillies. The Cubs, by contrast, were a club in disarray. Manager Joey Amalfitano, who had replaced Preston Gomez in midseason, led a weak-hitting club that was in last place (54-83), 20½ games behind the Expos.

One of the reasons for Montreal's success was its pitching staff. Longtime ace Steve Rogers was joined by 23-year-old righty Scott Sanderson and Gullickson to form one of baseball's best starting trios. Gullickson was a sturdy 6-foot-3, 200-pounder whom the Expos chose second overall in the 1977 amateur draft. He proved his big-league readiness by going 6-2 with a stingy 1.91 ERA with the Triple-A Denver Bears in the American Association in 1980, earning his call-up in mid-May. After some initial rough outings, Gullickson entered his historic game against the Cubs as one of the hottest pitchers in the league. In his previous start he had tossed a sparkling three-hit shutout against the San Francisco Giants (the Expos' first of three consecutive shutouts against the Giants at Candlestick Park) to record his sixth win in his last seven starts, while striking out 50 in 56 innings and posting an impressive 2.09 ERA. He relied on breaking pitches, changing speeds, and good control for his success. "His fastball hits 84 mph on a good day—nothing more than a batting-practice pitcher unless he cuts or sinks it," read one scouting report. "Keeping hitters off balance is the key for Gullickson."[3]

Given the pennant race, the Expos drew a sparse crowd of 17,874 to Olympic Stadium on an autumnal Wednesday evening, about 10,000 fewer than the night before when Rogers blanked the New York Mets on five hits to win his 100th big-league game. Gullickson came out strong, breezing through the first three innings, striking out six. That number could have been higher save for a controversial call in the first inning. Bill Buckner appeared to have swung on a "sweeping curve" in the dirt.[4] The wily veteran, however, took off for first claiming that he was hit by the pitch. After the umpires conferred, third-base ump Bill Williams ruled inexplicably that Buckner had neither swung nor was hit. Buckner went back to the plate, and popped up. "It was a lot of play acting," fumed Carter after the game.[5] Chicago starter Rick Reuschel, a durable nine-year veteran who had amassed an impressive 125-111 record despite playing for awful Cubs teams in the 1970s, yielded only a single in the first three frames.

In the fourth inning the Cubs tallied the game's first run. Buckner, easily the Cubs' best hitter, who went on to capture the NL batting crown in 1980 with a .324 average, smashed a double to deep center that drove in third sacker Lenny Randle, on first via a single. Buckner scampered to third on a wild pitch before Gullickson escaped the jam by punching out the next two batters. In the fifth, Gullickson struck out the side for the second time in three innings to bring his strikeout total to 11.

Carter and first baseman Warren Cromartie led off the fifth inning with back-to-back homers to give the Expos a 2-1 lead. It did not last long. In the sixth, shortstop Ivan de Jesus drew the first of Gullickson's two free passes, stole second, and scored on Buckner's single to right to tie the game. Gullickson ended the frame with yet another strikeout, his 14th of the game, which matched Bill Stoneman's team mark for most in a nine-inning game.

In danger of squandering Gullickson's gem, the Expos took a 3-2 lead in the sixth on center fielder Andre Dawson's one-out single to drive in right fielder Rowland Office, subbing for the injured Ellis Valentine. Carter and Cromartie walked to load the bases, but third baseman Larry Parrish hit into an inning-ending double play. Montreal tacked on another run off eventual loser Reuschel in the next frame when shortstop Chris Speier scored on second baseman Rodney Scott's single.

Fans "roar[ed] approval after every whiff," reported Expos beat writer Ian MacDonald.[6] Gullickson whiffed his 15th and 16th batters in the seventh to establish a new team record, breaking Mike Wegener's mark of 15 set in an 11-inning outing in 1969. Fans realized that Gullickson had a chance to tie the big-league record of 19 strikeouts in a nine-inning game held by Steve Carlton, Nolan Ryan, and Tom Seaver. "I was trying to keep the strikeout record out of my mind," said Gullickson after the game. "I was aware of what the crowd was doing and it was wonderful but I was trying to concentrate on the game."[7]

"What impressed me the most was that even after 15 strikeouts, he wasn't trying for more," said pitching coach Galen Cisco.[8] After not recording a strikeout in the eighth inning, Gullickson yielded a double to his nemesis Buckner to start the ninth. The Expos

bullpen remained silent as Williams had decided it was Gullickson's game to win or lose. Unfazed by a man in scoring position, the rookie whiffed center fielder Jerry Martin, induced Larry Biittner to ground out to first, and on his 133rd pitch of the evening struck out left fielder Jim Tracy to end the game in 2 hours and 30 minutes.

Gullickson's teammates mobbed him on the mound. "The big thing was he was getting ahead in the count all the time," said an obviously ecstatic Carter after the game. "He had excellent control and he had an excellent slider, and that's what most of the guys were striking out on."[9] With 18 strikeouts, Gullickson tied Bob Feller and Ron Guidry for the second highest total in a nine-inning game. "We struck out guys on bad pitches because he was always ahead in the count," exclaimed Carter, who had inherited Johnny Bench's mantle as arguably the best backstop in baseball.[10] The umpire's blown call in the first inning was a point of contention after the game. "[Gullickson] stands just one controversial call away from being at the top of baseball's all-time strikeout record," noted the *Montreal Gazette*.[11] Gullickson, who was not used to pitching

Bill Gullickson

so late in the season as a minor leaguer, revealed after the game that he felt fatigued during his pregame preparation. "When I warmed up tonight," he said, "my arm felt tight and I didn't feel like I had the stuff."[12]

Gullickson's record-setting four-hitter helped the Expos maintain a precarious half-game lead over the Phillies. But it was another heartbreaking finish for Montreal, which lost the division crown on the last weekend of the season. Gullickson concluded the campaign with an impressive 10-5 record and 3.00 ERA in 141 innings and was runner-up to reliever Steve Howe of the Los Angeles Dodgers for the Rookie of the Year Award.

In his rookie season, Gullickson discovered that he suffered from type 1 diabetes. "I decided that I'm not going to let this (diabetes) ruin what I have worked for," said Gullickson not long after his epic performance.[13] Though the disease could have ended his career, he persevered and learned to control it by staying in excellent physical shape and monitoring his injections.[14] He went on to win 162 games and log 2,560 innings in his 14-year big-league career, but never came close to having another game like the one he had against the Cubs in September 1980. Gullickson was right—he wasn't a strikeout pitcher. In 390 big-league starts, he reached double figures only seven times.

SOURCES

In addition to the sources listed in the notes, the author consulted:

BaseballReference.com.

Retrosheet.org.

SABR.org.

NOTES

1 Ian MacDonald, "Gullickson fires masterpiece as Expos maintain NL lead," the *Montreal Gazette*, September 11, 1980.

2 "Joliet's Gullickson 1 off record. Expos' rookie's 18 strikeouts stifle Cubs," *Chicago Tribune*, September 11, 1980.

3 Bill James and Rob Neyer, *The Neyer/James Guide to Pitchers* (New York: Touchstone, 2008).

4 *The Sporting News*, September 27, 1980.

5 MacDonald.

6 Ibid.

7 Ibid.

8 Ibid.

9 *Chicago Tribune*.

10 MacDonald.

11 Ibid.

12 Catherine Wolf (UPI), "Gullickson Sets Rookie Record With 18 K's; Astros Win in 12," *Tyrone* (Pennsylvania) *Daily Herald*, September 11, 1980.

13 Ron Martz, "Diabetes doesn't deter Gullickson," *St. Petersburg Times*, September 15, 1980.

14 Gullickson never used diabetes as an excuse for a poor outing or pitching woes. While playing in the Japanese Professional League in 1988 and 1989, he impressed his teammates and the media with his dedication to baseball despite his diabetes. Subsequently, the Japan Diabetes Mellitus Society established the "Gullickson Award" to recognize those people with diabetes who have made great contributions to society.

LEA PITCHES A GIANT NO-HITTER

May 10, 1981: Montreal Expos 4, San Francisco Giants 0 At Olympic Stadium

By Gregory H. Wolf

MONTREAL'S 24-YEAR-OLD RIGHT-HANDER Charlie Lea was an unlikely candidate to toss the first no-hitter in the history of Olympic Stadium. Pounded in his first two starts in 1981 (nine runs in 6⅔ innings), Lea held the San Francisco Giants hitless on Mother's Day. "I'm not the type of person who jumps up and down," he said. "Everything fell into place. We had an excellent defence. It was a team effort."[1] Lea's dominance was not lost on his batterymate, Gary Carter. "No one would have thought he'd do it," said the NL's best backstop. "He was getting his fastball over and he had command of all his stuff. He was just super."[2]

On Sunday, May 10, the Expos arrived at *Stade Olympique* to conclude an 11-game homestand with a doubleheader. Skipper Dick Williams's bunch had an impressive record (16-9) and was one game off the lead in the NL East; however, they had lost five of their previous eight games and had fallen out of first place. Manager Frank Robinson's Giants were in fourth place in the NL West (14-16), six games off the pace, and had taken the first two games of the series.

A good crowd of 25,343 turned out for an afternoon of baseball, but had little to cheer about in the first game. Tom Griffin fired a four-hitter, and Enos Cabell and Darrell Evans belted home runs to lead the Giants to a 5-1 victory.

Given a spot start in the second game, the 6-foot-4, 200-pound Lea surprised everyone. One year earlier, Lea was burning up the Double-A Southern League, winning all nine of his starts for the Memphis Chicks. After two starts in Triple-A, he was summoned to the parent club in June during a heated, season-long pennant race. "He came in and pitched like hell when we needed him last year," said pitching coach Galen Cisco of the rookie who went 7-5 with a 3.72 ERA in

104 innings.[3] Despite Lea's potential, Expos beat writer Ian MacDonald thought he'd be in Triple-A to start the 1981 season in light of the club's signing of free agent Ray Burris. "Some of the people thought I was getting on Lea too heavily last year," said Williams, whose hard-driving reputation was well-known. "I know he has the potential to be a big winner."[4] Given his 7.36 ERA in 11 innings thus far in 1981, Lea recognized that he was pitching to keep his spot on the team.

A popular player during his six-year tenure with the Expos, Lea was born in France to American parents stationed in the military. The family moved back stateside when he was three months old, and Charlie grew up in Memphis, Tennessee. He spoke with a pleasant Southern drawl, and made it known, "I don't talk any French," much to the dismay of the French-speaking Québécois.[5] "I'm a Southern guy and yes, it was a different culture for me," he said in retirement. "There were some different things there and French was the preferred language. But I never had any trouble communicating with anybody and everybody worked hard to make it a nice place to be and I enjoyed every bit of my time there."[6]

On a cool, cloudy afternoon with the threat of rain looming, the second game shaped up as a classic pitchers' duel. Lea faced the minimum number of batters through seven innings; he yielded only a leadoff walk to center fielder Bill North in the fourth, but the speedster was promptly thrown out by Carter in a steal attempt. The Giants' 26-year-old righty Ed Whitson, an All-Star the previous season, held the Expos scoreless through six innings. The Expos loaded the bases with two outs in the second inning on a single, a hit batter, and a walk, but Whitson escaped the jam by inducing 21-year-old leadoff hitter Tim Raines, who entered the game batting .356, to hit a grounder and force out Darrell Evans at third base to end the inning.

The Expos scored all four of their runs in the seventh inning. Third baseman Tim Wallach clubbed Whitson's first pitch for a home run. With right fielder Rowland Office on second via a single and Raines on first courtesy of an intentional walk, second baseman Rodney Scott smashed a two-out double driving in both of them. Andre Dawson followed with a run-scoring double to make it 4-0.

The Expos' offensive outburst re-energized the crowd, which, according to the *Montreal Gazette*, had thinned out to about 8,000 with the "temperatures dropp[ing] markedly."[7] Shunning superstition, Lea talked about his no-no with teammates. "I knew it, and everybody in the ballpark knew, so there was no need to keep quiet."[8] Ian MacDonald reported that fans "cheer[ed] every pitch Lea fired from the eighth inning until the end" of the game.[9]

When Lea walked Darrell Evans and Larry Herndon to start the eighth inning, relievers Woody Fryman and Elias Sosa began warming up. Lea got a big boost when second baseman Scott fielded catcher Milt May's one-hop grounder to initiate a double play. "If that ball May hit is five feet right or left, it's a hit," said Lea after the game.[10] Lea issued his third walk of the frame, to Dave Bergman, before Billy Smith flied out. "He was pumped up," said Carter about Lea's wildness in the inning.[11] "I was tired because that's the longest I've gone this year," explained Lea honestly. "If they got a hit, then (Williams) would take me out."[12] Dick Williams looked at the situation in context. "There's a natural letdown," he said. "We were watching him closely. He regained control. Besides if we hadn't scored those runs, maybe he wouldn't have walked anyone."[13]

Lea, who became known as an excellent curveball pitcher, relied on his heater with a four-run lead in the final two innings. "I was just laying the ball across the plate," he said.[14] After pinch-hitter Jim Wohlford grounded out for the first out in the ninth, Lea showed some signs of nervousness. He bounced the ball on the pitching mound, drawing the ire of Giants manager Robinson, who asked third-base umpire Ed Runge

to check the ball. With a 3-and-0 count on North, Lea tossed "three straight strikes," including a hotly-contested called third strike, for the second out. First baseman Enos Cabell hit a "soft fly ball to short center" to end the game.[15] As Dawson caught the ball, teammates mobbed Lea on the mound. The *New York Times* reported that Robinson continued his argument with Runge after the game. "I felt the umpire should have taken the scuffed ball out of the game," said Robinson. "But Runge told me that bouncing the ball on the turf is the same as batting the ball on the turf."[16]

"(Lea) had some smoke in the ninth and he came through in tight situations," said an ebullient Williams after the game. Lea whiffed a then-career-high eight to pick up his first win of the season. "I've had a lot of confidence in him," said Cisco. "He has the arm and the know-how."[17] Lea's no-hitter was the third in franchise history; Bill Stoneman tossed the other two, in 1969 (in Philadelphia) and 1972 (in Montreal).

"We needed this," said Lea. "I just want to sit back and let this sink in for a while."[18] In his first big-league complete game in his 22nd start since the beginning of 1980, Lea did not yield any hard-hit balls and was quick to credit his catcher for his success. "I didn't have to shake off Gary once," he said.[19] His teammates seemed genuinely excited for his accomplishment, and gave him a "makeshift royal treatment" in the clubhouse by laying towels on the floor and lining up cans of beer beside his stool and locker instead of bottles of champagne.[20]

Notwithstanding his no-hitter, Lea was unsure when his next start would be. "I have no idea if this will get me back in the rotation," he said matter-of-factly. "Maybe they'll want me for long relief."[21] But Lea's wait was short. Six days later, he tossed a four-hitter to blank the Giants at Candlestick Park as part of a career-high streak of 29⅓ consecutive scoreless innings. He was named NL pitcher of the month in May, during which he won four consecutive starts and yielded just one earned run in 35⅓ innings.

Lea's once promising career was derailed by back and shoulder problems. After winning 43 games over a three-year stretch (1982-1984) and averaging more than 200 innings per season over that period, Lea missed the 1985 and 1986 seasons. He had an abbreviated comeback in the American League with Minnesota, and retired at the age of 31 in 1988.

SOURCES

In addition to the sources listed in the notes, the author consulted:

BaseballReference.com.

Retrosheet.org.

SABR.org.

NOTES

1 "Good Ol' Charlie: He's Expos' Second No-Hit Pitcher," the *Montreal Gazette*, May 11, 1981, 1.

2 "Lea Hurls No-Hit Gem," *Logansport* (Indiana) *Pharos-Tribune*, May 11, 1981, 6.

3 Ian MacDonald, "Lea throws Big O's first no-hitter," the *Montreal Gazette*, May 11, 1981, 21.

4 Ibid.

5 Ibid.

6 Kevin Glew, "Former Expo Charlie Lea Dies at 54," *Coopertowners in Canada*, November 12, 2011.

7 MacDonald.

8 "Expos Lea belies his 7.36 ERA by throwing no-hitter at Giants," *San Bernardino* (California) *County Sun*, May 11, 1981, 17.

9 MacDonald.

10 Ibid.

11 Ibid.

12 Ibid.

13 Ibid.

14 "Expos Lea belies his 7.36 ERA by throwing no-hitter at Giants."

15 Ibid.

16 "Expos' Charlie Lea Pitches 4-0 No-Hitter," *New York Times*, May 11, 1981.

17 MacDonald.

18 "Good Ol' Charlie: He's Expos' Second No-Hit Pitcher."

19 MacDonald.

20 Ibid.

21 Ibid.

THIS GAME HAD IT ALL

September 21, 1981: Montreal Expos 1, Philadelphia Phillies 0 At Olympic Stadium

by Norm King

THIS GAME HAD EVERYTHING THAT MAKES baseball great — nail-biting tension, great pitching, playoff implications, two rival teams, 17 innings, you name it. Throw a record-setting achievement and a walk-off hit to send the home team off happy, and you'll get an idea of the marvelous, maddening 1-0 affair between the Expos and the Phillies played in the heat of the 1981 pennant race.

The 1981 season was unlike any other in the history of baseball. On June 12, players began the first midseason strike in history (the only previous work stoppage to affect the schedule occurred at the beginning of the 1972 season) which resulted in a unique split-season format and an extra round of playoffs involving the division winners for each of the season's two halves.[1] The Phillies were guaranteed a playoff spot by virtue of being in first place in the National League East when the strike started. At game time on September 21, the Cardinals led the division by 1½ games over Montreal. The division was so tight that the Phillies were only four games out yet they were in fifth place.

Montreal's Ray Burris (9-7 in 1981) faced off against future Hall of Famer Steve Carlton (13-4 in 1981), and it was clear from the get-go that runs would be at a premium. Burris got into trouble in the top of the second when he walked third baseman Mike Schmidt to lead off the frame, then gave up a single to catcher Keith Moreland. A potential big inning was nipped in the bud when right fielder Bake McBride fouled out to first and shortstop Larry Bowa grounded into a 4-6-3 double play.

The Expos' first chance to crack the goose egg came in the bottom of the third. Shortstop Chris Speier led the inning off with a single. After second baseman Jerry Manuel popped out to first, Burris sacrificed Speier to second. Then Fate's flair for the dramatic entered

the picture. Carlton walked first baseman Warren Cromartie and left fielder Jerry White to load the bases and bring the dangerous Andre Dawson to the plate. Carlton got behind the Expos' center fielder, 2-1, then evened the count before making Dawson look silly as he flailed away weakly at strike three. This was no ordinary strikeout for Lefty, because it not only kept the game scoreless, but it also made him the National League's all-time strikeout king, surpassing former teammate Bob Gibson's total of 3,117. After the game Burris, who received two standing ovations of his own, commented eloquently on how the Expos faithful reacted to Carlton's achievement.

"I especially appreciate the courtesy of the fans in recognizing my effort," he said. "But the ovation they gave Carlton tells me something about the integrity of the game and the fans."[2]

From that point on the two starters paraphrased Irving Berlin and played "Any Pitch You Can Throw I Can Throw Better" for the next seven innings. Sure, there was a hit here, or a runner or two left there, but after 10 innings, neither pitcher had given up a run. At this point the managers started earning their money and began shifting personnel in an effort to win the game. Expos skipper Jim Fanning, who had replaced Dick Williams on September 8, made a double switch, inserting reliever Jeff Reardon into Manuel's spot in the order — Manuel was the last out in the 10th — and bringing Rodney Scott in to play second base. This latter move proved especially significant.

Ron Reed took over for Carlton in the bottom of the 11th. Maybe Phillies manager Dallas Green was anxious to go out and enjoy Montreal's famous night life because he pulled off an unusual move in the inning. Scott singled to left and advanced to second on a groundout by Cromartie. After White flied out to center for the second out, Reed walked Dawson intentionally to get to catcher Gary Carter, the Expos' leading RBI man. The move worked because Carter grounded into a fielder's choice.

The Phillies' best chance to take the lead came in the 14th with Woodie Fryman on the mound. Left fielder Gary Matthews led the inning off by doubling to right. A great opportunity seemed doomed when Schmidt struck out and Moreland grounded to third. With two out, Green sent Dick Davis in to pinch-hit for McBride. This was no half-baked idea because Davis singled to left; Matthews, who could run, was sent home but White's throw cut him down at the plate. The marathon continued.

Stan Bahnsen took the mound in the 15th for the Expos. Bowa greeted him with a single to right. After second baseman Manny Trillo popped up, Bowa gave the Expos an out when Carter gunned him down trying to steal second. Del Unser, pinch-hitting for pitcher Sparky Lyle, who had come on in the 13th inning, got on base with a walk; Green put Bob Dernier in to pinch-run for Unser and he lived up to his name–the word "dernier" is French for "last"—by getting caught stealing by Carter for the last out of the 15th.

Bahnsen walked center fielder Lonnie Smith to lead off the 16th. It was clear that Smith hadn't paid attention during the previous frame because he too tried to steal on Carter and the result was the same. That out was crucial to the Expos because Bahnsen walked Rose and Schmidt, sandwiching a flyout by Matthews. Moreland came up with two out and two on instead of with one out and the bases loaded, and he flied out to end the inning.

The Expos' bench was getting pretty thin by the bottom of the 17th. Bryn Smith, who had replaced

Bahnsen in the top of the frame when Bahnsen pulled his hamstring, batted for himself and grounded out. Scott singled and then showed the Phillies how it was done by stealing second. Phillies pitcher Jerry Reed walked Cromartie and Terry Francona, who had replaced White in the 12th, to load the bases for Dawson. The Hawk hit a dribbler to third, and in yet another example of the Expos' dangerous speed, Scott beat Schmidt's throw to the plate to give the Expos the win. It was Smith's first major-league victory; he had faced only two batters.

The victory gave the Expos the momentum they needed to overtake St. Louis and win the second-half East Division crown. They went 9-4 the rest of the way, while the Cardinals went 7-6. In what is now called the National League Division Series, the Expos defeated the Phillies in five games to gain a measure of revenge for losing the division to them in 1980. Montreal went on to lose the 1981 NLCS to the Dodgers in five games.

SOURCES

In addition to the sources listed in the notes, the author consulted:

CNN.com.

Baseball-reference.com.

Gettysburg Times.

New York Times.

NOTES

1   If a team won the division title for both halves, that team would have played whoever came in second during the second half. That scenario never happened.

2   Ian MacDonald, "Dawson's 17th-inning hit lifts Expos over Phillies," the *Montreal Gazette*, September 22, 1981.

WE'RE GOING TO THE PLAYOFFS

October 3, 1981: Montreal Expos 5, New York Mets 4 At Shea Stadium

By Mark S. Sternman

WITH A 1½-GAME LEAD OVER THE ST. LOUIS Cardinals and just two games to go in the second half of the bastardized 1981 split season, the Montreal Expos needed just one more win to clinch their first postseason berth. Montreal would have to triumph on the road, but had the good fortune to face the sad-sack New York Mets, a team against which the Expos had gone 8-2 thus far in the strike-interrupted campaign.

"The Expos … had wasted opportunities the last two years to win the National League East on the final weekend," wrote Dave Anderson. "Two years ago they were one game behind the Pittsburgh Pirates with three to play in Montreal and were eliminated on Sunday; last year they were tied with the Phillies with three games to play in Philadelphia and were eliminated on the final Saturday."[1]

Mike Scott, finishing up a dismal 5-10 season, started for the Mets and retired Warren Cromartie, Jerry White, and Andre Dawson in order in the top of the first. Cromartie hit leadoff because wunderkind rookie Tim Raines had broken a bone in his right hand[2] nearly three weeks earlier.

Montreal manager Jim Fanning tapped fourth-year righty Scott Sanderson to start. Sanderson had faced a season-low 15 batters in his previous outing, a 6-2 loss at St. Louis, and would last just one batter longer against New York.

Sanderson got into trouble immediately by walking leadoff hitter Lee Mazzilli and giving up a one-out single to future Expo Hubie Brooks that sent Mazzilli to second. Sanderson escaped (this time) by retiring Dave Kingman and Rusty "Le Grand Orange" Staub on fly balls.

Ed Lynch came on for the second inning to replace Scott, who after his September 27 start against Montreal "said his pitching elbow tightened."[3] Lynch gave up a hit to Larry Parrish but stranded him at first. The Mets took the lead in the bottom of the frame after consecutive singles by Alex Trevino and the light-hitting future Expo Doug Flynn that put runners on first and third with one out and Lynch coming to the plate. Unable to fan his opposing hurler, Sanderson gave up the only sacrifice fly Lynch ever hit in his 248-game career to drive home Trevino. New York led 1-0 after two innings.

Chris Speier led off the Expos' third with a single, but failed to advance. Brooks started another Mets rally in the bottom of the frame with a single. After a walk to Kingman, Staub's RBI double increased the New York lead to 2-0. When Trevino singled to make the score 3-0, Fanning hooked Sanderson in favor of rookie Bryn Smith, who retired Flynn to end the inning.

After Lynch got the heart of the Expos (Dawson, Gary Carter, and Parrish) in the top of the fourth, Smith pitched around a walk to Lynch and a wild pitch in the bottom half. The rookie Smith's 1⅓ innings of scoreless relief kept the New York margin manageable.

The comeback commenced in the top of the fifth. With one out, Jerry Manuel and Speier singled and each advanced on an error by the defensively challenged Kingman in left. Brad Mills, pinch-hitting for Smith, knocked in his only run of 1981 with a ground-out. The Expos trailed 3-1 midway through the game.

Bill Lee came in from the bullpen in the bottom of the inning. Working on only three days' rest after a subpar start, Lee began badly but recovered quickly. After a Kingman single and steal, Staub bunted, but Lee threw out Kingman at second. "'The turning point today was when I nailed Kingman,' quipped Spaceman Lee."[4] A fly ball to right by Ellis Valentine proved harmless. Lee hurled two scoreless frames and unwittingly made a prophet of Dick Williams, Montreal manager for most of 1981, who in spring training had told the *Boston Globe*, "Lee still can be a very valuable man to the Expos if he is healthy, but not necessarily as a starter."[5]

In the sixth, Carter's 16th homer of the year closed the gap to 3-2. Flynn opened the bottom of the sixth with a single. Lynch had pitched well, but rather than have him bunt, New York manager Joe Torre pinch-hit Bob Bailor to sacrifice. While the conservative play moved the runner this time, the Mets did not score, and the New York bullpen could not preserve the lead.

"Torre did not worry about his starters going more than five or six innings when he had [closer Neil] Allen in the pen for the last two," wrote Jack Lang.[6] Here, on the next-to-last day of the season, Torre tried to stretch Allen for the final three. In what became the lucky Montreal seventh, Terry Francona reached on an error, but was out when Manuel hit into a fielder's choice. Batting for Speier, pinch-hitter John "The Hammer" Milner singled to move Manuel to second and bring up Lee. Fanning tapped Rodney Scott to run for Milner and turned to rookie Wallace Johnson to hit for Lee. The matchup seemed to represent a mismatch for the Expos, as a strong reliever faced an unknown who had begun 1981 in Double-A Memphis before moving up to Triple-A Denver. Johnson had made his major-league debut during the same September 8 game as Bryn Smith when he batted for his fellow rookie.

To this point in his career, Johnson had one single in six at-bats with one RBI. Another single would tie the game and might put the Expos ahead. Johnson delivered magnificently. He "went to a 2-and-2 count before driving a 350-foot triple to right-center for two runs and the lead," reported the *New York Times*.[7] Montreal now led 4-3. Allen escaped additional damage by intentionally walking Cromartie, inducing a popup from White, and fanning Dawson.

To terminate the game, Fanning turned to former Met Jeff Reardon, who had "escaped the dungeon of Shea Stadium and the shadow of Neil Allen by way of a trade to the Expos in June for Ellis Valentine," wrote Peter Gammons. "Reardon had been an issue in the firing of Dick Williams. Then, when he had been used [more frequently] down the stretch … Reardon was the best short reliever in the National League

Jeff Reardon

East, better than Bruce Sutter or Tug McGraw or Neil Allen."[8]

"When this season becomes history, the trade in which the [Expos] acquired … Reardon from the Mets … for outfielder Ellis Valentine may turn out to be one of the biggest and best the team has ever made," wrote Ian MacDonald.[9] After allowing a double to Staub, Reardon closed the seventh otherwise unscathed.

In the top of the eighth Allen yielded a critical insurance run with two outs on an RBI double by Manuel. Reardon quickly gave the run back on a homer by pinch-hitter Mike Cubbage, the only homer he ever hit in the National League and the 34th and last of his eight-year career, to trim the lead to 5-4.

The Expos went down in order in the top of the ninth, Reardon returned for his third inning to face Mike Jorgensen, who had played 670 games for Montreal. Pinch-hitting for Frank Tavares, Jorgensen popped out. The Expos stood two outs away from the playoffs. Brooks bounced a comebacker to Reardon, who tossed to Cromartie at first. One out remained for Montreal. Reardon "retired Dave Kingman on a fly ball for the final out after throwing two curves for strikes and then wandering around the back of the mound as if he wanted to do anything but throw another pitch," wrote Michael Farber.[10] The rookie Francona, who 23 years later would cross paths with Torre in managing the Red Sox to a historic playoff comeback against New York's other baseball team, caught the ball to ensure that the Expos would experience the glories and agonies of postseason baseball for the first and, alas, only time in the franchise's star-crossed history.

NOTES

1   Dave Anderson, "The Expo's Torch," *New York Times*, October 4, 1981. Montreal actually trailed Pittsburgh by 1½ games with three to go in 1979.

2   Ian MacDonald, "Raines Injury a Jolt to Expo Playoff Bid," *The Sporting News*, October 3, 1981.

3   Michael Strauss, "Mets Stop Expos, 2-1; Lead Is Cut to 1½," *New York Times*, September 28, 1981.

4   Bob Logan, "Gary Rookie Gives Expos Title," *Chicago Tribune*, October 4, 1981.

5   Larry Whiteside, "He's Same Old Lee; He's 34 Years Old Now, and Still in Doghouse," *Boston Globe*, March 17, 1981.

6   Jack Lang, "Mets: Look Out Below," *The Sporting News*, September 19, 1981.

7   Joseph Durso, "Expos, Astros, Brewers Clinch in Divisional Races," *New York Times*, October 4, 1981.

8   Peter Gammons, "He's Finally Getting Some Expo-Sure," *Boston Globe*, February 13, 1982.

9   Ian MacDonald, "Expo Fans Hail Their Half-Title," *The Sporting News*, October 17, 1981.

10   Michael Farber, "The Phillies Can Wait/It's Champagne Time for Our Thirsty Expos," *The Montreal Gazette*, October 5, 1981.

ROGERS LEADS EXPOS TO NLCS

October 11, 1981: Montreal Expos 3, Philadelphia Phillies 0 At Veterans Stadium

By Norm King

FOR GAME FIVE OF THE 1981 MINI-SERIES playoff between the Montreal Expos and the Philadelphia Phillies, Expos manager Jim Fanning unleashed his best pitching weapon, Steve Rogers. He also unleashed his secret offensive weapon— Steve Rogers?

The 1981 major-league season was interrupted by a 50-day midseason players' strike that divided the campaign into two halves. In order to determine the division champions, Major League Baseball decided that the division leaders at season's end would meet the teams that led when the strike started in best-of-five mini-series.[1] In the National League East, this arrangement pitted first-half winner Philadelphia against second-half leader Montreal.

This setup suited the Expos just fine because they wanted revenge for October 4, 1980, when the Phillies' Mike Schmidt blasted an 11th-inning home run that eliminated Montreal from the pennant race and vaulted Philadelphia to the World Series title. It was payback time.

Montreal won the first two games at Olympic Stadium by identical 3-1 scores. When the series moved to Veterans Stadium, Philadelphia rebounded to even the series with 6-2 and 6-5 wins. With the series tied at two games apiece, it all came down to a winner-take-all matchup between the teams' aces. Rogers had gone 12-8 in the truncated campaign, while Steve Carlton was 13-4. Rogers went 8⅓ innings in besting Carlton in Game One, so he had every reason to be confident going into this pressure-packed finale.

Carlton and the Phillies weren't ready to concede anything, either, despite the distraction of rumors that manager Dallas Green was moving on to the Chicago Cubs after the season. (He took over as Cubs general manager on October 15, 1981, four days after the Phillies

were eliminated.) "Actually, the Expos thought they had the division title iced when they left Montreal with a two-games-to-none lead over Philadelphia," wrote Steve Wulf in *Sports Illustrated*. "They should have known about Phillie Ball, though. Last year's champs play best when they haven't a prayer."[2]

The Lord may work in mysterious ways, but so did Carlton's slider, as he struck out the Expos' Warren Cromartie, Jerry White, and Andre Dawson to lead off the game. Pitching dominated the first four innings, which were not only scoreless, but included some bizarre baserunning. After leading off the second with a single to left, the Expos' Gary Carter tried to steal second off his opposite number, Phillies catcher Bob Boone. Now, the Expos had a lot of fast players in 1981; they even led the league in stolen bases with 138. Carter, however, contributed only one steal and was caught stealing five times. If he was trying to catch Boone off guard, it didn't work, because Boone gunned him down.

Doing the unexpected was clearly behind Phillies third-base coach Lee Elia's decision to wave Gary Matthews home in the fourth inning. After singling with two out, Matthews was off with the crack of the bat on a single to center by Manny Trillo. Perhaps sensing that runs would be at a premium that day, Elia channeled his internal Tasmanian Devil, wildly waving his right arm as a signal for Matthews to head for home instead of stopping at third. Dawson, meanwhile, corralled the ball and gunned it to cutoff man Jerry Manuel, who rifled it to Carter in time for the out at home.

"I thought he had a good shot at it, and I was going with the element of surprise," Elia explained.[3]

If Carter wasn't already having a rough enough day after getting caught stealing, it got worse during the

Warren Cromartie (left), Steve Rogers (center), and Gary Carter celebrate a win.

play at the plate because instead of sliding, Matthews ran into him in an attempt to knock the ball out of his hand. In doing so, Matthews elbowed Carter in the head, which caused the Expos catcher to play the next three innings with blurred vision.

"I thought it was pretty dirty when it happened," Carter said. "Later, he apologized. I have no hard feelings. I commend him. You have to play hard like that when everything is on the line."[4]

The Expos broke through in the fifth. Larry Parrish led things off with a single and went to second when Carlton walked Tim Wallach. Chris Speier reached on a fielder's choice that erased Wallach and moved Parrish to third. Manuel walked to load the bases for Rogers. The career .138 hitter used his self-described "bail and wail" hitting style to smack a hanging slider up the middle — his second hit of the game — to bring Parrish and Speier home with, as it turned out, all the runs he would need.[5] Of course they didn't know that at the time, so the Expos padded their lead in the sixth when Dawson singled and scored on a Parrish double.

Philadelphia made some noise in the bottom of the sixth with Montreal leading 3-0. Leadoff hitter Lonnie Smith singled and moved to second on a walk to Pete Rose. George Vukovich hit into a fielder's choice that forced Rose at second, and brought up the ever-dangerous Schmidt with one out and runners on first and third. Schmidt hit 57 career home runs against Montreal, and had popped one the previous day off

of Scott Sanderson. He caused the Expos so much concern that they walked him intentionally in Game Two, even though that meant breaking the cardinal rule of not putting the tying run on base. This time, though, Rogers pitched to him and got him to hit into a double play, ending the threat.

Schmidt, Matthews, and Trillo batted for Philadelphia in the bottom of the ninth. Schmidt and Matthews lined out quickly. With the count 1-and-1 on Trillo, the right-handed-hitting Phillies second baseman lined the ball toward right, but Cromartie jumped up, grabbed it for the third out, then ran to the hugfest convening at the mound as Expos players piled on top of Rogers and one another in celebration. Then he wandered over toward the Phillies dugout, took a Canadian flag from a Montreal fan and waved it in the air. The Philadelphia fans, infamous for once booing Santa Claus, responded as would be expected.

"I made the last out of the playoff game [a reference to his putout on Trillo's liner] and I think holding up the Canadian flag after we won was kind of [memorable] for me," Cromartie said.[6]

The series win was also a vindication of sorts for Rogers, who was often criticized by former Expos manager Dick Williams for not being able to pitch well under pressure. He defeated one of the all-time great left-handers twice in the series, pitching two complete games and allowing only one earned run in 17⅔ innings against the team that scored the most runs (491) in the National League that season.

"Rogers has pitched two games just about as well as any pitcher can pitch against the Philadelphia Phillies," said Tom Seaver, the NBC color commentator for the series.[7]

SOURCES

In addition to the sources listed in the notes, the author consulted:

Baseball-almanac.com.

Baseball-reference.com.

Usereau, Alain. *The Expos in Their Prime: The Short-Lived Glory of Montreal's Team 1977-1984* (Jefferson, North Carolina: McFarland & Company, 2013).

NOTES

1   MLB referred to these series as Division Series as per the current name, but at the time the media called them "mini-series." What baseball fans now call the division series only came into existence in 1995.

2   Steve Wulf, "The Gang Of Four Shoots To The Top," *Sports Illustrated*, October 19, 1981.

3   Jerome Holtzman, "Rogers double trouble for Phils, gives Expos title," *Chicago Tribune*, October 12, 1981.

4   Ibid.

5   Ibid.

6   *Les Expos Nos Amours*, produced by TV Labatt, 1989 (Video series).

7   NBC telecast of Game Five of the 1981 National League Division Series, Youtube.com.

ROGERS WINS GAME THREE OF NLCS

October 16, 1981: Montreal Expos 4, Los Angeles Dodgers 1 At Olympic Stadium

By Norm King

STEVE ROGERS WAS PREPARING FOR A SHOW-down against the Pittsburgh Pirates in the heat of the 1979 National League East Division pennant race when a reporter told him that manager Dick Williams had just said he would have preferred to start one of his good pitchers but that he had to go with Rogers.

This kind if comment was typical of the Rogers-Williams mutual animosity society that went on when the latter was the skipper, due in part to Williams's belief that Rogers couldn't do it in the clutch.

"He [Rogers] couldn't win the big one," Williams said. "If you needed a big game, he couldn't give you that total effort."[1]

Fast-forward to the 1981 National League Championship Series between the Expos and Dodgers. The Expos were in the NLCS due mainly to Rogers' pitching in the Division Series against the Phillies that resulted from the 50-day players' strike earlier in the season. Rogers had defeated Philadelphia ace Steve Carlton twice in the five-game matchup, including a 3-0 complete-game shutout performance in the clincher. Big-game pitcher indeed.

Rogers' next assignment came on October 16, 1981, as Montreal hosted the first League Championship Series game played outside the United States in chilly (46 degrees at game time and dropping) Olympic Stadium. "The Expos spiritedly took batting practice wearing their official team ski caps," wrote Dick Kaegel in *The Sporting News*. "Young men in the grandstand stripped to the waist, thus advertising the balmy clime to television viewers. Santa Claus appeared and the stadium organist, in high good humor, hit the chords to *Jingle Bells*."[2]

The cold weather promised a hot showdown, just like the Old West. Well, the Old Midwest, actually,

as Rogers and Dodgers starter Jerry Reuss continued a pitching rivalry that began in state high-school tournaments in Missouri. Like Rogers, Reuss was undefeated in the 1981 playoffs; he pitched nine scoreless innings in the Game One of the Division Series against the Houston Astros, although the Astros won 1-0 in 11 innings. Reuss held the Astros scoreless for nine innings again in Game Five, except this time the Dodgers won 4-0, without needing extra frames, to win the series.

Game Three of the NLCS started as one might expect in a game between two pitchers who between them had given up one earned run in their last 35⅔ innings. (Rogers gave up a run in Game One of the Division Series against Philadelphia.) Reuss and Rogers both breezed through the opposing lineups the first time around without breaking much of a sweat, which would have been difficult anyway, considering the temperature. Reuss was particularly nasty, as his slider was acting like a buzzsaw.[3]

The Dodgers opened the scoring in the fourth inning. In a manner reminiscent of the punchless Dodgers teams of the 1960s, they scored without benefit of an extra-base hit. Dusty Baker led off with a single, raced to third on a Steve Garvey single, then scored on Ron Cey's groundout. No doubt former Dodgers manager Walter Alston approved.

Reuss's pitching so far in the playoffs indicated that one run could have been enough, but no one told that to Jerry White. When Williams managed the Expos, he called White the best fourth outfielder in baseball, which is the baseball equivalent of winning Miss Congeniality in a beauty pageant. Even after the Expos traded away right fielder Ellis Valentine for Jeff Reardon in May 1981, White still did not play every day. That is until the Expos fired Williams on September 7 and replaced him with Jim Fanning. Fanning gave White more playing time, first in left to replace an injured Tim Raines, then in right when Raines returned. He was in right field for this game, which was fortunate for Montreal.

The bottom of the sixth inning started off well for Reuss. Despite getting behind the first two hitters, Raines and Rodney Scott, he got them out easily, Raines on a grounder to third and Scott on a popup to second. Andre Dawson singled, then reached second when Reuss walked Gary Carter. With two on, Larry Parrish singled to score Dawson and tie the game. Then up came White using, ironically, a bat left behind by Valentine.

White was no power hitter, as attested by his 18 home runs in 512 games to that point. But Reuss got a 2-and-1 pitch up in the strike zone; White swung and a no-doubter flew over the left-field wall. As he watched the ball in flight, White started skipping sideways toward first base, just as Carlton Fisk did after he hit his famous home run in Game Six of the 1975 World Series. White, though, didn't need the body English. The high fives he received when he arrived at home almost hit the Richter Scale. The fans, to say the least, were ecstatic.

"Montreal, or at least the part of it that jammed Olympic Stadium, went slightly wild. ... Men kissed each other. Some others took their shirts off. Jerry White, a little surprised himself, just stood and watched it go."4

That ended the scoring for the game, but the Dodgers wouldn't go quietly. Steve Garvey and Ron Cey led off the ninth with back-to-back singles, but Rogers got Pedro Guerrero to ground into a 5-3 double play when Parrish nabbed his grounder at third, touched the bag, then threw to first. Rogers finished with a flourish by striking out Mike Scioscia to end the game.

The Expos won the game with all the elements of winning baseball. They got the pitching they needed, power when they needed it, and great defense, particularly from Parrish. In addition to the double play he started in the ninth, he also initiated a twin killing in the fifth when Reuss attempted a sacrifice

Jerry White

bunt with Bill Russell on first. Parrish grabbed it and threw it to shortstop Chris Speier covering third, who in turn gunned the ball to Rodney Scott covering second. Parrish's defensive gems complemented a fine day at the plate; he went 2-for-4 with an RBI and a run scored.

Rogers, for his part, gutted it through despite not having his best stuff. "I can look back on it with a little bit of a smile, but it certainly was a lot harder work," he said of his outing. "I had a good sinker and I was able to get a lot of groundballs. My curve was only fair."5

The Expos also employed some subterfuge, which is a fancy way of saying they were sneaky.

"The Expos suspected that [Dodger] First Base Coach Manny Mota was tipping off the Dodgers as to what pitches were coming—he could tell, for instance, that a fastball was on the way if Catcher Carter set up on the inside of the plate with a righthander up," wrote Wulf. " 'We messed up their minds,' Carter said triumphantly after the game. What he did was simply call for an inside pitch and set up on the outside."[6]

After the game, Expos players laid a path of red towels from their clubhouse entrance to White's locker. Pretty damn good for a fourth outfielder.

SOURCES

In addition to the sources listed in the notes, the author consulted:

Los Angeles Times.

Milwaukee Journal.

youtube.com.

NOTES

1   *Les Expos Nos Amours* (video) produced by TV Labatt, copyright 1989.

2   Dick Kaegel, "Dodgers Weather Rain, Cold, Expos," *The Sporting News*, October 31, 1981.

3   According to Steve Wulf in his roundup of the series for *Sports Illustrated*, one estimate had nine Expos broken bats in the game.

4   "White's Rare Home Run Turn Dodgers Blue," *Milwaukee Sentinel*, October 17, 1981.

5   "Fanning Cautions Expos on LA's Comeback Ability," *Evening Sun* (Hanover, Pennsylvania), October 17, 1981.

6   Steve Wulf, "LA Gets the Last Ha-Ha-Ha-Ha-Ha-Ha," *Sports Illustrated*, October 26, 1981.

SPEIER GOES CRAZY WITH EIGHT RBIS

September 22, 1982: Montreal 11, Philadelphia 4 At Olympic Stadium

By Brian P. Wood

MONTREAL EXPOS MANAGER JIM FANNING returned to the dugout on September 22, 1982, after missing five games with severe migraines. But it was Expos shortstop Chris Speier who gave the visiting Philadelphia Phillies headaches that night, driving in eight runs in an 11-4 Expos win.

Expectations for the Expos ran high at the beginning of the 1982 season, but their chances of winning the National League East were fading as late September rolled around. On September 22, with 12 games to go, they were in third place, 6½ games behind the National League East-leading St. Louis Cardinals. Their opponents, the Phillies, were in second place, 4½ games back.

In addition to Speier, the Expos lineup contained two future Hall of Famers, center fielder Andre Dawson and catcher Gary Carter, as well as basestealing threat Tim Raines. The Phillies, two years removed from their first-ever World Series championship, listed future Cooperstown inductee Mike Schmidt and all-time hits leader Pete Rose on their roster. Two pitchers with similar records faced each other: Bill Gullickson (11-12, 3.54 ERA) for the Expos and Dick Ruthven (11-10, 3.51) for the Phillies.

Speier's enchanted evening began in the bottom of the second inning. Gary Carter and Tim Wallach singled, then Warren Cromartie walked to load the bases. Speier, hitting .262 at game time, stepped to the plate and sent a bases-clearing triple to the center-field wall, giving the Expos a 3-0 lead. Speier remained at third as Ruthven retired the next three batters.

Montreal continued its offensive output in the third. Al Oliver and Carter both singled with one out and moved up on a grounder by Wallach. Ruthven walked Cromartie for the second time, this time intentionally, to load the bases and bring up Speier. Again the shortstop came through, this time driving

in two runs with a single to center to make the score Speier 5, Phillies 0. Philadelphia manager Pat Corrales decided Ruthven was done for the night, and brought in reliever Ed Farmer, who ended the inning by striking out Doug Flynn.

Gullickson retired the first 10 batters he faced but lost his perfect game, no-hitter, and shutout in the fourth. With one out, Pete Rose walked (perfect game gone) and Gary "Sarge" Matthews tripled to center (goodbye, no-hitter), plating Rose (farewell, shutout). Gullickson settled down to get the next two batters.

Speier's teammates showed they could score some runs without his help. They tallied a run in the bottom of the fourth when Tim Raines singled to center with one out, stole second, and advanced to third on catcher Ozzie Virgil's errant throw. Andre Dawson knocked in Raines with a sacrifice fly to center field for a 6-1 Montreal lead. Carter led off the fifth with his 29th home run of the season, making it a 7-1 game for the Expos.[1]

Philadelphia finally broke the code on Gullickson in the seventh inning, roughing him up for three runs. John Vukovich started off with a single to center and Virgil walked with one out. Ivan de Jesus tripled to center, knocking in both runners. Pinch-hitter Greg Gross scored de Jesus on a grounder to first.

Southpaw pitcher Tug McGraw entered the game for Philadelphia in the bottom of the seventh. With one out, Wallach and Cromartie singled. With Speier coming up, Corrales played the percentages and brought in righty Porfi Altamirano. Speier greeted Altamirano with a three-run home run, scoring both Wallach and Cromartie. The homer made the score 10-4 and gave Speier eight RBIs for the night. "I didn't think the ball was going out," Speier said of his homer.[2]

After the home run, the crowd of 18,123 showed their approval with an extended standing ovation that became more intense until Speier acknowledged it from the dugout, a first in his career. "I've made a couple of defensive plays that brought a standing ovation, but never anything like that before," he said.[3]

The Expos put one more on the board in the bottom of the eighth. Jay Baller, in the second outing of his career, became the Phillies' sixth pitcher of the game. Joel Youngblood, in the game for Oliver, reached first on a one-out error by de Jesus. Carter moved Youngblood to second on a single to left, his fourth hit of the game. After Wallach struck out, Cromartie drove in Youngblood with a single to right field. Speier stepped to the plate with two on and a chance to add to his RBI total. However, he hit into a fielder's choice to end the inning with the score 11-4.

The Phillies came up short in the ninth as Gullickson again set them down in order to end the game. The Expos' slim hopes to win the National League East remained alive, with 11 games remaining in the season, but they didn't gain any ground on the Cardinals, who beat Pittsburgh 2-1.[4]

After his three-hit, eight-RBI outburst, Speier's batting average stood at .265 with 60 RBIs, including 22 in September.[5] He remarked, "I don't think I did that even in Little League. I'm not big on statistics, but offensively, it's probably the best game I've ever had."[6]

"My pitchers served him up three easy pitches right across the plate," Phillies skipper Corrales said.[7]

Speier's eight RBIs established a team record as well as being the most allowed by the Phillies in a game.[8] Speier said that he had "started picking up some bad habits," but Billy DeMars, Montreal's hitting coach, "has straightened me out and he's worked with me all year long."[9]

This would be the high-water mark of Speier's season. He went 4-for-32 (.125) in the last 10 games he played that season, his final year as an everyday player.

The Cardinals won the division, the National League pennant, and eventually the World Series

in 1982. Speier blamed the Expos' shortcomings on inconsistency. "That's the way we've been, we're so inconsistent," he said. "That's probably the reason we're in the situation we're in now. If we had played consistent baseball, I don't think we'd be where we are. You can't win divisions by being inconsistent. I don't think you can figure out why we've been inconsistent. If you could come up with a reason, there would be a lot of people willing to spend an awful lot of money to get it. It's one of those intangibles; you can't put your finger on it."[10]

For one day, Chris Speier was "tangible" and you could put your finger on his eight RBIs in one game.

NOTES

1   Carter was attempting become the fourth catcher to hit 30-plus home runs in a season while batting over .300. After this game he stood at 29 home runs and a .303 average. However, he hit no more home runs and his average sank to .293 by season's end. In 1993 Mike Piazza, then with the Los Angeles Dodgers, joined Gabby Hartnett, Roy Campanella, and Joe Torre as the only catchers with 30 or more homers and a .300-plus batting average. As of 2015 four more catchers have since reached those marks (Ivan Rodriguez, Mike Lieberthal, Charles Johnson, and Javy Lopez).

2   "Expos 11, Phillies 4," *Washington Post*, September 23, 1982.

3   Larry Millson, "Speier's amazing bat routs Phillies 11-4," *Globe and Mail*, September 23, 1982.

4   The Phillies fell to 5½ games behind the Cardinals.

5   In addition to the eight RBIs in this game, Speier also had two four-RBI games that September, against the Cubs on the 12th and the Mets on the 15th.

6   Millson.

7   "Sports News," United Press International Morning Cycle.

8   Speier surpassed John Bateman, Bob Bailey, Willie Davis, and Larry Parrish, all of whom had seven RBIs.

9   "Sports News," United Press International, Evening Cycle, September 23, 1982.

10 Larry Millson, "What happened? Expos refuse to dig for also-rans' excuses," *Globe and Mail*, September 25, 1982.

PETE ROSE GETS HIS 4,000ᵀᴴ MAJOR LEAGUE HIT

April 13, 1984: Montreal Expos 5, Philadelphia Phillies 1 At Olympic Stadium

By Bill Schneider

AS PETE ROSE STOOD ON SECOND BASE, BASKING in the cheers of the Expos faithful on hand for the 1984 home opener, it's reasonable to think that he was feeling pretty good. He had made it through the most difficult offseason of his major-league career to that point, with the Expos the only team to express interest in employing him for the 1984 season after the Phillies declined to offer him a new contract. This day belonged to Charlie Hustle, as he reached a milestone only one other major leaguer, Ty Cobb, had accomplished—4,000 hits.

The Expos and Phillies squared off on April 13, 1984, on the 21st anniversary of Rose's first major-league hit. Each team had high expectations for the season; the Phillies were coming off a loss in the 1983 World Series and the Expos were hoping to reverse a disappointing third-place finish the previous season. Those high expectations, along with the chance to witness history—not to mention the opportunity to hear a young Montreal chanteuse named Celine Dion sing the Canadian and American national anthems—enticed 48,060 fans to *Stade Olympique*. As writer Brian Kappler noted, "The Big O had a festive atmosphere for Rose's big day."[1]

That festive atmosphere came compliments of the Cincinnati Reds pitching staff. Rose had had a chance to get the milestone hit in his hometown of Cincinnati in the last game of the Expos' season-opening road trip, but Reds pitchers walked him four times; he saw only two strikes in his four plate appearances.[2]

The Phillies sported a 5-2 record heading into the game, while the Expos got off to a middling 4-4 start. The Phillies sent 41-year-old left-hander Jerry Koosman to the mound for his second start of the

season, while the Expos countered with right-hander Charlie Lea. As for Rose, his hit total stood at 3,999 at the start of the game. Rose had accumulated nine hits in the season's first eight games, and was batting .273 with a .368 on-base percentage.

Philadelphia threatened in the first, as Mike Schmidt and Joe Lefebvre reached on a single and a walk. Lea worked out of the jam by striking out Glenn Wilson, and the Olympic Stadium crowd swelled with anticipation as Rose crouched in the batter's box to lead off the home half of the first. The swelling went down quickly as Rose grounded out to second.

Lea again held the Phils scoreless in the top of the second, and Rose got another chance at 4,000 in the bottom of the inning. Tim Wallach reached on a single to lead off the inning, but was erased on a fielder's choice by Bobby Ramos. After number-8 hitter Angel Salazar flied out, Lea hit a grounder to shortstop that Ivan de Jesus muffed. Ramos scored and Lea wound up on second. Rose stepped in for another shot at history, but grounded weakly to Koosman, who mishandled the ball for another error that allowed Lea to reach third. Lea then scored when Bryan Little singled. Tim Raines walked but Koosman got Andre Dawson to fly out to left fielder Glenn Wilson. The Expos led, 2-0.

The Phils got one run back in the top of the fourth. Wilson doubled to center field and scored from second on a single by Bo Diaz, making it 2-1 Expos.

Montreal got that run back and more in the bottom of the fourth. Lea led off with a walk, and Rose again faced Koosman. Rose struck a hard liner to the right-field corner, over the glove of outfielder Joe Lefebvre. Rose ran out from under his batting helmet on the way to second base, as was his custom.

Pete Rose

Lea advanced to third on the play. The game was halted for two minutes as the crowd celebrated Rose's achievement. Rose described the Olympic Stadium ovation as "special to me because I'm new here."[3] Phillies shortstop Ivan de Jesus presented the ball to Rose, who walked it over to Expos hitting coach Billy DeMars. None of the Expos players came out of the dugout to congratulate Rose, but that doesn't mean they weren't pleased for him.

"I wasn't cheering as much as I would if I hadn't been pitching," said Lea. "I had to think of the next inning and things like that. But everyone was pulling for him. We wanted to see him get it in Cincinnati."[4]

When play resumed, Little grounded out. Then Rose, displaying the basepath aggressiveness for which he was well known, scored from second on Tim Raines' soft single to center as Phils center fielder Von Hayes

played the ball nonchalantly. With Lea having preceded Rose home on Raines' single, the inning ended with the Expos up 4-1.

The Expos got one final run in the seventh, as Andre Dawson tripled to right and was doubled home by Gary Carter. Lea held the Phils until two walks and a hit batsman loaded the bases with two outs in the top of the ninth. Reliever Gary Lucas retired Phils pinch-hitter John Wockenfuss on a grounder to third baseman Tim Wallach to end the threat, and the historic game was in the books.

The day ended triumphantly for Rose and the Expos, but Rose's Montreal career proved to be short and not very sweet. The team traded him to the Reds on August 6 after he had played 95 games, in part because he wasn't the versatile type of player that manager Bill Virdon liked. Rose ended his time in Montreal having contributed a .259 batting average, with a .334 on-base percentage and .295 slugging percentage for an OPS of .629. He did not hit a home run, and had only eight extra-base hits. The failed Rose experiment typified the Expos' season, as they finished at 78-83, with April being their only winning month. While the signing of Rose did not have the outcome either he or Expos general manager John McHale had envisioned, Pete's 4,000th hit made the Phillies-Expos contest on April 13, 1984, one of the most notable games in Montreal Expos history.

NOTES

1   Brian Kappler, "48,000 Cheer the Expos' New Star," the *Montreal Gazette*, April 14, 1984.

2   Alain Usereau, *The Expos in Their Prime: The Short-Lived Glory of Montreal's Team, 1977-84* (Jefferson, North Carolina: McFarland & Company, 2013), 211.

3   "Rose reaches milestone, says ovation was 'special,'" *Kokomo* (Indiana) *Tribune*, April 14, 1984.

4   Ian MacDonald, "Rose Gets 4,000th Hit as Expos Win Opener," the *Montreal Gazette*, April 14, 1984.

DAWSON HITS THREE HOME RUNS

September 24, 1985: Montreal Expos 17, Chicago Cubs 15 At Wrigley Field

By Tom Heinlein

WRIGLEY FIELD HAS SEEN ITS SHARE OF WILD games over the past 100-plus years, and the September 24, 1985, contest between the Montreal Expos and the hometown Chicago Cubs ranks right up there. Andre Dawson belted three home runs — two in one inning — to help the Expos build a 13-run lead, only to see the tying run for the Cubs come to the plate in the ninth before the final out was recorded in a 17-15 Expos victory.

"In this ballpark the game isn't over until the very last out," Dawson said. "We needed each one of those home runs."[1]

Eight home runs were hit in the game, five by the Expos and three by the Cubs, aided by a 17-mph wind blowing out.

Fittingly, Dawson had started the scoring by hitting a home run in the opening frame, a two-run blast that also brought Mike Webster home to score. Montreal added a run in the third, as Webster singled home Sal Butera, who had reached base on a fielder's choice and moved to second on an error by third baseman Keith Moreland.

The Cubs got on the board in the fourth inning, taking advantage of an Expos miscue, as Ryne Sandberg reached first after an error by Hubie Brooks at shortstop. Sandberg stole second, moved to third on a fly out by Moreland, and scored when Jody Davis went deep off Expos starter Bryn Smith for a two-run shot.

The victors did most of their scoring in just one inning, crossing the plate 12 times in the fifth to take a commanding 15-2 lead. Webster and Vance Law set the stage for the first of two Dawson homers in the inning by singling in front of him to start the inning. Dawson followed with his first blast of the frame, off Cubs starter Ray Fontenot, to put Montreal ahead 6-2. Brooks struck out, but Tim Wallach got things going again with a single, chasing starter Fontenot from the game.

Andres Galarraga greeted reliever Jon Perlman with a single, moving Wallach to third base while Galarraga scampered to second on an error by Cubs center fielder Bob Dernier. After an intentional walk to Jim Wohlford, Butera singled to score Wallach and Galarraga. Smith bunted Wohlford and Butera over, and then Webster doubled both runners in to make it 10-2.

After the next batter, Vance Law, walked to put runners on first and second, "The Hawk" stepped in again. Dawson drilled a Perlman pitch out of the park for his second round-tripper of the inning — becoming only the 19th player to perform the feat since 1900 and the second to do it twice.[2] The other time came on July 30, 1978, against the Braves at Atlanta-Fulton County Stadium. "This was the second time I've done it, so it was no big deal," he said afterward.[3]

It was Dawson's sixth home run in his last four games, and it was a preview of the many fine seasons he would have later at Wrigley Field as a member of the Cubs. In his first season in Chicago, in 1987, Dawson would hit 49 home runs with 137 RBIs and be named the NL's Most Valuable Player despite the Cubs' sixth-place finish (of six teams) in the NL East.

After Dawson's second home run, the Expos added two more runs in the big inning. Brooks singled and Wallach socked a two-run homer, his second hit of the frame, to put the Expos up 15-2 and end Perlman's day. Dave Beard replaced Perlman and mercifully ended the inning for the Cubs by striking out Galarraga.

After the Expos' onslaught in the fifth, the Cubs added a run in the sixth that looked harmless enough at the time, with Moreland scoring on a sacrifice fly to left by Thad Bosley. Trailing by 12 runs, the

Cubs unloaded their bench in the seventh, replacing four starters, including their first (Dernier), third (Sandberg), and fourth (Moreland) hitters, as well as number-six hitter Davis—a move that later would have importance.

However, the Cubs were about to be inspired by announcer Harry Caray, "who came out to sing 'Take Me Out to the Ballgame' at the seventh-inning stretch, and just as sure as Caray urged 'Let's Get Some Runs!' that's what the Cubs did."[4]

The hosts scored three times that inning off John Dopson. Dopson had relieved Smith, who would get the win, having gone six innings while giving up three runs—only one earned—and five hits. Billy Hatcher led off the inning with a home run. Gary Woods followed with a double and advanced to third base on a groundout by pinch-hitter Richie Hebner, before scoring on a single by Dave Owen. Owen moved to third on a single by Chris Speier and came in when Leon Durham hit into a force play at short.

The Expos responded right away, though, adding two more runs in the top half of the eighth on a

Andre Dawson

two-run homer by Butera, scoring Doug Frobel, who had drawn a leadoff walk off the Cubs fifth reliever of the day, Steve Engel. That put the lead back up to double digits, 17-6, and none of the 6,947 in attendance who might have had their hopes raised in the seventh would likely have imagined that those two extra runs would be all that meaningful.

But meaningful they were, as the last two Cubs at-bats turned this rout into one of Wrigley's most memorable games. The North Siders got four runs back in the eighth. Bosley led off with a single, moved to second on a groundout by Shawon Dunston, advanced to third on a wild pitch, and scored on a single by Hatcher. Another hit, this time by Gary Woods, put runners at first and third, setting the table for pinch-hitter Gary Matthews, who drilled a three-run homer to cut the visitors' lead to 17-10. Randy St. Claire replaced Dopson, and he immediately gave up back-to-back singles to Owen and Speier to put runners on first and third, before squashing the threat by striking out Durham and retiring Steve Lake on a popup to short.

After the Expos squandered a leadoff double by Brooks in the top of the ninth, the Cubs started quietly in the bottom half, as Bosley flied out to left. After the next two batters, Dunston and Hatcher, both singled, Woods grounded out to third, and the end seemed near. But Ron Cey scored Dunston and Hatcher with a pinch-hit single, Owen walked, and Speier singled to score Cey and trim the lead to four.

That was the day for St. Claire, as Jack O'Connor came on to finish things. Instead, Durham greeted him with a double to score both Owen and Speier, cutting the lead to just two runs and, incredibly, bringing the tying run to the plate. Expos skipper Buck Rodgers wasted no time bringing in his closer, Jeff Reardon, who was on his way to a league-leading 41 saves that year.

"I wasn't even planning on pitching," Reardon said. "They had to come into the locker room to get me."[5]

Reardon faced Cubs backup catcher Steve Lake. Lake, a .151 hitter in 1985, had replaced the strong-hitting Davis—who had homered earlier in the game—after the sixth inning, when it seemed Davis's bat would no longer be needed. Reardon got Lake to ground to first as the Montreal closer covered the bag for the final out, recording his 36th save and ending this 3-hour, 32-minute affair and one of Wrigley's zaniest games ever. The 32 runs scored by both teams was a record for an Expos game, eclipsing the 27 scored in a 19-8 Expos win over the Mets on July 3, 1973. The 12-run fifth was also a team record.

"It got kind of scary, didn't it?" Brooks said. "Playing at Wrigley Field is no day at the beach. We almost lost. If it wasn't for Andre's day, I don't think we would have come out on top. And thank God for Reardon 'The Terminator.'"[6]

SOURCES

In addition to the sources listed in the notes, the author consulted:

The *Montreal Gazette*.

Mlb.com.

NOTES

1   Fred Mitchell, "Cubs dodge blowout, but lose 17-15," *Chicago Tribune*, September 25, 1985.

2   Willie McCovey did it on April 12, 1973, and June 27, 1977.

3   Mitchell.

4   bleacherreport.com/articles/429282-the-chicago-cubs-and-the-10-craziest-box-scores-since-1950.

5   Mitchell.

6   Mitchell.

RAINES MAKES GRAND RETURN TO EXPOS

May 2, 1987: Montreal Expos 11, New York Mets 7 At Shea Stadium

By Mark Simon

IT IS KNOWN IN EXPOS HISTORY AS "THE TIM Raines Game" and if ever there was a game meant to be named after a player, it was this one.

The 1986-1987 offseason was an odd one in Major League Baseball as it lacked business and busy-ness. Prominent free agents like Raines, Ron Guidry, and Jack Morris, who normally would have been hotly pursued by free-spending owners, couldn't find any takers. Something fishy was going on.

That, an arbitrator later ruled, turned out to be collusion among the owners, who in an effort to keep salaries down, instructed their management not to make any big-money offers despite the presence of those high-quality players.[1]

This froze those players because the rules at the time didn't permit them to negotiate with their original teams after January 8 through the end of April.

Raines was coming off a 1986 season in which he hit an NL-best .334, with a league-leading .413 on-base percentage and 70 stolen bases. Nowadays, that would merit a deal of five years or more (especially considering that Raines was only 27 years old).

"He was exactly the kind of player teams would want in the game today," said a former teammate, Tim Wallach.[2]

"He would have been a superstar anywhere else," said former teammate Bob McClure. "He was a good teammate and as talented a player as I've run across. Guys loved him and loved playing with him. He had fun and he played extremely hard."[3]

But instead of playing, Raines was stuck. And though Raines may have been ticked, he wanted back in the lineup … immediately. Raines kept in shape while waiting to sign by working out at Palmetto High School in Sarasota, Florida. He signed a three-

year deal on May 1 for a much smaller raise than he deserved.

"I was disappointed," Raines said. "I was upset with the way the process went down, to be a player of my ability and not able to (really) become a free agent."[4]

Expos manager Buck Rodgers put Raines right into the thick of things, batting him third against the Mets on Saturday afternoon, May 2, at Shea Stadium. The Expos needed a jolt as they entered the day with an 8-13 record and stood in fifth place in the NL East. After a mediocre batting practice ("I think I hit one ball out of the cage," Raines said in an interview 20 years later), Raines flipped the switch once the game began.[4] His first swing against Mets starter David Cone resulted in a triple off the right-field wall.

"I almost missed second base," Raines said.[5]

Cone escaped the jam caused by that hit, but allowed a run in the second inning on a Tom Foley double, then ran into more trouble after walking Raines in the third inning. The speedster stole second and scored the first of two Expos runs in the inning on a base hit by Andres Galarraga. Galarraga scored on a hit by backup catcher John Stefero.

The Expos had a 3-0 lead, but starting pitcher Neal Heaton couldn't hold it. Tim Teufel cut the lead to 3-1 with a third-inning RBI double. Darryl Strawberry's two-run home run in the fourth inning tied it and Dave Magadan's RBI single put the Mets ahead, 4-3.

The Expos tied the game in the sixth inning, as Foley doubled and scored on an error by Mets reliever Terry Leach. But the Mets got two runs back in their half to lead 6-4. Strawberry set that up with a single and two stolen bases. He scored on Magadan's sacrifice fly and the Mets added another run when Howard Johnson walked, stole second, and scored on a pinch hit by Lee Mazzilli. That lead held for two innings and Raines led off the ninth inning looking to start a rally.

He did by beating out a groundball to shortstop for an infield hit. A single by Tim Wallach pushed Raines to third. He scored on a groundout by Andres Galarraga. The Expos tied the game with two out on a single by Vance Law that scored Wallach and forced extra innings. Sparked by that rally, the Expos went to work in the 10th against Jesse Orosco. Singles by Reid Nichols, Casey Candaele, and Herm Winningham loaded the bases with nobody out. It's as if it was scripted for Raines to show his ultimate worth, despite being 3-for-20 with 10 strikeouts against Orosco entering that at-bat.

After Orosco missed with his first pitch, he tried to hit the outside corner with a fastball. Raines was right on it. The ball cleared the left-field wall by a good 20 feet and landed in the Expos' bullpen.

In a career marked by clutch hits, this might have been the most clutch.

"Would you believe a grand slam for Tim Raines?" said Vin Scully, broadcasting the game on NBC. "That has to be one of the most incredible stories of the year in any sport."[6]

"If you wrote it for television they'd say it's too corny, it would never work," said Scully's analyst, Joe Garagiola, as Raines returned to the dugout with teammates bowing to him.[7]

Said Raines: "At that point I was feeling pretty good about myself. I wasn't looking to hit a home run in that situation. I was just looking for a good pitch to hit. He threw me a fastball. I took a good swing and it went out of the ballpark. In that situation, in that game, in that moment, it was quite exciting for me. It was like, 'Welcome back, Tim Raines. I'm ready to go.'"[8]

The Expos scored once more in the inning, and when Randy St. Claire and Andy McGaffigan held the Mets to one run in the home half, the Expos had a season-changing 11-7 win.

Raines finished 4-for-5 with the only out coming on a nice play by Mets second baseman Tim Teufel. It marked the first time in Raines' career that he had four hits and four RBIs in the same game. It was also the second extra-inning grand slam in franchise

Tim Raines

history, the first since Dave Cash hit one to beat the Cardinals in 1979.

"I think I'm still a little rusty," Raines told reporters after the game.[9]

Raines was more trusty than rusty. The next day, in his first at-bat he homered again, this one off Mets lefty Bob Ojeda in the first inning. The Expos won that game, 2-0.

Raines hit .330 in 1987 and set career highs in home runs (18), on-base percentage (.429), and slugging percentage (.526). He stole 50 bases, with a 91 percent success rate, the most efficient he'd been to that point in his career. Raines also won All-Star Game MVP honors with an extra-inning go-ahead triple. He finished seventh in the NL MVP voting.

"He could hit rolling out of bed, from both sides of the plate," said his former teammate Mitch Webster, who spent most of the season hitting in front of Raines and had a career-high 101 runs scored. "He had a tremendous feel for the barrel and sweet spot and incredible strong legs."[10]

"I took a lot of pride in my hitting," Raines said. "People talk about me as a guy who could steal bases. But people don't realize I was almost a .300 hitter. I read *The Art of Hitting* by Charlie Lau and I put in a lot of work to become the hitter that I became. I studied the guys that he illustrated. George Brett was one of my favorites. I patterned myself after those type of hitters. I think I made a good choice."[11]

Beginning with Raines' debut, the Expos went 83-58. Over 162 games, that's a 95-win pace. The Cardinals won the NL East with those 95 wins. The Expos finished third, a game behind the Mets, with 91. Had the Expos had Raines the full season, might things have turned out differently? Perhaps, but we'll never know.

We do know this. The game's memories will last a lifetime.

"That's a day I will never forget," Raines said.[12]

SOURCES

In addition to the sources listed in the notes, the author consulted:

Keri, Jonah. "Raines: I played the game with excitement, focus," *ESPN.com*, December 30, 2007.

Wulf, Steve. "More Bang for More Bucks," *Sports Illustrated*, May 11, 1987.

NOTES

1 On August 31, 1988, arbitrator George Nicolau ruled that clubs had colluded to restrict free-agency movement. The victimized players were declared free agents at season's end, though Raines waived his right to free agency by signing a three-year deal with the Expos.

2 Tim Wallach interview with ESPN.com, April 21, 2015.

3 Bob McClure interview with ESPN.com, April 25, 2015.

4 Tim Raines phone interview, April 21, 2015.

5 Raines interview.

6 NBC broadcast: Expos vs. Mets, May 2, 1987.

7 NBC broadcast (Scully and Garagiola).

8 Raines interview.

9 John Jackson, "Raines Pours it On, Sinks Mets with Slam," *The Record*, Bergen, New Jersey, May 3, 1987, S1.

10 Mitch Webster, e-mail interview, April 21, 2015.

11 Raines interview.

12 Raines interview.

TIM RAINES HITS FOR THE CYCLE

August 16, 1987: Montreal Expos 10, Pittsburgh Pirates 7 At Olympic Stadium

By Tom Heinlein

THE MONTREAL EXPOS COMPLETED A FOUR-game sweep of the Pittsburgh Pirates on Sunday, August 16, 1987, by rallying from a three-run deficit to defeat the Bucs 10-7 in front of 26,134 fans at Olympic Stadium. Tim Raines hit for the cycle while Tom Foley delivered the big blow with a three-run home run to lead the home team to victory. The win improved the Expos' record to 66-51 and kept them within four games of the first-place St. Louis Cardinals.

"The tide has turned for us," Raines said after the game. "They have to count us in the race. We are proving we can come back and win."[1]

With the Expos trailing 7-4 in the seventh inning, Raines led off with a double down the right-field line and then scored on a single up the middle by Mitch Webster to cut the Pirates' lead to two runs. After a walk to Herm Winningham put runners on first and second, Pittsburgh brought in Brett Gideon to face Tim Wallach. Gideon struck out Wallach, and looked to have escaped the jam when Andres Galarraga hit a groundball to second that might have been an inning-ending double play. Instead, the ball was misplayed by second baseman Johnny Ray, and Webster scored. That set the stage for Foley, whose blast gave the Expos a 9-7 lead.

"It's a great feeling to know that you can trail in a game like this and still come back and win," Raines remarked. "And every day, somebody else is doing the job. Today was Tom Foley's turn."[2]

Early on, it did not appear that the Expos would need a comeback, as they jumped to a 2-0 lead in the first inning. Raines led off with a triple off Pirates starter Rick Reuschel. After Reuschel retired Webster on a popup to shortstop, Winningham drilled a double down the right-field line to score Raines. Reuschel

retired Wallach on a fly to center, but Galarraga delivered a two-out single to left field to drive in Winningham.

The Pirates, whose roster featured a young nucleus that would go on to win three consecutive division titles from 1990 through 1992, quickly sprang to life. Their lineup included the outfield of Barry Bonds, Andy Van Slyke, and Bobby Bonilla, and catcher Mike LaValliere—the core of the team's future success—as well as Sid Bream, R.J. Reynolds, and Rafael Belliard, all members of the first of the Pirates division-winners in 1990. Pittsburgh tied the game in the second with two runs off Expos starter Floyd Youmans, who lasted only 3⅓ innings. Belliard got the Pirates on the board, tripling to left-center field to score Bream, who had singled, then scored himself on a single to center by Reuschel.

The Pirates took the lead in the third on three consecutive hits. Ray and Bonilla both singled, and scored on Reynolds's double to right-center field. Pittsburgh extended the lead in the fourth, again led by Belliard. The Pirates shortstop singled to center, stole second, advanced to third on an error by catcher Mike Fitzgerald, then scored easily when Bonds deposited an opposite-field double down the left-field line.

Montreal trimmed the Pirates lead with runs in the fourth and fifth innings. A single to right field by Fitzgerald in the fourth plated Tom Foley, who had doubled to left-center field with one out, cutting the deficit to two runs. In the fifth the Expos registered four hits but came away with only one run. Raines and Webster started the inning with singles to right to put runners on first and third, but the Pirates turned a 5-4-3 double play off the bat of Winningham and, having held Raines at third on the play, looked as though they would escape the inning unscathed. With two outs, though, Wallach dropped a bunt single down to third to score Raines. An infield single by Galarraga again put two Expos on, but Reuschel induced Foley into a groundout to end the threat.

Having minimized the damage in the fifth, Pittsburgh wasted no time in again answering back, scoring two unearned runs on just one hit in the sixth. Joe Hesketh, who had relieved Youmans in the fourth, loaded the bases by walking two and making an error on a groundball by Bonds. Bonilla made him pay, stroking a a two-run single between short and third to push the lead back to three tuns. That, however, would be the last of the scoring for the Pirates. Reliever Jeff Parrett entered the game in the seventh and shut down the visitors the rest of the way for the win, while his team mounted its comeback in the bottom of the inning.

With Parrett keeping the Pirates at bay in what had been a see-saw game, the drama continued in the bottom of the eighth when Raines came to the plate with a second chance to hit for the cycle. He had tripled to right-center in the first, doubled in the third, singled in the fifth, and doubled again in the seventh. The perennial all-star did not disappoint, sending a pitch into the seats off Mark Ross to cap his incredible performance, which included scoring four times.

"I wasn't even thinking about the cycle when I came up in the eighth," Raines recounted. "I just wanted to hit the ball hard."[3]

Hitting for the cycle would normally be the highlight of any hitter's season, but for Raines his stellar 1987 campaign featured an equally spectacular performance. He was forced to sit out the first month of the season, having not received a single offer from any other team as a free agent, despite winning the 1986 batting title with a .334 average. (This lack of offers was widely believed to be due to collusion by owners to restrict the size of contracts.) Raines eventually signed a three-year deal with the Expos, his original team, for $4.8 million on May 1. In his first game, the next day, a nationally televised contest against the defending World Series champion New York Mets, he went 4-for-5, scored three runs, and, as reported in the *Washington Post*, "he capped a storybook, four-hit day with a 10th-inning grand slam that gave the Expos an 11-7 comeback victory … at Shea Stadium."[4] Later in the season, Raines was named MVP of the All-Star Game after his game-winning two-run triple in the top of the 13th inning lifted the National League to a 2-0 win.

Before Raines returned, the Expos were 8-13 and languishing in fifth place in the National League East. With "Rock" back in the lineup, the Expos played at an impressive .586 clip the rest of the way, and were in the division race until the last week of the season. Raines batted .330 with a .429 on-base percentage and .955 OPS, and led the league with 123 runs scored. "The way our team keeps fighting back to win you feel you have do your share," Raines said after the August 16 game, "so hitting for the cycle was the way I did it best."[5]

NOTES

1   Dan Hafner, "National League Roundup: Raines Hits for Cycle in Expos' 10-7 Win," *Los Angeles Times*, August 17, 1987.

2   United Press International, "Tim Raines says hitting for the cycle is just…," upi.com/Archives/1987/08/17/Tim-Raines-says-hitting-for-the-cycle-is-just/4829556171200/, Aug. 17, 1987.

3   Hafner.

4   miscbaseball.wordpress.com.

5   "Tim Raines says hitting for the cycle is just…"

DENNIS MARTÍNEZ' PERFECT GAME

July 28, 1991: Montreal Expos 2, Los Angeles Dodgers 0 At Dodger Stadium

By Rory Costello

"EL PRESIDENTE! EL PERFECTO!"

That was broadcaster Dave Van Horne's call on July 28, 1991, at Dodger Stadium, after Dennis Martínez completed the only perfect game in Montreal Expos history.

Other Montreal pitchers had thrown no-hitters—Bill Stoneman in 1969 and 1972, and Charlie Lea in 1981. Also, just two days before Martínez's gem, Mark Gardner went nine no-hit innings against Los Angeles—but Montreal could not score. Gardner then lost his no-no and the game in the 10th inning.[1] But Martínez became just the 13th man to throw a perfect game in major-league history.

Martinez's masterpiece symbolized his personal redemption. The pitcher, whose father was an alcoholic, became one too. It nearly derailed his career. As early as 1976, in Triple A, there were warning signs.[2] In 1983 his alcohol problem came to a head, and he got help. "It was a bad year," he later said, "but I got a new start."[3]

Though it took more than three years for Martínez to re-emerge fully, he became a master craftsman on the mound. The Expos acquired him from Baltimore in June 1986, and from June 1987 through 1993, Martinez was consistently among the best pitchers in the National League.

In 1988 he had said, "Before, when I was drinking, I used to think I was good. I didn't think about pitching. … I used to just try to throw the ball past the hitter. Now I think. I don't say it makes it easy, but it makes it easier."[4]

That thinking process made him a very crafty pitcher. He moved the ball around, changed speeds, focused on the weaknesses of the hitters, and made constant adjustments, setting up batters based on their reactions from pitch to pitch. He also hid the ball well with his motion and threw from varied arm angles. In some respects, Martinez had his finest season in 1991. He led the NL in ERA at 2.39—never rising above 2.42—and finished fifth in the Cy Young Award voting.

"He's been this way all year," catcher Ron Hassey remarked after the perfect game. "There's been only one or two games when he hasn't had the kind of stuff he had today."[5]

However, as *El Presidente* took the hill at Dodger Stadium on July 28, he hadn't won since a complete-game 4-3 victory at Pittsburgh on July 5. In three starts after that, he had two no-decisions, sandwiched around one of his few shaky outings in '91, a loss to San Diego at home.

It was a typical summer Sunday afternoon in Los Angeles: 95 degrees and hazy. A big crowd of 45,560 was at the game. Martinez had attended Mass that morning, as he did each Sunday. "To me, that was the key point to the day," he later said.[6]

Never overpowering, Martinez fooled the Dodgers "with curveballs and sinkers and guts."[7] As Expos historian Jonah Keri wrote, "Though there weren't advanced pitch-tracking systems back then … you'd swear he threw 50 of his trademark knee-buckling curveballs."[8] Ken Singleton, the color commentator who teamed with Dave Van Horne on the TSN (Canada's only sports network at the time) telecast, said, "It's not your run-of-the-mill curveball that's coming up there today."[9]

Two of those benders came at critical junctures. As Bill Plaschke of the *Los Angeles Times* put it, "Hassey and Martinez combined on two big, bold pitches that may have saved the perfect game. With two out in the seventh inning and a full count on Eddie Murray, Martinez dared to throw a curveball. Murray jumped at it, grounding it to second base. With one out in

Dennis Martinez

the eighth inning and a full count on Kal Daniels, Martinez threw another curveball. Daniels swung through it for a strikeout."[10]

The Dodgers came close to a hit several times. With one out in the fourth, Montreal third baseman Tim Wallach handled Juan Samuel's smash on the lip of the infield grass. With one out in the fifth, Daniels grounded to second base. Delino DeShields backed onto the outfield grass, waiting for a big hop. Daniels—once a fast runner, but slowed by several knee operations—got out of the box slowly but was still out by just half a step.

El Presidente also helped himself with one out in the seventh. The speedy Samuel pushed a bunt up the first-base line, but Martinez raced over, barehanded the ball, and threw out Samuel while falling forward. In the fourth inning, he had fought off a sore hip, caused by landing in a hole on the slippery mound dug by opposing pitcher Mike Morgan.

There was a play that almost led to an error. With one out in the sixth, DeShields fielded Alfredo Griffin's grounder, but his low throw to first nearly pulled Larry Walker off the bag.

Morgan also had a perfect game through five innings until Hassey led off the sixth with a single. The Expos' two runs—both unearned—came in the top of the seventh inning. Griffin, the Dodgers' shortstop, committed an error, and after a sacrifice bunt and a groundout, Walker got Montreal's big hit, a triple. Walker scored when Griffin made his second error of the inning on a Hassey groundball. Morgan went on to throw a complete game himself, allowing just four hits while walking one.

The last man between Martinez and perfection was pinch-hitter Chris Gwynn, younger brother of Tony. The lefty swinger almost ended the dream when he slapped a 1-and-1 pitch barely foul down the third-base line. Expos center fielder Marquis Grissom said, "I don't think anybody wanted the ball hit to them. I was so overexcited out there. I was just thinking, 'Please, no line drives, nothing hard.' I don't want to be the one to ruin history."[11]

Martinez left the 1-and-2 pitch up, and Gwynn lifted it to right-center. "I hit it well," said Gwynn, "but I knew it wasn't enough to get out."[12] Grissom said, "It was a routine fly ball. But I had to get over there and get it. I had to forget what was at stake."[13]

After Grissom gloved the ball, celebration ensued, led by Wallach. When the swarm abated, Martinez then enjoyed an interlude alone in the dugout. "There was nothing in my mind," he said. "I had no words to say, I could only cry. I didn't know how to express myself. I didn't know how to respond to this kind of game."[14]

Martinez's command was exceptional. He needed just 96 pitches, 66 of which were strikes. He went to a two-ball count on only eight hitters, and of these, only three went to a three-ball count. There were 17 groundouts, five strikeouts, two foul outs, and just three fair balls hit out of the infield.[15]

Hassey, who also caught Len Barker's perfect game of May 15, 1981, became the first major-league catcher to handle two of them. "This was a lot different than Lenny's," Hassey said. "Lenny was … a wild pitcher. Dennis is a pitcher's pitcher."[16]

The catcher added, "We had a game plan, and we went out and did it. You give the credit to Dennis. He's the guy who had to throw the pitches. I'm just the guy who's catching them and helping him."[17] Other Expos said, however, that Hassey was being too modest.[18]

Jonah Keri wrote, "In the clubhouse afterwards, Walker showered Martinez with beer, and the conquering hero carefully wiped it off his face. Later that night, teammates and friends toasted him with champagne; Martinez raised his glass, then set it down without taking a sip."[19] After the game, the sober man offered hope to others with drinking problems, saying, "It's never too late to do something about it."[20]

Martinez, the first player from Nicaragua to reach the majors, was already a hero in his homeland. He got the nickname *El Presidente* in 1979 from Ken Singleton, then a teammate with the Orioles. Tito Rondón, who in 1991 was sports editor of the Nicaraguan newspaper *La Prensa*, said, "Dennis Martínez was already the most popular man in the country before he pitched a perfect game. Now he's just more popular."[21]

"I thank God for this game that He gave me late in my career," said Martinez.[22] As it turned out, the veteran remained active through the 1998 season, when he turned 44. He threw eight more shutouts, including two of his six career two-hitters (he also had a one-hitter in 1985). He amassed 245 regular-season victories in the majors, still the record for Latin American hurlers as of 2015, but win number 174 was his finest hour.

SOURCES

In addition to the sources listed in the notes, the author consulted:

"Perfect Sunday," *Washington* (Pennsylvania) *Observer-Reporter*, July 29, 1991.

NOTES

1   Also worthy of mention are two rain-shortened performances. On April 21, 1984, David Palmer retired the first 15 St. Louis Cardinals he faced, but the game was called. On September 24, 1988, Pascual Pérez pitched five hitless innings against the Philadelphia Phillies, but that game was called in the top of the sixth. In September 1991 the Committee for Statistical Accuracy issued a retroactive ruling that these, among 50 games that had been listed as no-hitters, no longer qualified as such. The irony is that the committee made this decision after being asked to rule whether Mark Gardner's achievement deserved to be called a no-hitter.

2   Brian Bennett, *On a Silver Diamond: The Story of Rochester Community Baseball From 1956-1996* (Scottsville, New York: Triphammer Publishing, 1997), Chapter 4.

3   Gary Washburn, "Where Have You Gone, Dennis Martinez?" MLB.com, September 12, 2002.

4   Ian MacDonald, "Heeding Expos' Call for Arms," *The Sporting News*, September 12, 1988.

5   Wendy Lane, "Dennis Martinez: Simply Perfect," *Lexington* (North Carolina) *Dispatch*, July 29, 1991.

6   James Buckley Jr., *Perfect: The Inside Story of Baseball's Twenty Perfect Games* (Chicago: Triumph Books, 2012), 160.

7   Bill Plaschke, "Martinez Perfect Against L.A.," *Los Angeles Times*, July 29, 1991.

8   Jonah Keri, *Up, Up and Away* (Toronto: Random House Canada, 2014), 267.

9   TSN broadcast of the perfect game, accessed via YouTube.com.

10 Plaschke, "Notebook: Perfect Game Not New to Hassey," *Los Angeles Times*, July 29, 1991.

11 Plaschke, "Perfection Brings Expos' Martinez to Tears." (This is an alternate version of "Martinez Perfect Against L.A.")

12 Lane.

13 Plaschke, "Perfection Brings Expos' Martinez to Tears."

14 Plaschke, "Martinez Perfect Against L.A."

15 Ibid.

16 Plaschke, "Notebook: Perfect Game Not New to Hassey."

17 Lane.

18 Plaschke, "Notebook: Perfect Game Not New to Hassey."

19 Keri, 268.

20 Lane.

21 Buckley, *Perfect*, 169.

22 Lane.

THE KID GOES OUT IN STYLE

September 27, 1992: Montreal Expos 1, Chicago Cubs 0 At Olympic Stadium

By Norm King

WITH DUE RESPECT TO TED WILLIAMS, FOR Montreal fans there was only one Kid. And if any player ever bled the colors of a franchise, it was The Kid, Gary Carter, who became the face of the Expos and led it through sometimes faltering steps from being an expansion novelty to a contender in the late 1970s and early 1980s. Even after mutual disappointments led to his being traded to the Mets after the 1984 season, he came back to the team and city he loved and not only retired as an Expo, but did so with a dramatic game-winning hit and an exit that was too corny for Hollywood but wonderful nonetheless.

The Expos claimed Carter off waivers from Los Angeles on November 15, 1991. He played in 95 games for Montreal in 1992, batting .218, with 5 home runs and 29 RBIs. He had announced his retirement due to bad knees at a tearful news conference on September 25, two days before his last game. "As the 38-year-old Carter announced that he would call it quits at the end of this season, his 18th major league campaign, in a career that began and will end with the Expos, a cloud replaced his trademark smile and he broke into sobs," wrote Robert McG. Thomas Jr. in the *New York Times.*[1]

The sobbing stemmed, in part, from the fact that the relationship between Carter and the city transcended that of a player and a town. It's one thing for an American player to move to Baltimore or Philadelphia. It's different for an American player to become a landed immigrant in Canada, especially when it's a California dude who chooses to put up with Canadian winters. There's also the cultural element that made Montreal unique among major-league cities. Most Expos players headed south once the season was over, but Carter endeared himself to Montreal's French

baseball fans by willingly learning some *français* and calling Montreal home.

The 1992 season was transformative for the Expos. After a mediocre 17-20 start, the team fired manager Tom Runnels and replaced him with Felipe Alou, who righted the ship and had the Expos playing very good baseball by September. They had an 85-70 record going into the game against the Chicago Cubs, who were 75-80 when they met in Montreal on September 27. The team's play and the chance to say goodbye to No. 8 brought 41,802 fans to Olympic Stadium that day. It was veteran Mike Morgan for the Cubs against Expos rookie Kent Bottenfield. Both pitchers had last gone to the mound on September 22. Morgan was having a fine season with a 15-7 record with a 2.65 ERA. He went five innings in his previous start, giving up five earned runs to the Mets in a game the Cubs lost 8-7. Morgan received a no-decision. Bottenfield, conversely, was making only his third major-league start and was still seeking his first big-league win. He went only four innings against the Phillies in his previous outing, giving up five runs, four earned, and taking the loss in a 5-2 Expos defeat to go 0-2.

Ah, the heck with it; let's get right down to the big moment. Morgan and Bottenfield had a good old-fashioned pitching duel going on for six innings. Neither was ever in serious trouble. Ryne Sandberg was the only baserunner to reach third base, which he did in the fourth inning, but former Expo Andre Dawson popped out to end the inning. The Cubs had two runners on in the sixth, but could not cash in. Morgan, meanwhile, was toying with the Expos; he was like some guy's first girlfriend because he wouldn't allow anybody to get to second base.

Mel Rojas replaced Bottenfield in the seventh, and he also allowed two baserunners, but Chicago again came up empty. The bottom of the inning started off like all the others for Morgan when he got two quick outs. He then walked Larry Walker, which brought Carter to the plate and the fans to their feet.

Now, Carter rubbed some people the wrong way during his career with his unbridled enthusiasm and "golly-gee willikers" persona. But that personality was genuine, and it hid a dogged determination to win regardless of the situation. For example, in the famous 10th inning of Game Six of the 1986 World Series, with two out and nobody on, it was Carter's seemingly inconsequential single to left that started the Mets' game-winning rally culminated by Bill Buckner booting Mookie Wilson's grounder.

This game wasn't the World Series, but Carter knew it was the last at-bat of his career, and damned if he wasn't going to make the most of it. The count went to—what else?—o-and-2, and with the fans going nuts, Carter drove an outside pitch to right-center field over Dawson's head for a double. Walker scored from first for the go-ahead run, but that seemed almost incidental. Carter stood at second with a Kid-like grin on his face, pumping his fist in the air and reveling in the moment.

"Holy Cow! What an emotional moment here in Montreal," roared legendary Cubs broadcaster Harry Carey above the din. "Enjoy it all, pal. You've earned it."[2]

"Maybe this will be a Hollywood ending for Gary Carter," added fellow broadcaster Steve Stone.[3]

Alou sent Tim Laker out to run for Carter, allowing him to jog to the dugout to the deafening applause of the fans. He hugged each of his teammates in the dugout, then came out for a curtain call, blowing kisses to the fans as they roared their final thank yous and goodbyes.[4]

The rest of the game was anticlimactic. After Rojas pitched the seventh (he got the win to make his record 7-1), Jeff Fassero pitched two-thirds of an inning, then closer John Wetteland came on for 1⅓ innings to earn his 36th save of the season. But all of these numbers and statistics were insignificant in light of Carter's farewell performance.

Gary Carter and Tim Laker hug.

"You couldn't write a Hollywood script for Gary Carter and let it come out like today was," said Cubs manager Jim Lefebvre. "The fans' reaction when he stood on second sent chills up and down my spine. Not too many players end their careers the way he did."[5]

Carter spoke briefly to the crowd after the game ended, then circled the field with his wife, Sandy, in a final *au revoir* to the fans. He also received gifts from the Expos as tokens of the team's appreciation.

"I wasn't going to go out on the field," said Carter's widow Sandy. "He was waving me down, so I walked down just to the tunnel to give him a big hug; he pulled me on the field and said, 'you've been in this career as much as me and I want you down here with me.' It was really his moment but, yes, we shared it together."[6]

The Expos went on a six-game road trip after this game, but Carter didn't play in any of them on the recommendation of Expos broadcaster Dave Van Horne.

"I saw Dave around six months ago," said Carter's widow Sandy in July 2015. "I said, 'you know Dave, Gary never forgot…that you're the one who told him not to have any more at-bats because [he] could not top that last at-bat in [his] whole career."[7]

No one realized it at the time, but Carter's hit was symbolic, almost mystical, in many ways. The 1992 season had started in disarray, righted itself when Felipe Alou took the reins as manager, and gave fans a taste of things to come. Carter's game-winning hit, especially over Dawson's head, was a metaphorical passing of the torch from the "Team of the '80s" to the burgeoning powerhouse of the early 1990s.

SOURCES

In addition to the sources listed in the notes, the author consulted:

Baseball-reference.com.

Hardballtimes.com.

Kuenster, John. *At Home and Away: 33 Years of Baseball Essays* (Jefferson, North Carolina: McFarland & Company, 2003).

Los Angeles Times.

NOTES

1   Robert McG. Thomas Jr., "BASEBALL; I'll Catch You Later, Says a Tearful Carter," *New York Times*, September 26, 1992.

2   Broadcast of September 27, 1992, game between the Expos and Cubs, mlb.com.

3   September 27, 1992 broadcast.

4   Carter later said it was appropriate that Laker came out to run for him because he was going to be the Expos' catcher of the future. It didn't work out that way, as Laker only played in 135 games for Montreal over three seasons.

5   "Carter Sinks Cubs in Farewell Game," *Pharos-Tribune* (Logansport, Indiana), September 28, 1992.

6   Telephone interview with Sandy Carter, July 30, 2015.

7   Telephone interview with Sandy Carter.

THREE CANADIANS IN EXPOS' STARTING LINEUP

September 6, 1993: Montreal Expos 4, Colorado Rockies 3 At Olympic Stadium

By Bill Young

MONDAY, SEPTEMBER 6, 1993, WAS LABOR DAY in Canada and the United States. The Expos were at home, and for the first time since Opening Day more than 40,000 patrons (40,066) had spun through Montreal's Olympic Stadium turnstiles anxious to take in the game. It was the last month of the season and the red-hot Expos were still in the hunt for the National League East Division title. The holiday could easily have been called "Canada's Day" in Montreal because for the first time in baseball history, a Canada-based major-league franchise had listed three Canadian-born players in the starting lineup.[1]

Anchoring the trio was right fielder Larry Walker from Maple Ridge, British Columbia, already a core member of the club. Joe Siddall of Windsor, Ontario, called up in July from the Ottawa Lynx, Montreal's Triple-A International League farm club, was behind the plate. But the starting pitcher was the game's star attraction: Denis Boucher, a local lad from Lachine, Quebec, was the first Quebec-born pitcher to start a game for the Expos, and the second to pitch for the team since Claude Raymond (1969-1971). It would also be the first time since 1883, when pitcher Tip O'Neill threw to catcher John Humphries for the New York Gothams, that any major-league team fielded an all-Canadian battery.

The Olympic Stadium crowd was hoping for a couple of outcomes. To begin with, the fans expected the team to win, as it had been doing all year with remarkable consistency. The 1993 Expos were among the best of all Expos clubs: They completed the season with 94 victories, second only to the 95 wins garnered by the 1979 team.

But more than delighting in how the team was faring, the gathered multitudes were there to cheer on Boucher, who had been acquired by Montreal from San Diego the previous July 10 in a minor-league deal that made him very happy. When first told he had been traded to Montreal, Boucher said, "I had tears running down my cheeks. I was so happy to be coming home."[2]

Boucher faced the expansion Colorado Rockies, a team still struggling through its inaugural season. When the Expos took the field in the top of the first, stadium announcer Richard Morency reeled off the

Denis Boucher

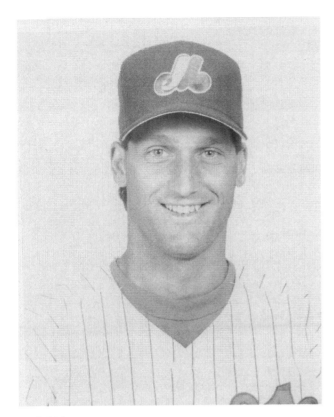

Joe Siddal

name and position of each player to polite applause. When it came time to announce the pitcher, he roared, "And now pitching for the Expos, [from] Lachine, Quebec…" Boucher's name could barely be heard over the standing ovation the fans gave him.

Quebecers have a long history of revering their sports heroes, and saw any success of a Francophone athlete as reflecting positively on themselves. Hockey has always been the unofficial Quebec state religion and players like Maurice Richard, Jean Beliveau, and Guy Lafleur are the deities. But to see one of their own succeed in an American sport, playing for their team in their city, that was a special treat.

If Boucher was nervous going into the game, he didn't show it, as both he and Rockies pitcher Kent Bottenfield (a former Expo) each delivered a three-up-three-down first inning. The Expos opened the scoring in the bottom of the second on back-to-back homers by Walker and Sean Berry to give Montreal a 2-0 lead. The Rockies' Andres Galarraga cut that lead in half in the fourth with a two-out solo home run of his own.

Boucher and Bottenfield battled through the sixth, after which both pitchers left the game with the score still 2-1 for Montreal. When the fans realized Boucher's night was over, they began cheering, and wouldn't stop until Boucher came out for a curtain call, which happened only because his teammates had to virtually throw him out of the dugout onto the field to acknowledge the tribute.

"It is very difficult to do what he did today," said Expos manager Alou after the game. "He was pitching in front of fans who wished him well, and it's very hard to overcome the kind of pressure that can create. Nevertheless, not only did he not give in, but he showed he was not afraid, and this is the kind of man we want with us."[3]

Mel Rojas took the mound for Montreal in the seventh. Rojas, normally a dependable set-up man, gave up a one-out double to Roberto Mejia, who then took third on a wild pitch and came home on a Daryl Boston groundout, tying the score and preventing Boucher from getting the win. The Rockies went ahead 3-2 in the eighth on a Dante Bichette home run off reliever Tim Scott, quieting the crowd and sending more than a few disappointed souls home. But the Expos still had two turns at the plate, and that gave Siddall the chance to show his mettle.

Randy Ready led off the bottom of the eighth with a walk, igniting new life up in the grandstand. Siddall followed and after failing on two bunt attempts, he got his pitch and hammered the ball deep on a line to center for a double, driving Ready home, which tied the score and sent the fans into a frenzy. Siddall took third on a Tim Spehr sacrifice bunt, then was lifted for pinch-runner John Vander Wal.

"I could see what Felipe was thinking," Siddall told baseball historian Jim Shearon. "If it's a sacrifice fly, on a close play, Vander Wal has a little more speed than I have."[4] As it turned out, Grissom, the next batter, singled and Vander Wal simply jogged home with what turned out to be the winning run.

Going into the ninth inning, manager Alou turned as usual to his closer, John Wetteland, to preserve the lead. Wetteland was coming into his own as one of the game's most dominant shutdown men and the confident way he wrapped up this game–two strikeouts and a lazy fly ball to right–proved it.

All in all, it was a good day for Montreal's Canadians. Boucher stayed out of serious trouble, allowing only six hits and one run, and collecting three strikeouts while surrendering no walks over six innings. Siddall handled his duties behind the plate with assurance, and helped to produce two runs. And once again Larry Walker was the catalyst, getting things going with his 18th home run of the campaign.

Boucher had a successful September, winning three games and losing only one, but after he surrendered the decisive run in an extra-inning loss at Houston on Opening Day in 1994, his stock plummeted. By the end of May he was back to Ottawa, never to see the major leagues again.

Joe Siddall got into 19 games in 1993 but was left off the '94 Expos roster. Briefly called up in 1995, he later touched down with the Marlins and the Tigers before returning to the minors. In 2014 he joined the Toronto Blue Jays radio/TV broadcast team.

Larry Walker continued to grow as a ballplayer through 1994. He was eligible for free agency after that strike-truncated season, and given the stoppage's crippling financial impact, the Expos let him move on to Colorado in 1995, where he developed into a superstar.

SOURCES

In addition to the sources listed in the notes, the author consulted:

Baseball-reference.org.

Retrosheet.org.

Youtube.com.

NOTES

1   It would appear that never before in major-league history had three or more Canadian players appeared in the starting lineup of a regular league game. This rarity would not be repeated until April 25, 2015, when the Toronto Blue Jays met the Tampa Bay Rays in St. Petersburg. That evening the Jays started youngsters Michael Saunders (Victoria, British Columbia) and Dalton Pompey (Mississauga, Ontario) in the outfield and the Toronto-born, Montreal-raised veteran catcher Russell Martin behind the plate. The Jays lost, 4-2.

2   Danny Gallagher and Bill Young, *Ecstasy to Agony: The 1994 Montreal Expos. How the Best Team in Baseball Ended Up in Washington Ten Years Later* (Toronto: Scoop Press, 2013), 98.

3   Jacques Doucet and Marc Robitaille. *Il était une fois les Expos; Tome 2: les années 1985-2004 (Once Upon a Time There Were the Expos; Volume 2: The Years 1985-2004)* (Montreal: Les Éditions Hurtubise, 2009), 341 (translation by author).

4   Jim Shearon, *Canada's Baseball Legends: True stories of Canadians in the Big Leagues Since 1879* (Kanata, Ontario: Malin Head Press, 1994), 224.

EXPOS PLAY WITH PRIDE

September 17, 1993: Montreal Expos 8, Philadelphia Phillies 7 At Olympic Stadium

By Norm King

BASEBALL FANS FEEL MANY EMOTIONS DURING the course of a game. They may feel joy, anger, euphoria, or despair. But rarely, if ever, does a single, ordinary play become a moving, lump-in-your-throat memorable event. It did on this night.

The 45,757 fans who attended the game at Olympic Stadium on September 17, 1993, felt all of these emotions and more as they watched the Expos roller-coaster their way to a thrilling 8-7 win over the Philadelphia Phillies in the heat of the pennant race. And they took to their hearts a 24-year-old minor leaguer named Curtis Pride as they saw him get his first major-league hit and acknowledge their thunderous applause—even though he couldn't hear it.

The Expos were so hot when play began that night that you could have fried a proverbial egg on them. After losing 4-2 to Cincinnati on August 20, the Expos were in third place in the National League East, at 64-59, 14½ games in back of Philadelphia. They then went on a 20-3 run, and at the start of play on September 17 the Phillies (89-57) were five games up on Montreal (84-62). The two teams were looking over their shoulders only to wave goodbye to the rest of the division.

Ben Rivera started for the Phillies. He had a 12-9 record going into the game; he had been hammered for five runs (four earned) in his previous start, a 9-2 loss to the Houston Astros on September 12. Dennis "El Presidente" Martinez (14-8) was his mound opponent. He had pitched well in his previous start, a no-decision against Cincinnati, in which he gave up only one run over seven innings in a 3-2 Expos win.

The crowd, the quality of the teams, and the tension of the pennant race all promised a tight, close ballgame, and that's how it went—at least in the beginning. The game was scoreless until the bottom of the fourth, when the fastest team in baseball—the Expos led the National League in stolen bases that year with 228—walked their way to their first run of the game. Larry Walker singled to center, but was forced out at second on a Darrin Fletcher fielder's choice. Fletcher then paraded around the bases to third after walks to Randy Ready and Wil Cordero, and scored when Rivera walked Martinez.

The Expos built on their 1-0 lead in the fifth. Rivera started the inning by issuing his fifth free pass of the game, this time to Delino DeShields. DeShields took all these walks as a personal insult, so he showed off some team speed by stealing second. He moved to third on a sacrifice bunt by Rondell White and scored on Walker's single. Walker himself moved to third on a Fletcher single, and that was it for Rivera. Roger Mason replaced him, and started off by—you guessed it—walking the first hitter he faced, Randy Ready. Sean Berry hit a sacrifice fly to score Walker and the Expos led 3-0.

The usually reliable Martinez, who gave up only three hits in the first five innings, fell apart in the sixth. Mariano Duncan started the inning with a single and moved to third on John Kruk's double. After Dave Hollins struck out, Darren Daulton smacked his 24th home run of the year, which tied the game at 3-3, but the Phillies' barrage was just beginning.

Martinez's first pitch to Jim Eisenreich found its way down the left-field line; Eisenreich headed to second and Martinez headed to the showers. Mel Rojas came in and was victimized by bad luck when Ready didn't live up to his name and made an error on Milt Thompson's grounder. Rojas didn't do nepotism's reputation any favors—Expos manager Felipe Alou was his uncle—by walking Kevin Stocker and pinch-hitter Mickey Morandini to score Eisenreich with the go-ahead run. A sacrifice fly by Lenny Dykstra and a two-run double by Duncan completed the carnage. It was 7-3 Phillies after 5½ innings.

The Expos got one back in the bottom of the inning off Bobby Thigpen. With two out, DeShields cracked a single to center. White hit an ordinary fly that Dykstra caught in center for the third out, yet nobody left the field. It turns out that Thigpen had balked on the play, sending DeShields to second. White then singled to center, scoring DeShields and making it 7-4.[1]

The bottom of the seventh started routinely enough. Fletcher singled and was forced at second on a Ready grounder. Berry beat out a high chopper to third and, with two runners on, Alou sent Pride up to pinch-hit for pitcher Chris Nabholz, who had come on with two out in the sixth. (This is the moment when this became more than just a ballgame.)

We are all inspired by the resiliency of the human spirit. Everyone loves to see people succeed after overcoming a physical or mental disability, especially in professional sports. Pride was born deaf, was a multi-sport athlete—he was named one of the top 15 youth soccer players in the world in 1985—and graduated from the College of William and Mary in 1990 with a degree in finance. When he made his Expos debut on September 14, he became the first hearing-impaired major leaguer since Dick Sipek, who played 85 games for the Cincinnati Reds in 1945.

Pride received the same polite applause when he was announced into the game that any other pinch-hitter would get. Thigpen threw his first pitch, and Pride swung and sent a liner to the gap in left-center for a double that scored two runs. Naturally the hometown crowd stood to cheer. Phillies manager Jim Fregosi came out to change pitchers, and while that was going on, Expos third-base coach Jerry Manuel walked over to Pride and through gestures got him to remove his batting helmet to acknowledge the crowd. The cheering got louder and continued all through Larry Andersen's warm-up tosses.

"The way they kept cheering, it's as if the crowd wanted to break a barrier," said Manuel after the game. "They wanted him to know how they felt, to get beyond the wall. That's the greatest thing I've ever seen."[2]

Not only was it emotional, it was also clutch because it brought the Expos back to within a run with a runner on second and only one out. The Expos tied the game at 7 when Marquis Grissom singled Pride home. Olympic Stadium was a happy nuthouse.

From that point on it became a war of attrition. The Expos almost took the lead in the eighth when they had the bases loaded with one out, but Sean Berry hit into an inning-ending double play. No one scored in the ninth, 10th, or 11th. Finally, with Mitch "Wild Thing" Williams on the mound in the 12th, Grissom doubled, stole third, and incited fan pandemonium when he scored on a DeShields sacrifice fly.

The victory brought the Expos to within four games of the Phillies, but for all intents and purposes they never got any closer. A 3-1 victory over Pittsburgh on the last day of the season brought them within three games of Philadelphia, but that was too little, too late. There was, however, lots of room for optimism. The team went 46-28 after the All-Star break and that record was a harbinger of things to come in 1994; that season they had the best record in baseball when the players strike wiped out the remainder of the season and the World Series.

As for Pride, he never really caught on at the major-league level, playing only 421 games for six different teams. He finished with a .250 career batting average, 20 home runs, and 82 RBIs, but his numbers didn't prevent his efforts from being acknowledged for his courage. In 1996 he won the Tony Conigliaro Award, which is given annually to a major-league player "who best overcomes a major, often life-altering obstacle and continues to thrive through adversity."

Pride continued working with the deaf after his playing career in many capacities, including as baseball coach at Gallaudet University, a school specifically for hearing-impaired students, and with his Together With Pride Foundation, which operates programs for hearing-impaired children.[3] Pride's contributions and achievements were even recognized at the highest levels, when President Barack Obama named him to the President's Council on Fitness, Sports, and Nutrition in 2010.

SOURCES

In addition to the sources listed in the notes, the author consulted:

Baseball-reference.com.

Baseball-almanac.com.

Fitness.gov.

Gallaudet.edu.

Redeafined Magazine.

Togetherwithpride.com.

YouTube.com.

NOTES

1 As of this writing, the entire game can be viewed on the Internet.

2 Jonah Keri, *Up, Up & Away, The Kid, The Hawk, Rock, Vladi, Pedro, Le Grand Orange, Youppi!, The Crazy Business of Baseball & the Ill-Fated but Unforgettable Montreal Expos* (Toronto: Random House Canada, 2014).

3 He was still the Gallaudet baseball coach as of 2015.

FLOYD GOLFS ONE OFF MADDUX

June 27, 1994: Montreal Expos 7, Atlanta Braves 2 At Olympic Stadium

By Rod Mickleburgh

MENTION 1994 TO A FAN OF THE MONTREAL Expos, and chances are his or her heart will immediately sink. It was the best of times, but it was also the worst of times, and the worst of times came at the end, when labor troubles shut down the season with the Expos far ahead in their division. For many, the heartache from that bittersweet season still lingers. Yet the best is often forgotten amid the tears.

On June 27 the Expos and their ever-hopeful fans, still waiting after 25 years for their first World Series berth, had only one matter on their minds: the division-leading Atlanta Braves. Although the Expos had been on a roll all month, taking 16 of 23 games, the Braves had been winning, too. As the two teams prepared to go at each other in a three-game showdown series in Montreal, the Braves retained a 2½-game lead. With the hockey season over, Montrealers were now focusing on their red-hot Expos. More than 45,000 boisterous rooters streamed into gloomy Olympic Stadium for Game One.

The Braves were a proven powerhouse, winner of the NL West for the previous three seasons, before a league realignment brought them properly back to the NL East. Their 103 victories in 1993 had been the most in the team's 122-year history, and, with Greg Maddux, Tom Glavine, John Smoltz, and Steve Avery, their starting rotation was easily the best in baseball.

But the young Expos, managed by the savvy Felipe Alou, were coming on. They, too, had had a good year in 1993, winning 94 games, their second highest total ever. Nonetheless, the team's success went almost unnoticed in a country caught up in the national hoopla over another World Series for the Toronto Blue Jays.

The Expos were even better in 1994. Alou had a set lineup that was the stuff dreams were made of. He rarely needed to juggle, sending the same eight position players out time after time. All played in at least 100 of the abbreviated season's 114 games except for catcher Darrin Fletcher, who chalked up 94 games. Third baseman Sean Berry was the oldest of the bunch at 28. The outfield of Moises Alou, Marquis Grissom, and Canadian Larry Walker was the envy of the league. Only one rookie managed to crack the regular lineup: prized prospect Cliff Floyd, at first base.

For the series opener, both teams sent their aces to the mound. Maddux and the Expos' Ken Hill were at the peak of their game. Each already had 10 wins, on the way to what would likely have been their best seasons if the strike had not intervened. As it was, Hill finished 16-5. Maddux also won 16, while winding up with a league-leading ERA of 1.56, the lowest since Dwight Gooden's minuscule 1.53 in 1985. On May 6 Maddux had shut out the Expos on four hits. Two days after that, Hill returned the favor, blanking the Braves on three hits over seven innings as the Expos eked out a 1-0 win in Atlanta. A pitchers' duel seemed certain.

Unsurprisingly, after six innings, the score was tied, 1-1. The Braves went scoreless again in the seventh. In the bottom of the inning, however, the Expos began to get to Maddux. Grissom singled for his third hit of the game. Taking advantage of perhaps the only flaw Maddux had—surrendering stolen bases—the speedy Grissom stole second, then third. Left fielder Lou Frazier, filling in for Larry Walker, worked a rare walk from the Braves' uber-control artist. Then he swiped second base, too. Moises Alou popped out, but Fletcher was intentionally walked to load the bases. The large crowd roared in anticipation as Wil Cordero came to the plate. With the count even at 1-and-1, the slick-fielding shortstop lined the ball to Ryan Klesko in left. Grissom tagged up and scored easily. The Expos were in front. Author Jonah Keri later wrote: "The resulting ovation was probably one of the five biggest ever for a Big O sacrifice fly."[1] Up stepped Cliff Floyd.

The Expos chose Floyd, an imposing, 21-year-old slugger from the working class South Chicago suburb of Markham, in the first round of the 1991 draft. Two years later, after a fence-busting stint with the Harrisburg Senators of the Eastern League and time with the Triple-A Ottawa Lynx, the 6-foot-5, 220-pound hulk was named *The Sporting News'* Minor League Player of the Year. Now he was with the Expos. His adjustment to the big leagues had not been easy. Although he was batting a respectable .277, his vaunted power had been missing in action, with only two home runs to show so far in the season.

In a preseason television interview, Floyd said his goal was to not think too much at the plate. "If you got a hundred things on your mind, how you going to hit the ball?" But facing Greg Maddux was a formidable task, thinking or not. In four at-bats against the future Hall of Famer back in May, the youngster had failed to get the ball out of the infield, striking out once. In a phone call before this game, his father cautioned him to concentrate on just getting any kind of a hit. Floyd retorted: "Nah, I'm swinging for the fences tonight."[2]

As he settled into the batter's box, however, the left-handed-hitting Floyd was mired in an 0-for-13 slump, having taken a called third strike against the Braves' Cy Young hurler only the inning before. As Frazier danced off third, the count went to 2-and-2. Catcher Javy Lopez called for Maddux's two-strike money pitch, a devilish changeup that dipped alarmingly as it crossed the plate.[3] This time the ball dropped so dramatically that it was down around Floyd's ankles by the time he had a chance to swing. No one, apart from maybe Cliff Floyd himself, could have predicted what happened next. He swung hard and low at the plummeting baseball, golfing at it, as if he were driving off on a par 5 at the course back home where he used to caddy as a teenager. The ball leapt off his bat like a rocket and slammed high up into the right-field stands, 400 feet from home plate. In the twinkling of an eye, the Expos led the Braves 5-1.

Maddux was stunned. Raw rookies don't homer off the great Greg Maddux, let alone blast the ball off his shoetops for a deep, deep moonshot. Atlanta manager Bobby Cox came out to the mound. His shaken pitcher handed him the ball, and was gone. Floyd's monster drive sent the Big O crowd into an absolute frenzy, sparking wave after wave of mock war chants and tomahawk chops that didn't let up until the final out.

Relief pitcher Tim Scott saw it all from the bullpen. "He golfed it out," he told author Danny Gallagher in 2011, still marveling at the memory. "It was unthinkable, considering that Maddux was pitching. Maddux was shocked, absolutely shocked."[4] Nor did Cliff Floyd forget his big moment. "That was the highlight of the season for me," he said in 2012. "The Braves … were our nemesis, the team of the 1990s. So when I did that, I felt I helped get us over the hump. There was a packed house. It was something."[5]

The rest of the game was anticlimactic. Atlanta nibbled a run off Hill in the eighth, but the Expos replied with two more in their half of the inning. They won in a breeze, 7-2. The 1994 Expos were on their way.

Floyd's electrifying home run remains a treasured remembrance of Expo fans, as well. When Montrealers packed the Big O for a Blue Jays preseason game in 2015, Olivier Pinsonneault tweeted: "Olympic Stadium hasn't been this crazy since Cliff Floyd's home run against Greg Maddux in 1994."

SOURCES

In addition to the sources listed in the notes, the author consulted: YouTube.com.

Gallagher, Danny. "Cliff Floyd, he of the Bunyanesque, Samson-style power, fully expects he will be hitting a few 500-foot dingers down the road in the majors," *The Globe and Mail* (Toronto), March 29, 1993.

NOTES

1   Jonah Keri, *Up, Up, & Away: The Kid, The Hawk, Vladi, Pedro, Le Grand Orange, Youppi!, The Crazy Business of Baseball & the Ill-fated but Unforgettable Montreal Expos* (Toronto: Random House of Canada, 2014), 303.

2   Jeff Blair, "Floyd powers Expos to win; Three-run homer key blow as Braves' lead chopped," the *Montreal Gazette*, June 28, 1994.

3   Keri, 304.

4   Danny Gallagher and Bill Young, *Ecstasy to Agony, The 1994 Montreal Expos* (Toronto: Scoop Press, 2013), 94.

5   Gallagher and Young, 94-95.

THE EXPOS ARE FOR REAL

June 28, 1994: Expos 8, Braves 7 At Olympic Stadium

by David Denomme

THE ATLANTA BRAVES CAME TO MONTREAL for a three-game series in late June of 1994 with a 2½-game lead in the NL East over the Expos and every reason to be confident. The Braves team was a juggernaut; they had finished first in their division for three consecutive years and had made it to the World Series in 1991 and 1992.[1] After 1994, the Braves would go on to finish first in the National League East an astonishing 11 straight years. The only time they did not finish first between 1991 and 2005 was in 1994, when the season ended prematurely because of the players' strike with the Braves in second place six games behind Montreal. The Expos were looking over their shoulders at Atlanta, but that was only to say goodbye.

The June 28, 1994, game was the second of the three-game set. In the opener, the Expos beat ace Greg Maddux, 7-2, with the help of a Cliff Floyd home run. In the second game, the Braves came back with Tom Glavine, another future Hall of Famer. Glavine had won 20 games three years in a row and had finished in the top three in the Cy Young Award voting each year, winning the trophy in 1991. So there was no reason for the Braves faithful to doubt that a comeback win was in the offing.[2]

The Expos fans were more than ready; while attendance at the Tuesday game was down about 5,000 from the Monday opener, it was still above 40,000, and the three-day weekday series averaged almost 44,000 per game. The Expos welcomed back All-Star Larry Walker, who had been suspended four games for charging a Pirates hurler earlier in the season.[3]

The Expos started 23-year-old lefty Kirk Rueter, who was 3-1 after 12 starts but with a less-than-sparkling 5.44 ERA. Things went bad quickly for Rueter in the top of the first; after striking out left fielder Dave Gallagher and getting shortstop Jeff Blauser to

ground out, he walked Roberto Kelly and then gave up back-to-back doubles to Fred McGriff and David Justice to score two runs.

The Expos got a run back off Glavine in the bottom of the inning when Walker singled home Rondell White. They scored two more runs on a single, double, groundout, and suicide squeeze to take a 3-2 lead after two innings.

It didn't take long for the Expos' new lead to evaporate. In the top of the third, Rueter gave up singles to Blauser and Kelly and walked McGriff to load the bases before uncorking a wild pitch that scored Blauser. David Justice's subsequent run-scoring groundout was all manager Alou needed to see and he yanked Rueter with one out and the Expos down 4-3. Gil Heredia, replacing Rueter, allowed a sacrifice fly to make the game 5-3.

Heredia and Glavine settled down into a brief pitchers' duel and there was no further scoring until the seventh inning. In the top of the seventh, right-hander Heredia, in his fifth inning of relief, gave up a single to the Braves' Bill Pecota, batting eighth. After Glavine sacrificed Pecota to second, Tony Tarasco (who had entered the game earlier as a pinch-hitter and left-field replacement for Dave Gallagher) singled to right field, but Moises Alou threw out Pecota at the plate for the second out of the inning, with Tarasco advancing to second. Manager Alou brought in Tim Scott, another righty, to pitch to the Braves' Jeff Blauser. Scott entered the game via a double switch; utility infielder Freddie Benavides entered the game to play second base and bat ninth, while Scott replaced Sean Berry in the seventh spot in the order and Mike Lansing moved from second to third base. Blauser rudely welcomed Scott with a single through the hole into left field to score Tarasco, but then got caught in a rundown

Cliff Floyd

trying to advance to second base and was put out in a rundown to end the inning with the Braves up 6-3.

Braves manager Bobby Cox brought in lefty Mike Stanton to start the bottom of the eighth and face the 4-5-6 hitters in the Expos lineup. The move proved disastrous for Atlanta, as Walker singled to center and Wil Cordero homered on a line to deep left field to delight the Olympic Stadium crowd and bring the Expos back into the game, trailing 6-5. That was enough for Cox and he called for righty Greg McMichael from the bullpen to face Lenny Webster, who lined out to deep right for the first out. The next spot in the order belonged to Scott because of the previous double switch. Continuing the chess match, Alou brought in Darrin Fletcher to pinch-hit for Scott and was immediately rewarded when Fletcher doubled to left. Alou called on Tim Spehr to pinch-run for him. The strategizing proved successful when Mike Lansing doubled to left on a 1-and-1 pitch, scoring Spehr and tying the game at 6-6.

So the rivals moved, tied, into the climactic ninth inning. Felipe Alou brought in his trusted reliever (and nephew) Mel Rojas to pitch. Rojas began well,

striking out eighth-place hitter Pecota on three pitches to bring up the pitcher's spot. Bobby Cox sent up Ryan Klesko, a young power-hitting lefty swinger who had had only 31 at-bats with the Braves before the 1994 season. Klesko took an 0-1 pitch down the right-field line for a solo homer, quieting the partisan crowd and giving the Braves a 7-6 lead. Stung, Rojas struck out Tarasco and induced Blauser to ground out to end the inning, but the Expos entered the bottom of the ninth with their backs to the wall.

Bobby Cox brought in reliever Steve Bedrosian to close out the game against White, Alou, and Walker. The 36-year-old Bedrosian was back with the Braves, having started there before moving on to great success with the Philadelphia Phillies. He had not recorded a save since the 1991 season, but in some ways seemed the perfect choice to try to put the game away—of his 184 career saves, 27 came against the Expos, more than against any other team. Cox couldn't have known that not only would Bedrosian not save this game, he would not record a save again before his 14-year career ended in 1995.

White took a 2-and-1 pitch to right field for a single, and then waited for the count to go to 3-and-1 on Alou before stealing second base. Alou walked on the next pitch, putting two runners on for Walker with nobody out. He responded with a single to right field to score White and move Alou to third, tying the game again. This blow gave Walker a 4-for-5 day on his return to the team. The delirious Expos fans didn't have time to appreciate this, however, before Wil Cordero worked Bedrosian to a 3-and-2 count and then hit the ball through the hole into left field for another single, scoring Alou and winning the game, 8-7. Bedrosian had given up three hits and two runs, losing the lead and the game without recording an out.

The Braves press called this game "easily their ugliest loss of the year"[4] because of the two blown leads. Two games of the 2½-game lead had been erased by Expos heroics, and it didn't escape attention that the Expos were doing it all with less than half the payroll of the lordly Braves.[5] The Expos lost the next day in the series finale (to a great pitching performance by yet another future Hall of Famer, John Smoltz) and wouldn't take the division lead for good until July 22, but the games of June 27 and 28 convinced the Braves, and the baseball world, that these Expos were for real.

SOURCES

In addition to the sources listed in the notes, the author consulted:

Gallagher, Danny, and Bill Young. *Remembering the Montreal Expos* (Toronto: Scoop Press, 2005).

Keri, Jonah. *Up, Up, & Away: The Kid, The Hawk, Rock, Vladi, Pedro, Le Grand Orange, Youppi!, The Crazy Business of Baseball, & the Ill-fated but Unforgettable Montreal Expos* (Toronto: Random House Canada, 2014).

NOTES

1   After competing in the National League West since the division alignment was instituted in 1969, the Braves were transferred to the National League East in 1994.

2   Glavine would finish his career with more wins against the Expos/Nationals franchise (33) than any other franchise.

3   Walker was not paid during the suspension and was none too happy about it: Joseph A. Reaves, "Expos' 'Fiscal Restraint' Doesn't Impress Walker," *Chicago Tribune*, July 3, 1994. Walker filed a grievance against the club through the players association.

4   I.J. Rosenberg, "More Bullpen Blues: Braves' Skid at 4," *Atlanta Journal*, June 29, 1994: D1.

5   I.J. Rosenberg, "Expos Get More Bang for the Buck," *Atlanta Journal*, June 30, 1994: F6.

INSIDE THE PARK FOR GRISSOM

August 1, 1994: Montreal Expos 3, St. Louis Cardinals 2 At Olympic Stadium

by David Denomme

WHEN BASEBALL'S 1994 CALENDAR FLIPPED from July to August, the clock was ticking towards the beginning of the infamous strike that ended what may have been the Montreal Expos' finest season and destroyed their last and best chance at glory.

When play began on August 1, the Expos had the best record in baseball at 65-38, one game better in the win column than the New York Yankees, and held a 3½-game lead in the National League East over the Atlanta Braves. The team's 37-16 record in June and July had caught the attention of the fans—30,359 attended the Monday day game in Montreal's *Stade Olympique*. By contrast, at 47-56 the St. Louis Cardinals were tied for last place in the NL Central with the Chicago Cubs, and had just completed a month in which they went 8-20, their worst July performance in 24 years.[1]

The starting pitchers for the August 1 game were right-hander Vicente Palacios for the Cardinals and lefty Butch Henry for the Expos. Palacios, 2-7, was making his 17th start of the year, having been used as a reliever in April before moving into the rotation in May. Henry, on the other hand, was 8-2 and had been used as a swingman early in the year, only settling into a starting job in late June. This was his 13th start overall and eighth in a row; in the previous seven starts he was 5-2. Henry's ERA was 2.47, in stark contrast to Palacios's 4.43.[2]

Both pitchers sailed through the early innings. Henry found himself in a jam in the top of the fifth inning when Mark Whiten, the Cardinals' right fielder, led off the inning with a single and left fielder Bernard Gilkey reached on an error by Expos third baseman Sean Berry. However, Henry extinguished the rally by striking out second baseman Geronimo Pena and inducing Terry McGriff, the Cardinals' catcher and eighth-place hitter, to bounce into his second double play of the game.

The Expos finally opened the scoring in the bottom of the sixth inning. Left fielder Lou Frazier walked to open the inning, and was forced at second by center fielder Marquis Grissom's groundball to short after Cliff Floyd's flyout to deep right field. With two out and Grissom on first, Larry Walker singled to move him to second. Catcher Darren Fletcher doubled to right, scoring Grissom and advancing Walker to third. Walker then scored when third baseman Todd Zeile mishandled Wil Cordero's grounder (St. Louis's only error of the game) to give the Expos a 2-0 lead.

The Cardinals immediately got one back when Whiten led off the seventh by homering off a tiring Henry, who was replaced by Mel Rojas after he walked Gilkey following Whiten's blast. Rojas's entry into the game did nothing to calm the nerves of Expos fans—Gilkey immediately stole second and went to third on a throwing error by Fletcher. Rojas walked Pena, putting runners on first and third with nobody out. Rojas quickly righted the ship, striking out pinch-hitters Gerald Perry and Luis Alicea in succession and causing center fielder Gerald Young to bounce harmlessly to first, ending the inning.

The Expos took their 2-1 lead to the top of the ninth inning and brought in their closer, John Wetteland, who at that point had 21 saves (he would finish the year with 25, fourth most in the NL). Wetteland quickly retired Whiten and Gilkey but then gave up a game-tying home run to Geronimo Pena, one of 11 homers Pena would hit in 1994, but one of only 30 in the second sacker's seven-year career in the majors. The game went into the bottom of the ninth tied 2-2.

The Expos threatened to win in the home half of the ninth when pinch-hitter Juan Bell walked and advanced to second on a Sean Berry sacrifice bunt. With one out, 22-year-old Rondell White was called on to pinch-hit and walked, causing Cardinals skipper Joe Torre to bring in Rich Rodriguez, his left-handed relief specialist. Rodriguez sent the game to extra innings by getting Frazier to pop up to the catcher and striking out Cliff Floyd.

Wetteland again took the hill in the 10th inning but continued to live dangerously. With one out he walked Ozzie Smith, who promptly demonstrated that he retained enough speed at age 39 to steal second off Lenny Webster, the Expos' third catcher of the day. But after an intentional walk to third-place hitter Gregg Jeffries, Wetteland induced Zeile to hit into the Cardinals' third double play of the game and end the inning.

Marquis Grissom led off the bottom of the 10th inning for the Expos. He hit a pitch low and away from lefty Rodriguez on a 1-and-2 count and sent it looping toward center field, to the right of the "404 pi./123 m" marking on the fence behind center fielder Gerald Young.[3] Young misread the hit, initially coming in but then realizing he had to get back. He tracked back with plenty of time to make an over-the-shoulder catch but saw the ball glance off the heel of his glove in front of him and roll away to his left. Compounding his hard day at the office, Young then reached down to barehand the ball as it hit the artificial turf but knocked it away, sending it rolling toward the base of the wall. Grissom, blessed with excellent speed (he stole 36 bases in 1994, but had had back-to-back seasons of 76 and 78 steals in 1991-92 for the Expos), went into another gear rounding second and decided to try for home. Pena took the relay when Young eventually retrieved the ball, but hesitated before throwing home. With Larry Walker behind the plate signaling for him to slide, Grissom made a head-first dive for home and crossed the plate before the relay throw could reach catcher Tom Pagnozzi.[4] It was Grissom's first inside-the-park home run, and would turn out to be the only one of his 17-year career.

Young was not given an error on the play, although it could be argued that he committed three serious misplays. He started only five games in center field

Marquis Grissom

in 1994, and in the 16 games he played that year, he got starts at all three outfield positions without being charged with an error. Although he had finished fifth in the Rookie of the Year balloting only seven years before with the Astros, his last major-league game would come 10 days after this one, on August 11, 1994, the last day before the players' strike ended the season.

Not only is this game notable because it took place toward the end of what is arguably the finest season in Expos history, and while the storm clouds of the players' strike were gathering, but it is also a rare opportunity to see two managers passing each other on the up and down escalators of their careers. The Expos' Felipe Alou had started his managerial career with the Expos (and in MLB) in 1992 and was the toast of the league for his performance—he would win Manager of the Year in 1994, and his record as manager in 1992-1994 was 238-163 (.594). While he would go on to manage six more full seasons and part of a seventh with the team after 1994, the cash-strapped Expos largely dismantled the team after the strike ended and in only one of those seasons did the ravaged team finish over .500.[5] On the other hand,

Joe Torre's tenure with the Cardinals was becoming shaky; he and the team would part ways early in 1995 when things failed to turn around after the disaster of 1994. This freed Torre to assume the helm of the Yankees in 1996; he promptly won AL Manager of the Year and guided the team to the first of four World Series titles and six AL pennants during his sparkling 12-year run with that club.

SOURCES

In addition to the sources listed in the notes, the author consulted:

Danny Gallagher and Bill Young. *Remembering the Montreal Expos* (Toronto: Scoop Press, 2005).

Jonah Keri. *Up, Up, & Away: The Kid, The Hawk, Rock, Vladi, Pedro, Le Grand Orange, Youppi!, The Crazy Business of Baseball, & the Ill-fated but Unforgettable Montreal Expos* (Toronto: Random House Canada, 2014).

St. Louis Post-Dispatch, August 2, 1994.

The Sporting News, August 15, 1994.

NOTES

1 Rick Hummel, "August starts off a bust for Cards," *St. Louis Post-Dispatch*, August 2, 1994, 1C.

2 According to baseball-reference.com, advanced statistics tell the same story: Henry in 1994 had 2.5 WAA (wins above average) and 3.3 WAR (wins above replacement), Palacios -0.1 and 0.8.

3 At Olympic Stadium, the markings were in feet and meters—but because the metric system was official in Canada, and because French is the official language in the province of Québec, the distance in feet was both much smaller than the distance in meters and used only the French abbreviation "pi." for pieds.

4 See video at http://m.mlb.com/video/v25607861/stlmon-grissoms-insidethepark-walkoff-home-run (accessed November 9, 2014).

5 Only 18 members of the 1994 40-man roster returned in 1995, and notable departures included Marquis Grissom, Ken Hill, Larry Walker, and John Wetteland.

PEDRO'S (NEARLY) PERFECT GAME

June 3, 1995: Montreal Expos 1, San Diego Padres 0 At Jack Murphy Stadium

By Danny Gallagher

HARVEY HADDIX DID THE IMPROBABLE BACK in 1959 when he pitched 12 perfect innings for the Pittsburgh Pirates against the Milwaukee Braves. But in the 13th, a throwing error, a sacrifice, and a double not only cost him the perfect game, but the victory as well.

Pedro Martinez was in almost the same boat as Haddix on June 3, 1995, when he threw nine perfect innings against the San Diego Padres. Unlike Haddix, Martinez had a chance to gain the victory and immortality with a perfect 10th, as his teammates had scored the go-ahead run in the top of the frame. But Bip Roberts ended Pedro's pursuit of perfection when he led off with a double that right fielder Tony Tarasco had no chance of catching. "It was a lucky hit to a lucky spot," Roberts told reporters.[1]

It was one of those classic pitchers' duels as Joey Hamilton of the Padres stayed in tune with Martinez, allowing no runs on three hits through nine innings. "That's big-league pitching at its best right there,'" San Diego's Tony Gwynn said of Martinez. "Not much you can say except superb and awesome. Tip your hat."[2]

Prior to Roberts' double, Martinez had pretty much breezed through the game, although he received some great defensive help from his teammates on four hard-hit line-drive outs—Roberts to second base in the fourth, Jody Reed to third base in the sixth, Brad Ausmus to right in the eighth, and Scott Livingstone, pinch-hitting for Reed, to deep right in the ninth, a blast that Tarasco caught as he banged into the wall.

"We went on to win but according to the rulebook, I could not be given credit for a perfect game even though I had gone nine perfect innings," Martinez said. "Reporters afterward told me that the last person to lose a perfect game in extra innings was Harvey Haddix. I really wasn't that upset about losing a perfect game according to a technicality. Everyone with the Expos thought I received some vindication.

"I know I'm still young but I've been around long enough now that I think I've shown some people what I can do. I'm not here to hurt anybody. But it seems like whenever I pitch, it's always the bad things that are brought up. It's never 'Pedro Martinez was 11-5 last year' or they never look back to how good I was in Los Angeles as a reliever. It's only the bad."[3]

That "bad" stemmed from Martinez's tendency to pitch just a little bit inside. Back on April 13, 1994, Martinez had pitched seven perfect innings against the Cincinnati Reds in Montreal before hitting Reggie Sanders with a pitch, prompting Sanders to charge the mound, and setting off a mini-melee. That was an example of the so-called "reputation" Martinez was gaining in only his second full season in the majors. Later that season, another brouhaha erupted after Martinez struck out Derek Bell of the San Diego Padres. Bell had barely made it back to the San Diego dugout when he turned around and ran to the mound to confront Martinez.

"This shouldn't be my first reputation as a pitcher because I have been here not very long, but long enough to show what I can do. When I'm fine, I can do a lot of stuff. I don't want to fight anybody. I'm here to play the game like I did tonight."[4]

Sitting in his manager's chair off to the side of the clubhouse after the game, manager Felipe Alou was impressed with Martinez's reply about vindication. "This was the best answer Pedro could give to all the harassment he's been going through," Alou said. "I'm not surprised that he threw this kind of game."[5]

Because of his tendency to go inside too often and keep batters on their toes, Martinez didn't think the near-perfect game would change things much as far as

Pedro Martinez

he was concerned. "I still had some control problems. Felipe didn't want me to stop pitching inside but he was in the middle of a jam, taking a lot of heat that I was generating," Martinez said.[6]

But back to that almost perfect game. In the Expos' half of the 10th inning, Shane Andrews singled to left off reliever Brian Williams, and after Martinez popped out attempting a sacrifice bunt, Andrews reached second when Lou Frazier drew a base on balls and scored when Jeff Treadway singled.

Manager Alou took Martinez out of the game immediately after Roberts got his hit. Martinez received a standing ovation from the crowd as he exited, and acknowledged the fans with a wave of his glove as he jogged toward the dugout. Mel Rojas took the mound and almost blew the lead when he threw a wild pitch that sent Roberts to third. After Steve Finley grounded out to first base unassisted, Rojas had to face the great Tony Gwynn. Gwynn grounded to Treadway at second; Roberts was off at the crack of the bat, but Treadway's throw to catcher Darrin Fletcher was in time for the out. Ken Caminiti fouled out to end the game.

"I'm still mad that I didn't get a big hit in that game to get Pedro the perfect-game victory," recalled Fletcher. "I had a chance in the top of the [ninth] to drive in a run with a man on [first] with [no] outs but I flew out to center. The thing I remember the most is feeling sorry for Pedro because we could not push a run across for him."[7]

Had Martinez been credited with a perfect game, it would have been the second in Expos history. His masterpiece came almost four years after Dennis "El Presidente" Martinez (no relation) threw a perfect no-no on July 28, 1991, against the Dodgers in Los Angeles that the Expos won 2-0.

NOTES

1   "Paradise Lost: Martinez Loses Perfect Game in the 10th," *New York Times*, June 5, 1995.

2   Ibid.

3   Pedro Martinez with Michael Silverman, *Pedro* (Boston: Houghton Mifflin Harcourt, 2015), 108.

4   *New York Times*.

5   Martinez, Silverman, 108.

6   Ibid.

7   Telephone interview with Darrin Fletcher, June 24, 2015.

RONDELL IS WHITE HOT

June 11, 1995: Montreal Expos 10, San Francisco Giants 8 At Candlestick Park

by Michael Huber

ON JUNE 11, 1995, THE 22,392 FANS ON HAND to watch the Montreal Expos battle the San Francisco Giants for 13 innings at Candlestick Park saw it all: lots of runs by both sides, the home side making a seemingly impossible comeback only to blow it in extra innings, and a player hitting for the cycle to boot. The two clubs combined for 18 runs, 36 hits, and 11 bases on balls, with the Expos emerging victorious. Rondell White, Montreal's center fielder, headlined the show by hitting for the cycle.

Second-year pitcher William VanLandingham was making his second start of the season for the Giants. His ERA was 1.29 when the game began, but a whole lot higher by the time he left. Opposing him was veteran Gil Heredia for the Expos, who brought a 5.11 earned-run average to the contest. The excitement started in the top of the second inning when White led off with a single to center field. On the very next pitch, Tony Tarasco doubled to center, sending White to third. Darrin Fletcher followed with a home run deep down the right-field line, and Montreal suddenly had a 3-0 lead. After the home run, VanLandingham settled down to retire the side, and even appeared to have found a groove when he worked a three-up, three-down third inning.

That groove only lasted one inning. White crushed a line drive over the left-center-field fence for a solo home run in the top of the fourth. Then the roof caved in in the fifth. After Mark Grudzielanek flied out, David Segui and Wil Cordero hit back-to-back singles. Moises Alou drew a walk, loading the bases for White. On a 1-and-1 count, White sent a line drive to center field for a double. Segui and Cordero scored, and Alou stopped at third base. Dusty Baker, the Giants manager, went to the mound and took the ball from VanLandingham. The call to the bullpen

brought Shawn Barton to the mound. Barton threw four straight balls to Tarasco. On ball three, the pitch got away from Giants catcher Kirt Manwaring; Alou tried to score but was tagged out at home, with White advancing to third on the play. Then Tarasco walked and Fletcher followed with an RBI single up the middle, plating White. White's run completed the line on VanLandingham; in 4⅓ innings, he gave up seven earned runs on eight hits and two walks, while striking out three Expos batters. His ERA had ballooned to 6.35.[1]

Manwaring led off the bottom of the fifth with a single, moved to second on a sacrifice by Barton, and scored on Darren Lewis's single. Lewis stole second and scored on Mike Benjamin's single. Benjamin also stole second, and scored on Glenallen Hill's double to center, cutting the Giants' deficit to 7-3.

The Expos added a run on three hits in the top of the seventh. White led off with his second double of the game, moved to third on a single by Tarasco, and scored on Fletcher's single. San Francisco answered in the bottom of the seventh with two-out singles by Benjamin, Barry Bonds, and Hill. Benjamin's run made it 8-4. Jeff Shaw replaced Heredia after Bonds' hit, and gave up Hill's single; Heredia was charged with the run.

San Francisco put together a gutsy comeback in the bottom of the ninth against Expos closer Mel Rojas. Benjamin led off with a line-drive single to center field. Bonds walked. Hill sent a line drive to deep left field for a double to score Benjamin, with Bonds going to third. Royce Clayton grounded out to shortstop, but got the RBI when Bonds came home. John Patterson, who had entered the game as a defensive replacement for Robby Thompson at second base in the sixth inning, fouled out to first baseman Segui. With two outs and two strikes, J.R. Phillips singled up the middle to score Hill, and suddenly Montreal's lead was down to one run, 8-7. Rojas now could not find the strike zone. With a 1-and-0 count, Rikkert Faneyte singled deep into the left-center-field gap, advancing Phillips to third base. Jeff Reed, who had replaced Manwaring in the seventh, walked on four pitches to load the bases. Tom Lampkin pinch-hit and also walked on four straight pitches, which brought Phillips in with the tying run. Alou replaced Rojas with Greg Harris, who got Benjamin to ground into a short-to-second force out to end the inning.

Neither team scored in the 10th, 11th, or 12th. White made some noise when he singled and stole second in the top of the 11th, but was stranded. Steve Mintz, the seventh Giants pitcher—he came on in the 12th—started the top of the 13th by quickly retiring Cordero and Frazier on three pitches. Then, on a 3-and-1 count, White drove the ball down the right-field line for a triple and the cycle. Mintz walked Tarasco intentionally, then gave up a two-run triple to Tim Laker, who had replaced Fletcher in the seventh.

Rondell White

Mintz walked Sean Berry and retired Shane Andrews, but the damage was done. The Giants went quietly in the bottom half of the inning against Gabe White, the Expos' sixth pitcher of the game, and the Expos had won, 10-8, in just over 4½ hours.

White had six hits in seven at-bats. He achieved the fourth cycle in Expos history (preceded by Tim Foli on April 22, 1976, Chris Speier on July 20, 1978, and Tim Raines on August 16, 1987). He had two singles, two doubles, the extra-inning triple, and a home run. He had a chance to complete the cycle in regulation, but he popped out in the top of the ninth.

White actually had ideas about trying for the triple in the seventh inning. "I felt I had a chance," he said after the game. "But I'm still a little sore in my hamstring and I didn't want to take the risk."[2] What was different in the 13th inning? The drive off White's bat was a dying liner that right fielder Glenallen Hill could not put a glove on, which allowed White to reach third base easily.

The Expos used 19 players in the game, including six pitchers. The Giants employed 20, with seven pitchers. Offensively, Benjamin led the way for the Giants, going 4-for-6 with two stolen bases; he was also hit by a pitch. For the Expos, White and Fletcher combined for a 10-for-12 afternoon with six runs scored and eight runs batted in. Both hit homers. The teammates were fated to be connected on this day. In fact, White remarked, "When you're hot, you're hot. I told Fletcher before the game that I just wanted one hit to enjoy the flight home. But when you get one, you want two. Two? You want three. After three, you're pretty satisfied."[3]

The whole team quite likely enjoyed the flight home. The victory over the Giants gave the Expos their first three-game series sweep at Candlestick Park in 11 years.[4] In the three games, White was 11-for-16 with a walk, and scored 10 runs for Montreal. His average rocketed from .299 coming to San Francisco to .373 after the series, and his slugging percentage leaped from .612 to .747.

SOURCES

In addition to the sources listed in the notes, the author consulted:

baseball-reference.com.

mlb.com.

retrosheet.org.

NOTES

1   VanLandingham finished the year with a respectable 3.67 ERA.

2   Jeff Blair, "A White Christmas for Run-dell; Expos blow lead, then bury Giants," the *Montreal Gazette*, June 12, 1995.

3   Blair.

4   According to Blair, the Expos' previous sweep of the Giants at Candlestick Park occurred on August 16-18, 1984.

EXPOS HIT TWO GRAND SLAMS, SCORE TEAM-RECORD 21 RUNS IN ROUT OF ROCKIES

April 28, 1996: Montreal Expos 21, Colorado Rockies 9 At Coors Field

By Frederick C. Bush

THE MONTREAL EXPOS OF THE 1990S OPERATED on a shoestring budget, but manager Felipe Alou—who took over the team during the 1992 season—still was able to mold his teams into contenders in the early years of his tenure. In 1993, his first full season at the helm, he guided the Expos to a 94-68 record and a second-place finish in the NL East. In 1994 Montreal's 74-40 record was the best in the majors when the players strike ended the season, but a fire sale of star players caused the team to regress to 66-78 in 1995.[1]

Most prognosticators expected Montreal to finish last in the division in 1996. The Expos ignored the so-called experts and stormed out of the gates to a 17-9 record in the season's first month. Victory number 17, a 21-9 rout of the Colorado Rockies at Coors Field on April 28, was punctuated by two grand slams, which paced the Expos to a new team record for runs scored in a game. Though the Expos lost their final game of the month to the New York Mets, they stood in first place on May 1, which prompted Alou to say, "At least we were the kings of April."[2]

Montreal entered the Colorado series on a seven-game winning streak that had included three walk-off wins against three different teams (Pittsburgh, St. Louis, and Cincinnati), and a victory in the first game of this series extended the mark to eight. Colorado ended the streak the next night by giving the Expos a taste of their own medicine with a 6-5 walk-off victory in 13 innings. Worse than the defeat for Montreal was the loss of center fielder Rondell White, a budding young star, who injured both a kidney and his spleen crashing into the outfield wall after a magnificent diving catch of a drive by Larry Walker in the sixth inning.

The Expos took out their anger over losing White in the third game. It began innocently enough with a groundout by leadoff batter Mark Grudzielanek, but the bottom then fell out for Rockies starter Bryan Rekar. After Mike Lansing singled and Henry Rodriguez doubled, Rekar hit Moises Alou with a pitch to load the bases, then walked Segui, forcing Lansing home for the Expos' first run. Darrin Fletcher stepped to the plate and launched a grand slam to deep right field to give Montreal a 5-0 lead. F.P. Santangelo extended the margin to 6-0 as he followed Fletcher's blast with a solo homer, but the Expos were still not finished. Dave Silvestri worked a walk, advanced to second on pitcher Kirk Rueter's sacrifice bunt, and scored on a single by Grudzielanek before Lansing flied out to end the top half of the inning.

Rueter set the Rockies down in order in the bottom of the first, and it appeared as though Rekar might fare better when he retired Rodriguez and Alou to start the second inning. That was not to be the case. Though the inning would not turn out quite as disastrously as the first, Rekar did not escape unscathed. Segui singled and scored when Fletcher followed with a double for his fifth RBI of the game, which tied his career high. Santangelo then singled to drive in Fletcher, giving Montreal a 9-0 lead.

After Colorado managed only a walk to Vinny Castilla in its half of the second, the Expos knocked the Rockies' starter out of the game in the third. Rekar did not help his own cause when he walked Rueter to start the frame. Rueter advanced to second on a single by Grudzielanek and scored two batters later on a hit by Rodriguez. When Rekar walked Alou to load the bases, Rockies manager Don Baylor pulled him and sent Lance Painter to the mound in relief. Painter allowed the Expos to go ahead 11-0 when he walked Segui to score Grudzielanek, but he retired the next two batters to end the inning.

The number 11 stood out because it recurred in several instances during the game. Not only was it the number of runs surrendered by Rekar, but the Expos also ended an 11-inning scoreless streak by sending 11 batters to the plate in the first inning.

The Expos' scoring barrage was so stunning that it damaged both Rekar's ERA and his psyche. The second-year starter's ERA ballooned to 13.97 for the season, and he was optioned to Triple-A Colorado Springs after the game.[3] Rockies pitching coach Frank Funk said, "He was relieved when we told him [he was being sent down]," and Baylor added, "His confidence probably sank to its all-time low."[4]

The Rockies managed to score their first run in the bottom of the fourth inning, but the Expos answered with three more runs of their own in the top of the fifth as Santangelo added to his RBI total with a double that drove in Rodriguez, Alou, and Fletcher. A solo homer by Rockies catcher Jayhawk Owens in the bottom of the fifth still left Colorado with a 14-2 deficit.

The Rockies dared to score another run in their half of the seventh, and the Expos responded with a new torrent of runs against reliever Mike Munoz in the top of the eighth. The fireworks began when Andy Stankiewicz hit a two-out double to knock in Silvestri, who had drawn a one-out walk. After Rodriguez walked, relief pitcher Dave Veres joined the hit parade with a bases-loaded single that scored Grudzielanek. Munoz found out how Rekar must have felt during the first inning when Segui smashed the Expos' second grand slam of the game to make the score 20-3 in favor of the visitors. The Rockies waited too long to turn the game into a typical two-team Coors Field slugfest, but they did manage two solo homers against Veres in the bottom of the eighth.

Montreal joined the 21 Club in the ninth when a single by Grudzielanek drove home Santangelo, who doubled to lead off the inning. Though the Rockies attempted to add some excitement for their fans by scoring four runs in the bottom of the ninth, Mel Rojas finally induced a double-play grounder from Vinny Castilla to end the game as a 21-9 Expos triumph. The Expos had pounded out a season-high 20 hits and had drawn eight walks and a hit batsman en route to scoring a team-record 21 runs that bested the previous franchise mark of 19 (accomplished six times previously). White's replacement in center field, F.P. Santangelo, responded with a 4-for-6 performance that included two doubles, a home run, and a career-best five RBIs. Fletcher matched Santangelo's RBI total, but both were outdone by teammate David Segui, who finished with six RBIs and hit Montreal's second grand slam of the day.

The game also marked Montreal's 17th victory in April, which set a club record for that month. David Segui and Henry Rodriguez had won back-to-back NL Player of the Week awards in April, and the Expos led the NL in batting average, runs scored, home runs, RBIs, and slugging percentage. Felipe Alou said, "We were picked to finish last with the lowest payroll in baseball, but we're having fun right now. I know that I'm having fun."[5]

Alou had earned his fun, having toiled for 12 years as a manager in the Expos' minor-league system and for an additional three years as an Expos coach before replacing Tom Runnells as the team's skipper after Runnells was fired 37 games into the 1992 season. Kevin Malone, Montreal's general manger in 1994 and 1995, praised Alou when he asserted, "As far as enabling young players to reach their potential and be the best they can be, he's the best in the business."[6]

Alou took his squad to greater heights in 1996 than most people had anticipated as he steered them to an 88-74 record, but they had to settle for second place, eight games behind the Atlanta Braves. As Alou had said after his team's 21-9 drubbing of Colorado, "We kicked some butt in April. You never know what May brings, but at least we had that."[7]

SOURCES

In addition to the sources listed in the notes, the author consulted:

Baseball-Reference.com.

Chicago Tribune.

NOTES

1   The team traded center fielder Marquis Grissom, as well as pitchers Ken Hill and John Wetteland. They also allowed right fielder Larry Walker to leave via free agency.

2   "Low-Rent Expos In Luxury Surroundings," *St. Louis Post-Dispatch*, May 1, 1996.

3   Rekar divided his time between Denver and Colorado Springs the entire season. He had an 8.95 ERA with the Rockies that year.

4   "Expos' Fletcher, Segui Slam Rockies, 21-9," *Los Angeles Times*, April 29, 1996.

5   "Low-Rent Expos In Luxury Surroundings."

6   Murray Chass, "The Manager as Alchemist: Alou Turns Young Players Into Gold for Expos," *New York Times*, April 29, 1996.

7   "Low-Rent Expos In Luxury Surroundings."

OH HENRY!

May 12, 1996: Montreal Expos 7, Houston Astros 6 At Olympic Stadium

By Brian P. Wood

HURLING BASEBALLS BACK AFTER OPPONENTS' home runs, flinging caps onto the rink after a hat trick in hockey, and tossing flowers onto the ice in honor of a figure skater's performance are three traditions where throwing things onto the field of play is acceptable behavior at sporting events.

However, take an unlikely baseball power hitter, fans hungry for a competitive team, and a candy bar, and a new form of accolade gained national notice at the game between the Houston Astros and Montreal Expos on May 12, 1996.

Henry Rodriguez, a 28-year-old outfielder for the Expos, "suddenly" found his home-run swing in 1996. Montreal manager Felipe Alou attributed his success to weight-lifting, adding 15 pounds of muscle, and having the initials "HR."[1]

In 1994, the Expos sported the best record in baseball, but had no postseason because of the players' strike. The following season found them at the bottom of the NL East. Seeing the 1996 incarnation of Roger Maris/Babe Ruth playing at *Stade Olympique* however, reinvigorated fan enthusiasm.

As the season progressed, fans handed Oh Henry! candy bars to Rodriguez after batting practice or home runs. Soon fans were tossing them onto the field. By May 6, Rodriguez had collected 16 bars. On June 10 left fielder Rodriguez swatted two home runs in a 5-2 win over Houston. Astros right fielder Derek Bell visited the Expos clubhouse after the game and yelled, "Yo! Henry: keep them (expletive deleted) chocolate bars out of right field now. They can throw them in left, I don't care. But keep them away from me; otherwise I'll be eating them during the pitching changes."[2]

"Hammerin' Hank" mania continued the next night. Despite striking out twice, Rodriguez returned to his position to cheers and a shower of chocolate bars in the fourth inning.

Montreal led the NL East (25-12) while Houston sat atop the NL Central with a sub-.500 record (18-19). On the mound, Houston's Mike Hampton faced Ugueth Urbina, just up from the Triple-A Ottawa Lynx.

The Astros featured the "Killer B's," consisting of future Hall of Famer Craig Biggio, four-time All-Star Jeff Bagwell, and Bell.[3] Rodriguez (15 home runs, 43 RBIs, and .352 batting average), Moises Alou (son of Felipe), and David Segui (son of former major-league pitcher Diego Segui) led Montreal's offense.

In the bottom of the first, Montreal's Mark Grudzielanek led off with an infield single. He advanced to third on a passed ball by Houston catcher Jerry Goff and a wild pitch by Hampton. After Mike Lansing walked, Grudzielanek scored when Alou reached first on an error by Biggio. With two outs Goff committed his second passed ball, moving the runners to second and third. F.P. Santangelo plated both with a double to left for a 3-0 Montreal lead.

Goff responded to his miscues in the top of the second with his first home run of the season to make it 3-1.

The offense continued for the Expos in the bottom of the second. Third baseman Shane Andrews doubled to left. Urbina singled to right, but right fielder Bell gunned down Andrews at the plate. Grudzielanek advanced Urbina to second with a single to right. After a groundout moved both runners into scoring position, Henry Rodriguez stepped to the plate. "Oh Henry!" did not disappoint, knocking in two with a double to center field, expanding Montreal's lead to 5-1.

The double led to a shower of candy littering the field. The umpires ordered the Astros off the field for safety and cleanup. Five minutes after the candy bars had been cleared, play had not yet resumed. Expos manager Alou, seeking an explanation for the delay,

Henry Rodriguez

strode out to speak to third-base umpire/crew chief Harry Wendelstedt, who ejected him from the game.

Wendelstedt commented afterward, "Alou didn't like my method of taking control. ... I told him, 'Settle down because your action, your body language indicates that you condone the throwing.' He got a little angrier and then I ejected him."[4] After the delay, Houston manager Terry Collins lifted Hampton in favor of Anthony Young, who recorded the last out of the inning.[5]

The Expos' scoring continued in the third. After Santangelo again doubled to left, Young intentionally walked Andrews. With Urbina up, Goff committed two more passed balls on consecutive pitches, the second scoring Santangelo with Montreal's sixth run.

Houston tallied one run in the fourth when Bell reached on an error by shortstop Grudzielanek, advanced to second on a single to right by Derrick May, and scored on a single by the still-atoning Goff. The

runners took second and third on a groundout, but Urbina stopped the Astros threat by striking out the next two batters. The Astros trailed 6-2.

In the fourth, Grudzielanek greeted new Houston pitcher Jeff Tabaka with an infield hit to shortstop and moved to second when Mike Lansing singled to left. Yet two more Goff passed balls, once more on consecutive pitches, allowed Grudzielanek to score and Lansing to reach third. But Bell again denied the Expos a run as he nailed Lansing attempting to score on a fly ball by Alou. Montreal now led 7-2.

The Astros plated another run on Craig Biggio's home run in the fifth inning to cut the lead to 7-3.

The Astros inched closer in the sixth. With two outs, Ricky Gutierrez reached base on Grudzielanek's second error and advanced on a wild pitch by Urbina. After pinch-hitter Sean Berry walked, Expos acting manager Jim Tracy sent in reliever Mike Dyer. John Cangelosi welcomed him with an RBI single to right. With Berry on third, catcher Lenny Webster threw out Cangelosi attempting to steal second. Montreal's lead shrank to 7-4.

In the bottom of the sixth, the Astros' Xavier Hernandez surrendered a pinch single to right by Andy Stankiewicz. Grudzielanek followed with his fourth single of the day and stole second before Rodriguez struck out to end the inning.

The Astros had a productive seventh inning. Biggio doubled to left field off Dave Veres, Montreal's third pitcher, Bagwell walked, and a wild pitch moved them 90 feet. Biggio scored on a grounder by Bell, making it a 7-5 game. New pitcher Omar Daal gave up an RBI single to pinch-hitter James Mouton, scoring Bagwell. Houston now trailed by one, 7-6. The inning ended when Goff struck out and Webster threw out Mouton trying to steal second.

In the eighth, Houston's Brian Hunter lined into an inning-ending double play, Lansing to Segui at first, which caught Gutierrez, who had singled.

A scoring chance fizzled for the Expos when Lansing struck out with runners on first and second after pinch-hitter Sherman Obando singled and Grudzielanek moved him to second with his fifth single of the night.

The Astros managed a single by Bagwell in the ninth before Mel Rojas, Montreal's sixth pitcher, closed out the game for his fifth save of the season. Urbina, who earned his first win of the year, would become Montreal's closer the following season.[6]

Two of the game's three big stories involved players having great days offensively and terrible days defensively.

Jerry Goff's only major-league appearance of 1996 was also the last of his six-year, 90-game career as he soon found himself with Triple-A Tucson. This day, he finished with a bang at the plate: 2-for-4 with a home run and two RBIs, but a whimper behind it, committing a National League record six passed balls[7] that accounted for five Montreal unearned runs.[8] "I don't have an answer," said Goff. "After the first one got by, I got a little tentative. It just snowballed from there. It was ugly. I'm not making excuses. I just wish I had an answer."[9]

Mark Grudzielanek recorded his second five-hit day, all singles.[10] However, his two errors led to two unearned runs.

And Oh Henry! Rodriguez? His double indirectly halted the game leading to his manager's ejection. He finished 1996 with career highs in home runs (36), RBIs (103), hits (147), doubles (42), and strikeouts (160) and was selected to the NL All-Star team for the first and only time. Colin Anderle of the Cauldron blogsite noted Rodriguez as having one of the "five wackiest power surges in the steroid era."[11]

Soon after this game, Rodriguez was signed as an Oh Henry! spokesman. Hershey's sponsored an Oh Henry! promotion at the June 24 game against Pittsburgh with tickets at a reduced price and free Oh Henry! T-shirts. Henry came through, going 3-for-3 with two more home runs—both bringing a rain of candy—a double, and four RBIs. After the 1997 season he became a Chicago Cub and "Oh Henry!" showers continued until 1999, when five Cubs fans were arrested for disturbing the peace. Although the Cubs had the charges dropped, it marked the end of the "Oh Henry" phenomenon.[12] Rodriguez returned to the Expos in 2002, at the age of 34, but managed

just one single in 20 at-bats before being released. The magic of 1996 was long gone.

SOURCES

In addition to the sources listed in the notes, the author consulted:

"1902 Enemies Within the Gate," thisgreatgame.com/1902-baseball-history.html.

Associated Press (AM cycle), "Alou Gets Birthday Present—Ejection, lexis-nexis.com, May 12, 1996.

Associated Press, "Major League Roundup," *Hamilton* (Ontario) *Spectator*, June 25, 1996.

Bill Beacon, "Oh Henry! Expo slugger sweet swinging surprise," *Calgary Herald*, May 7, 1996.

Jeff Blair, "Mr. Nice Guy: Rodriguez quickly becoming fan favorite," The *Montreal Gazette* , May 11, 1996.

Sam Carchidi, "A Sweet Season For Henry Rodriguez," *Philadelphia Inquirer*, July 8, 1996.

Mike Downey, "Rodriguez Is a Favorite in Montreal, Bar None," *Los Angeles Times*, May 13, 1996.

"NL Roundup," *Chicago Tribune*, June 25, 1996.

"Passed Balls Trivia," retrieved July 21, 2015.

Wayne Scanlan. "Pitter-patter of parade begins for Expos fans," *Ottawa Citizen* May 12, 1996.

Paul Sullivan, "Wild Bunch. Henry On Crackdown: Oh, No!" *Chicago Tribune*, June 3, 1999.

NOTES

1   Jeff Blair, "Oh Henry! strikes again for Expos: Rodriguez sinks sweet tooth into Astros with two homers," the *Montreal Gazette*, May 11, 1996: C1.

2   Terry Blount, "Astros summary," *Houston Chronicle*, May 12, 1996.

3   Third baseman Sean Berry, who would become a fourth Killer B, had come to Houston from Montreal after the 1995 season. He walked as a pinch-hitter in the Oh Henry! game.

4   Ian MacDonald, "Umps warn Expos about littering," the *Montreal Gazette*, May 13, 1996.

5   Hampton was removed because of a sore shoulder. Terry Blount, "Expos 7, Astros 6," *Houston Chronicle*, May 13, 1996.

6   Urbina saved 237 games in his career.

7   Goff tied the record set by pitcher (turned catcher for the day) Rube Vickers of Cincinnati (October 4, 1902) and Geno Petralli of the Texas Rangers (August 30, 1987).

8   Goff had 21 passed balls in 71 games behind the plate. In the minors he had 174 passed balls in 767 games caught.

9   "Expos 7, Astros 6," Associated Press, May 12, 1996.

10 Grudzielanek's first five-hit game came in a 21-9 Montreal victory over the Colorado Rockies on April 28, 1996, just two weeks before the Oh Henry! game. His third was as a Dodger on July 22, 1999, in a 12-11 loss to the Rockies. Grudzielanek ended 1996 with a career-high 201 hits.

11 Colin Anderle, "The five wackiest power surges of the steroid era," aol.com/article/2015/03/08/the-five-wackiest-power-surges-of-the-steroid-era/21150945/, March 8, 2015 (from the Cauldron blogsite), retrieved July 21, 2015.

12 Rahula Strohl, "Wrap This One Up: Outcome Is Sweet for Oh Henry!," *Chicago Tribune*, July 29, 1999: 5.

EXPOS SCORE RECORD 13 RUNS IN SIXTH INNING

May 7, 1997: Montreal Expos 19, San Francisco Giants 3 At 3Com Park

By Alan Cohen

"IF THE WHEELS COME OFF, IT'S BETTER THEY come off all at once" —Giants manager Dusty Baker.[1]

"A lot of balls were not hit very well, just grounders and balls in the gap. The balls managed to get through." —Expos manager Felipe Alou.[2]

Scoring was the name of this game, as about 9,600 fans made their way into San Francisco's Candlestick Park (then also known as 3Com Park) on May 7, 1997, for a Wednesday afternoon game. The best thing they could say once the carnage was over was that the Expos, after the biggest scoring inning in their history, restrained themselves from piling on to their 19-3 lead during the last three innings.

Osvaldo Fernandez started for San Francisco. The native of Cuba was in his second season with the Giants and brought a 3-2 record and 2.95 ERA into the contest. He held the Expos to one run through the first four innings as Rondell White led off the third with his eighth homer of the season.

The Giants jumped on Expos starter Jeff Juden for three runs in the first two innings. Juden did not help himself in the first as he hit Jeff Kent, gave up a bases-loaded walk to Glenallen Hill, and allowed a run-scoring single by J. T. Snow. It could have been worse, but Expos right fielder Vladimir Guerrero gunned down Kent as he tried to score from second on Snow's hit. In the second inning, Marcus Jensen doubled, went to third on a sacrifice by Fernandez, and scored on a fly ball by Rich Aurilia. The Giants' 3-1 lead lasted into the fifth inning. After that, things changed.

Mike Lansing and White singled for the Expos with one out in the fifth, but things looked good for the Giants when David Segui sent a groundball toward second baseman Kent. But Kent bobbled the potential double-play grounder and the bases were jammed

with Expos. "I forced it and I got bit. I was trying to stick my hand in the snake pit and got bit," said Kent after the game.[3] Expos left fielder Henry Rodriguez hit a grand slam to left-center field on a 1-and-2 count—his eighth home run of the season—giving the Expos a 5-3 lead. Guerrero followed with a double and was plated by a Doug Strange single that brought Giants manager Dusty Baker to the mound to replace Fernandez with Joe Roa. Roa temporarily stopped the bleeding, and kept the score at 6-3 by getting Chris Widger on a popup to short and Juden to ground out to third.

The Expos' turn in the sixth inning resulted in Baker saying, "It was a crazy inning. No matter who we sent in (the Giants used three pitchers in the inning), it was like throwing gasoline on the fire."[4] It unfolded like this: With leadoff hitter Mike Grudzielanek on second base by virtue of a single and a balk, Mike Lansing homered to extend the lead to 8-3. A single by White and a double by Segui put runners on second and third and ended Roa's work for the day.

Jim Poole came on and was clearly out of his depth, as he allowed four straight singles, which meant that each of the first eight batters in the inning had reached base safely. Juden, who had already struck out twice, was the ninth Expo to bat, and Poole chalked up strikeout number three. Juden, who had made the Expos' last out in the fifth, made their first out in the sixth. Unfortunately for the Giants, not every Expos batter was named Jeff Juden.

The Expos resumed the slaughter after Juden whiffed. Grudzielanek's second single of the inning scored Doug Strange with the seventh run of the inning and put runners on the corners. The single by Grudzielanek ended Poole's day.[5] Julian Tavarez got the task of trying to stop the mess from getting worse. He failed. Lansing came up again and hit a three-run shot that put the Expos up 16-3, making him the 18th National League player and 31st major leaguer since the beginning of the 20th century to hit two home runs in one inning. He also doubled his home-run count for the season.

Tavarez, after inducing a groundball from White for the second out of the inning, then loaded the bases on a single, double, and hit batter. Strange, who had singled earlier in the frame, drove a base-clearing double to right field. That ended the scoring., as Chris Widger grounded out to first for the third out. Tavarez could only say, "I've never seen anything like that in baseball, even in Little League. Those guys hit every pitch, good or bad, they chased every pitch, high pitch, fastball away, slider away. Everything was a blooper, base hit,

Mike Lansing

home run. There's nothing you can do about that. It was amazing. I've never seen anything happen like that in my life. You have to see that to believe it—26 hits, 19 runs? I'm still thinking like, I'm dreaming right now."[6]

Writer Neil Hayes, noting that "Giants fans stood and cheered as the home team ran off the field after the top of the sixth inning," wrote that, "It may have been the most united, spontaneous, and appropriate display of sarcasm in baseball history."[7]

The sixth-inning eruption lasted 30 minutes, saw 17 men bat, produced 13 runs on as many hits, and put the Expos ahead 19-3. Afterward, Lansing commented, "There were some cheap hits, and you kind of go, 'Gee! When is it going to stop?' It's one of those fluke things that happens, and luckily we were on the offensive side."[8]

Juden, having control problems, was relieved in the bottom of the sixth when the Giants loaded the bases with a pair of singles, and a walk. During his 5⅓-inning stint, Juden walked four and hit three batters. The Expos' bullpen shut the door the rest of the way and Juden was credited with his third win of the season.

The Expos' 12th win in 17 contests brought their season's record to 17-14. They were in second place, 5½ games behind division-leading Atlanta. However, they would not continue their winning ways, finishing the season with a 78-84 record, fourth in the five-team National League Eastern Division. During their hot streak, the Expos twice victimized the Giants, beating them 10-3 on the day before the 19-3 win. Giants manager Dusty Baker, somewhat agitated, and also battling the flu, accused the Expos' F.P. Santangelo of stealing signs from Giants catcher Marcus Jensen, a charge that the Expos vehemently denied.[9] Santangelo himself got two hits in the sixth after replacing Henry Rodriguez in left field for defensive purposes in the bottom of the fifth.

Lansing got the rest of the game off after walking in the seventh inning. The 1997 season was his last with the Expos; after career highs in home runs (20) and RBIs (70), he was dealt to Colorado.

After the game, Kent noted, "It was pretty much a disaster, but it's something you have to deal with in baseball. It's disappointing because we were in this game. It isn't like they did it from the beginning."[10]

SOURCES

In addition to the sources listed in the notes, the author consulted:

Baseball-Almanac.com.

Baseball-Reference.com.

mlb.com.

NOTES

1 Nick Peters, "S.F. Pitching Crumbles in Nightmarish Sixth," *Sacramento Bee*, May 8, 1997.

2 Vincent Cinisomo (Associated Press), "Expos Bury Giants with Record 13-Run Inning," *Daily Herald* (Chicago), May 8, 1997.

3 Joe Roderick, "Giants' Indecent Exposure," *Contra Costa Times* (Walnut Creek, California), May 8, 1997.

4 Nancy Gay, "Giants Give Up 13 Runs in Sixth—Expos Punish S.F. Pitching," *San Francisco Chronicle*, May 8, 1997.

5 Poole's ERA jumped from 1.74 to 5.91 that day. His ERA for the season was 7.11.

6 Gay.

7 Neil Hayes, "Give It Up for Those Giants," *Contra Costa Times* (Walnut Creek, California), May 8, 1997.

8 Cinisomo.

9 Mark Gonzales, "Expos Blast Giants 19-3, 13-Run 6th Sets Records," *San Jose Mercury News*, May 8, 1997.

10 Cinisomo, "Montreal's 19 run Performance Highlights a High Scoring Day," *St. Albans* (Vermont) *Messenger*, May 8, 1997.

WIDGER HELPS EXPOS WIN WILD ONE

May 16, 1997: Montreal Expos 14, San Francisco Giants 13 At Olympic Stadium

By Thomas Ayers

FANS ARRIVING AT MONTREAL'S OLYMPIC Stadium on Friday, May 16, 1997, likely never suspected that they were about to witness the largest comeback victory in the Expos' history to date. Although they faced a nine-run deficit after 2½ innings, the Expos never gave up. Behind a light-hitting catcher who would spend most of his career as a backup, the Expos clawed their way back and won a wild 27-run contest, 14-13 over the San Francisco Giants.

The Giants were in first place in the National League West. However, their lead over the Los Angeles Dodgers had slipped to only one game after the Dodgers beat the Cincinnati Reds on Thursday night and the Giants lost to the Expos, 8-7. The Expos were in third place in the National League East with a 21-16 record.

The pitching matchup saw a relatively new Expos hurler opposing a former Expo who had been dealt to San Francisco less than a year earlier. Jim Bullinger, who had signed with Montreal before the season as a free agent, started for the Expos. Bullinger spent the first five years of his major-league career with the Chicago Cubs, with whom he compiled a 27-28 record in 148 appearances as starter and reliever.

San Francisco's starter was southpaw Kirk Rueter. Rueter was Montreal's 18th-round draft pick in 1991 and spent the first 3½ years of his major-league career with the club. On July 30, 1996, Rueter and reliever Tim Scott were traded to the Giants for pitcher Mark Leiter. It was a trade the Expos likely regretted, as Leiter left the club at the end of the 1996 season and Rueter proceeded to win 105 games over 10 seasons for the Giants.

While this was a game to remember for the 22,365 in attendance, it was one to forget for the starting pitchers, who were both gone before recording an out in the fourth inning.

The first six batters for the Giants reached base on four hits, a walk, and an error. Among the hits were an RBI single by shortstop Jose Vizcaino and outfielder Glenallen Hill's fifth homer of the season, a two-run blast that gave San Francisco a 3-0 lead. Right fielder Vladimir Guerrero made two errors, one of which led to an unearned run, and after a pair of sacrifice flies, the Giants were leading by five runs before Montreal's first hitter stepped to the plate. Bullinger looked so ineffective during this stretch that manager Felipe Alou had reliever Salomon Torres warming up after Bullinger had only thrown 14 pitches.[1]

The Expos began to work their way back into the game in the bottom of the second inning, as first baseman David Segui hit his fifth homer of the season. This homer ended a streak of 21⅓ scoreless innings for Rueter, which spanned four starts.

With one out, the free-swinging 22-year-old Guerrero drew a rare walk and scored when catcher Chris Widger hit the first triple of his career, with two out. Never known for his batting talent, Widger hit only seven triples in 1,998 career plate appearances. His smash cut the deficit to 5-2, and it wasn't his last important offensive contribution in the game.

Any momentum the Expos had gathered in the bottom of the second was erased in the top of the third. J.T. Snow and Bill Mueller led off the inning with singles. With two outs, center fielder Daryl Hamilton delivered a big single to center, scoring both runners.

By this point Alou had seen enough from Bullinger and brought in Salomon Torres. However, Torres fared no better and, after walking a batter, he surrendered an RBI single to Hill that increased San Francisco's lead to six runs. Then Barry Bonds, who had already reached base twice in the first two innings, hit a three-run homer to deep right-center field that gave the Giants an 11-2 lead after only 2½ innings.

The Expos began to show signs of life in the bottom of the fourth. Consecutive singles by Henry Rodriguez, Guerrero, and Doug Strange loaded the bases with none out for Widger, who came through in the important at-bat with a two-run double. Alou summoned pinch-hitter Sherman Obando, who also delivered with a two-run single. This knocked Rueter out of the game before he had retired a single batter in the inning.

Reliever Anthony Telford retired the Giants in order and the Expos continued to try to work themselves back into the game in the bottom of the fifth. White was hit with a pitch by reliever Joe Roa, who then surrendered singles to Segui and Rodriguez. On Rodriguez's hit, Segui advanced to third. After the game he recalled, "[When] I got to third base in the fifth … Pete (Mackanin, the third-base coach) said, 'We're going to win this game.'"[2]

Segui scored on a sacrifice fly and then, with two out in the inning, Widger had another clutch hit, a single, scoring Rodriguez and cutting San Francisco's lead to two runs.

Even though the Expos had cut into San Francisco's lead significantly, there was no reason for Mackanin to be so optimistic. The Expos had never come back from an eight-run deficit before, let alone when trailing by nine runs. The largest comeback wins in franchise history had been two seven-run comebacks. The first occurred in 1980, when Montreal beat San Diego 12-9 after trailing 9-2, and the second came in 1986 when the Expos trailed the Phillies 8-1, before coming back to win 10-9.

In the bottom of the sixth San Francisco manager Dusty Baker replaced Roa with Julian Tavarez, but Tavarez fared no better at stopping Montreal's comeback. Mark Grudzielanek reached base when Vizcaino booted a groundball. Grudzielanek stole second base and, two pitches later, White drove him home.

With two out, Strange singled to center field, scoring White and Segui, who had both singled, and

Montreal had a 12-11 lead only 3½ innings after facing a nine-run deficit. The inning ended when Widger grounded out, failing to reach base for the first time in the game.

If Expos fans thought the excitement had finished with Montreal now in the lead, they soon found out that the game was far from over. Dave Veres replaced Telford and gave up a single to Rick Wilkins. After two wild pitches, Wilkins had advanced to third base.

After Veres walked Mark Lewis, Alou summoned southpaw Omar Daal as part of a double switch. Daal surrendered two singles, and San Francisco regained the lead, 13-12.

In the bottom of the eighth, Guerrero singled with one out and pinch-hitter Joe Orsulak walked on four pitches. Choosing to ignore the oft-heard advice that a hitter should wait to see a strike before swinging after a pitcher has walked the last batter, Widger drove the first-pitch fastball to center field to tie the game.

Baker called on closer Rod Beck in the bottom of the ninth, hoping to take the game into extra innings. However, Mike Lansing singled and advanced to second on a sacrifice bunt by White. Segui then hit

Chris Widger

a line drive single to left field, scoring Lansing with the game-winning run.

The Giants hadn't blown a lead of that size since the club moved to San Francisco. The New York Giants led the St. Louis Cardinals 11-0 on June 15, 1952, after four innings, but lost 14-12, which set a major-league record for largest blown lead at the time.[3]

It was clear that the Expos had never given up on the game. Segui, who contributed four hits, said, "It's funny, because, in the dugout everybody thought we were going to win."[4] Segui also said, "It shows you what this team is made of. We're scrappy. We're not going to roll over. That's the attitude of this team."

The offensive star for the Expos was one of the most unlikely names in the lineup. Better known for his defensive skills, Chris Widger went 4-for-5 with five RBIs. It was one of the best offensive performances of his career; he had four hits in a game only one other time.

Widger said, "I'm happy with the way I'm swinging the bat right now, but honestly, I'm just happy that we won the game." Widger said it was one of the most memorable experiences he'd had playing baseball. He continued, "That's the biggest game I've ever been a part of."[5]

NOTES

1   Jeff Blair, "Expos rally for a wild victory," the *Montreal Gazette,* May 17, 1997, F2.

2   Blair.

3   Associated Press, "Expos 14, Giants 13," May 17, 1997, apnews-archive.com.

4   Blair.

5   Associated Press.

THE MONTREAL-TORONTO RIVALRY FINDS A NEW OUTLET

June 30, 1997: Montreal Expos 2, Toronto Blue Jays 1 At Skydome

By Norm King

THE OLD-TIMERS STILL TALK ABOUT THE MELEE that broke out at the 1932 Canadian Tiddlywinks Championships between the Toronto Twinkers and the Montreal Squidgers.[1] Fists, tiddlys, and winks were flying everywhere—even fans got involved. The cops had quite the time breaking things up.

That story is, of course, fictional. There is no known record of any Canadian tiddlywinks championship in 1932, but such is the rivalry between Montreal and Toronto that the idea of a brawl breaking out in any sporting endeavor between the two cities would not surprise the residents of either metropolis.

One would be hard pressed to find two cities in the same country as culturally and linguistically diverse as Montreal and Toronto. Montreal has its European air, Gallic flair and *joie de vivre*. Toronto has a reputation for being English in both language and outlook.

It was this *nous* against them mindset that permeated the country's most heated sports rivalry, between the Montreal Canadiens and the Toronto Maple Leafs hockey teams. These teams had many great battles over the years, both with the pucks and the fists. On December 9, 1953, for example, all the players from both teams took part in a bench-clearing brawl that resulted in the referee ejecting everybody from each side except for three skaters and a goaltender. The brouhaha exploded at the 18:12 mark of the third period and became known as the War of 18:12.

Bench-clearing brawls and the enmity between the two cities were probably not on the minds of the Montreal Expo and Toronto Blue Jay players who took to the Skydome field for the first matchup between the two teams that affected the standings. After all, except for Jays' Canadian relievers Paul Quantrill and Paul Spoljaric, all of the players for both teams were either from the United States or Latin America.

"For the people who live here, I guess it's nice," said Jays' reliever Dan Plesac. "I don't care who we're playing."[2]

"We only have to play one anthem," added Jays' manager Cito Gaston.[3]

But it was not the first time they faced each other during the regular season. From 1978 to 1986, the two teams played an exhibition game during the season to raise money for amateur baseball in Canada.[4] Each team won three games and two ended in ties. No game was played in 1981 due to the players' strike.

Fans would have looked forward to this game even if it didn't have historical significance because it offered a mouth-watering pitching matchup between a reigning Cy Young Award winner (Toronto's Pat Hentgen) and a Cy Young winner to be (Montreal's Pedro Martinez). Martinez had a 9-3 record with a 1.58 ERA. He had gone nine innings in his previous start, against the Reds at Olympic Stadium, but wasn't involved in the decision as Cincinnati won 2-1 in 11 innings. Martinez was the leader of a starting staff that pitched seven shutouts in June as the team went 17-11 for the month. Hentgen's previous start was a disaster: He allowed 11 runs, all earned, over eight innings in a 13-12 loss to the Boston Red Sox at Skydome. Despite that debacle, he came into this game with an 8-4 record and a respectable 3.18 earned-run average.

The first inning looked as if the 37,430 in attendance would be in for a goose-egg convention on the scoreboard as both pitchers set the side down in order. In the second, Expos rookie Vladimir Guerrero took matters into his own bat as he smacked the first pitch he had ever seen from Hentgen for a home run to give the Expos a 1-0 lead.

Martinez, meanwhile, was showing the form that would win him the first of his three career Cy Young Awards. He retired the first 12 batters he faced, and broke that streak when he walked Carlos Delgado to start the bottom of the fifth. Martinez struck out the next two hitters and induced Benito Santiago to hit a groundball that forced Delgado at second and prevented any further damage.

Every pitcher likes to have more wiggle room than a 1-0 margin could give him, and the Expos padded their lead for Martinez in the top of the sixth. Mark Grudzielanek led off with a single and two outs later, David Segui hit a fly ball that Jays center fielder Otis Nixon misplayed into a triple that scored Grudzielanek, giving the Expos a 2-0 lead. The way Martinez was pitching, that appeared to be enough.

"This one might have gone the Jays' way except that Montreal's David Segui lifted a harmless-looking fly ball … that Otis Nixon lost in the twilight—or maybe it was the ozone—for a run-scoring triple," wrote Jim Byers in the *Toronto Star*.[5]

The Jays missed an opportunity in the bottom of the sixth. Alex Gonzales ended Martinez's no-hit bid when he singled to open the inning, but was forced at second on a double play ball hit by Carlos Garcia. This proved costly because the bases were empty when Nixon hit a line-drive single to right. Orlando Merced grounded out to prevent any further threat.

Toronto wasn't ready to give up just yet. Delgado homered with one out in the bottom of the seventh to narrow the score to 2-1. Martinez decided enough was enough after that and shut the door the rest of the way for a complete-game win. Pedro gave up three hits and struck out 10. Hentgen also pitched a complete game, although he gave up six hits and struck out only

one. Nonetheless he acquitted himself well and would have won on most nights, but such are the vagaries of baseball. Nixon's squinting proved very costly.

Even though the players themselves didn't feel the rivalry before the game, they knew that the fans were into it.

"You come here to play the Blue Jays and it feels like you're playing in the World Series," said the Expos' Henry Rodriguez.[6]

"We felt the emotion out there," said Gonzales. "There's no question that affects the players."[7]

The game sped by in 2 hours and 3 minutes and fans leaving the stadium could still see the sun setting. The players didn't duke it out and no new lore was added to the history of Montreal-Toronto sports competition. But the game was a dandy.

SOURCES

In addition to the sources listed in the notes, the author consulted:

Tiddlywinks.org.

baseballhalloffame.ca.

NOTES

1   The squidger is the big disk used to propel the smaller disks in tiddlywinks.

2   Dejan Kovacevic, "Baseball, eh," *Pittsburgh Post-Gazette*, July 1, 1997.

3   Ibid.

4   The winner was awarded the Pearson Cup, named after Lester Pearson, prime minister of Canada between 1963-68. In addition to being a politician and a Nobel Peace Prize-winning diplomat, Pearson was a baseball fanatic and was the Expos' honorary president between 1969 and 1972.

5   Jim Byers, "First Strike to the Expos," *Toronto Star*, July 1, 1997.

6   Ibid.

7   Ibid.

A CANADA DAY CLASSIC

July 1, 1997: Montreal Expos 2, Toronto Blue Jays 1 At Skydome

By Thomas Ayers

ON TUESDAY, JULY 1, 1997, CANADA CELEBRATED its 130th birthday and the major leagues' only two Canadian franchises met in the second game of the first regular-season series between the clubs. It was the inaugural season of interleague baseball, which meant this was baseball's first All-Canadian series. Unsurprisingly, the game drew a sellout crowd of 50,436 to the Skydome. It was the Blue Jays' first sellout since Opening Day of the strike-shortened 1995 season, which was a stretch of 195 games.

The hometown fans were undoubtedly happy to see Roger Clemens on the mound that afternoon. It was the first of his two seasons in Toronto after his acrimonious departure from the Boston Red Sox, and the 34-year-old Clemens entered the game with a 12-2 record and a 1.79 ERA. In 1997 Clemens would lead the American League with 21 wins, a 2.05 ERA, 264 innings pitched, and 292 strikeouts. He won the first of consecutive Cy Young Awards he would win in Toronto and the fourth of the seven he would win in his career.

Opposing Clemens was Jeff Juden, a 26-year-old right-handed pitcher in his first full season with Montreal. The Expos had acquired Juden off waivers from the San Francisco Giants the previous season. An imposing presence on the mound, the 6-foot-7 hurler had thrown a complete-game victory over the Florida Marlins in his previous start, which boosted his record to 9-2.

The game was a special occasion for Juden: Clemens had been his boyhood hero while growing up in Salem, Massachusetts. Juden remarked, "I dreamed of [the chance to face Clemens] for a long time and it finally came true."[1] Juden also had a Canadian connection, as his father, Fred Juden, was born in Kingston, Ontario, and was sitting in the sellout crowd.

With a combined record of 21-4 between the starters, the game looked as if it would be a pitchers' duel. Clemens retired the first two batters he faced in the first inning before surrendering a single to F.P. Santangelo. Santangelo scored when David Segui was credited with a double on a fly ball to short left field.

After the game, Toronto left fielder Shawn Green admitted he had misplayed Segui's hit. The ball fell into shallow left field and Green, after hesitating on the ball initially, was caught by surprise by an in-between hop, watching helplessly as the ball bounced off Skydome's Astroturf over his head. "I did mess it up," Green said. "I didn't want to back up and play it off too big a hop knowing that [Santangelo] was on base with two outs and running hard. ... I should have gone in, jumped up and blocked it."[2] Green knew the ball tended to bounce high off the artificial turf in warm weather and it was 81 degrees at game time. If Green had been able to block the ball, Santangelo likely wouldn't have scored.

It was the second straight game in which an outfielder's miscue had cost the Blue Jays a run. Otis Nixon lost a fly ball in the twilight on Monday night, which resulted in a run-scoring triple in a game the Jays lost 2-1 to Montreal.

Nixon led off the bottom of the first with a walk and immediately stole second. After Nixon advanced to third on a grounder, Juden struck out Joe Carter. He walked Carlos Delgado, then got Ed Sprague to hit a foul popup that third baseman Santangelo caught despite having to reach two rows into the stands to make the grab.

The Expos scored another two-out run the next inning when Rondell White hit a homer to deep right-center field. The damage could have been worse for Toronto if catcher Charlie O'Brien hadn't gunned down Ryan McGuire on a stolen-base attempt during White's at-bat.

After White's home run, nobody reached base for either team through the fourth inning. In the top of the fifth, White reached base with a one-out single, but was picked off by Clemens. This was important, as catcher Chris Widger followed with a single and Mark Grudzielanek drew a walk. However, Clemens escaped the inning, getting Mark Lansing to ground out.

Juden continued to breeze through Toronto's lineup, striking out Green and O'Brien in the bottom of the fifth. In the top of the sixth, Clemens struck out a pair of batters, but Juden was even more impressive in the bottom of the frame, striking out the side. Clemens struck out another two batters in the top of the seventh.

At this point, Clemens had retired 15 of 19 batters since surrendering the home run to White. However, Juden continued his dominance, as well. After he struck out two batters in the bottom of the seventh

Jeff Juden

inning, he had retired 19 batters in a row, 10 of them by strikeout.

More importantly, Juden hadn't given up a hit in the game. As he left the mound at the end of the inning, the Expos fans in the ballpark cheered him off, chanting, "Ju-den! Ju-den! Ju-den!"[3]

In the top of the eighth inning, the Expos had runners on second and third with one out on a single by Grudzielanek and a double by Lansing, but Clemens escaped without further damage.

Juden got two straight strikes on Shawn Green to begin the bottom of the eighth. Then Green ended the no-hit bid and shutout with one swing, hitting a home run to deep right-center field.

Later Juden said, "It was a curveball I was trying to backdoor on him and it slid over. He hits the ball well on the inner half of the plate and I was trying to stay on the outer half and it slid a little bit inside."[4] Juden got out of the inning with two more strikeouts and a fly ball.

In the top of the ninth, Blue Jays catcher O'Brien threw out his second runner of the game when he nabbed Guerrero, who had singled, on a stolen-base attempt. Ryan McGuire then singled deep into the hole between shortstop and third base to break an 0-for-12 slump.

With McGuire on first, Blue Jays manager Cito Gaston brought in reliever Paul Quantrill. Born in Port Hope, Ontario, Quantrill became the first Canadian to pitch in a regular-season game between baseball's two Canadian franchises. He did exactly what he had been asked to do; he induced a double-play groundball from White.

After striking out Nixon to start the bottom of the ninth, Juden surrendered a single to Orlando Merced to put the tying run on base for Carter. Even though Carter had struck out three times in three at-bats, Expos manager Felipe Alou decided to replace Juden after 114 pitches due to his pitch count and the afternoon heat.

Juden left the mound to a standing ovation. He tipped his cap to acknowledge the crowd. It was described as "one of the loudest ovations ever given a visiting player at Skydome."[5] Another reporter commented, "[T]he ovation [Juden] got was louder than the applause for Clemens."[6] Juden said, "I just had a feeling of pride, you know. How good it was to see all the people up in the stands watching the ballgame on a special day for Canada."[7]

Carter fared no better against closer Ugueth Urbina and struck out for the fourth time. Carlos Delgado stepped to the plate with the game in the balance and hit a fly ball to the warning track that momentarily excited the home crowd before falling into White's glove.

During the afternoon, Juden allowed only two hits and struck out 14, tying teammate Pedro Martinez for the most in a National League game so far that season. The victory was his best start as an Expo, as he was 30 days away from being traded to the Cleveland Indians for left-handed reliever Steve Kline.

Santangelo was among the many players who were initially skeptical of interleague play. However, this series caused him to reconsider his view, particularly given how far Montreal was from other National League franchises: "I'm changing my opinion on it a bit. This is sweet, the way the fans have responded to us in Toronto," Santangelo said.[8]

The series with the Blue Jays was also an opportunity to reflect on what baseball in Montreal might have been in a more ideal situation. After watching Montreal fans go into bars in downtown Toronto after the club's victory on Monday night, Expos marketing director Richard Morency remarked, "It's beautiful, isn't it? This is what it will be like with a downtown ballpark in Montreal."[9]

SOURCES

In addition to the sources listed in the notes, the author consulted:

Baseballalmanac.com.

Baseball-reference.com.

Retrosheet.org.

NOTES

1 Mark Zwolinkski, "An Idol Time for Big Expo," *Toronto Star*, July 2, 1997.

2 Larry Millson, "Green Wishes He Had Second Shot at Segui Fly," *Globe and Mail* (Toronto), July 2, 1997.

3 Jack Todd, "Expos Win Hearts in Toronto," the *Montreal Gazette*, July 2, 1997.

4 Millson, "Expos Hurler a Treat to Watch Against Jays," *Globe and Mail*, July 2, 1997.

5 Jeff Blair, "Juden Has Blue Jays Seeing Red," the *Montreal Gazette*, July 2, 1997.

6 Todd.

7 Zwolinski. .

8 Blair.

9 Todd.

VLAD IMPALES HIS 40TH

October 2, 1999: Montreal Expos 13 — Philadelphia Phillies 3 At Veterans Stadium

By Norm King

HE WAS NICKNAMED VLAD THE IMPALER, AND while he isn't a bad guy--his 15th-century namesake, on the other hand, came by his nickname honestly-- Vladimir Guerrero did some pretty mean things to baseballs thrown by National and American League pitchers during his playing career.

The Expos were going through a terrible period in 1999, as they were completing the second of four straight seasons of 90 or more losses. Management had sold off the stars who made the team so promising earlier in the decade, but the farm system could still produce a gem like Guerrero. He was a five-tool player when he came up to the Expos for good in 1997 (he had 27 plate appearances in 1996). He had power, hit for average, and ran like a deer. And on October 2, 1999, he became the first Expo to hit 40 home runs in a season as the Expos pasted the Phillies 13-3.

"He's in a league all his own," said teammate Trace Coquillette. "If there was a league better than this league, he'd be in it."[1]

Prior to Guerrero's arrival in Montreal, no member of *Nos Amours* had hit 40 home runs in a season.[2] Guerrero set a new mark in 1998 with 38, breaking the record of 36 set by Henry Rodriguez in 1996, and he surpassed his own record when he hit number 39 on October 1 off the Phillies' Mike Grace in a 7-4 Expos win.

If Guerrero could have chosen the team he wanted to face to try for his 40th home run, it might very well have been the Phillies because their pitching staff was awful, and a major reason why the team ended up with a 77-85 record in 1999. They were 13th out of 16 teams in the league in both team ERA (4.92) and home runs allowed (212). Guerrero was known for loving his mother's home cooking. The Phillies' pitching staff made his mouth water almost as much.

Paul Byrd started for Philadelphia. His last name was appropriate because many of his pitches took off on long flights. Despite a 15-10 record going into the game, he had a 4.60 ERA and he was third in the National League in home runs allowed with a whopping 31. Byrd had gone seven innings and given up two earned runs in his last start for the victory in a 3-2 win over the New York Mets. Jeremy Powell (3-8) started for Montreal, having given up eight earned runs in 5⅔ innings of a 10-0 Expos loss to the Braves.

Maybe Byrd was having sympathy pains over his opponent's previous start because from the get-go he seemed intent on duplicating Powell's pitching line from that game. Byrd began by walking leadoff hitter Rondell White, but got the next batter, Peter Bergeron, to hit into a fielder's choice that forced White at second. Bergeron himself moved to second on a wild pitch, then to third when Michael Barrett singled to deep short. This brought up Guerrero, as free a swinger as ever batted in the majors. He took Byrd's first pitch and deposited it deep in the left-field stands for milestone home run number 40. The next batter, Fernando Seguignol, proved to be a more patient hitter than Guerrero; he let one pitch go by for a ball before blasting a home run to right-center field. The Expos led 4-0 after one.

Philadelphia got one back in the bottom of the first, when Mike Lieberthal doubled to drive home Bobby Abreu, who had singled, but the Expos blew it open in the top of the second. Powell led off by hitting the first of his two career doubles, followed by White's second consecutive free pass. Bergeron attempted to sacrifice the runners ahead by bunting to third, and Byrd misplayed the throw for an error that brought Powell home. Barrett walked to load the bases. Byrd seemed poised to get out of the jam when Guerrero flied out and Seguignol struck out, but the next batter—this is the City of Brotherly Love, remember—was Vladimir's older brother Wilton, and he drove Byrd's second pitch into the right-field bleachers for a grand slam to give the Expos a 9-1 lead. This marked the second time the Guerrero brothers homered in the same game; they had done it on August 15, 1998 at Cincinnati.

Powell was probably pinching himself as he took the mound for the top of the third, because he was not used to an eight-run lead; his average run support in 1999 was 4.26 runs per game. A young pitcher like Powell, who was 23 at the time, often lets up with such a cushion, especially if he's making his last start of the season. Powell may have let his concentration sag a bit in the bottom of the second, when some sloppy pitching led to two runs. With one out, he walked Marlon Anderson, then hit number-eight hitter Alex Arias with a pitch on a 2-and-2 count. Chad Ogea, who had replaced Byrd in the top of the inning, bunted the runners ahead, and they both scored when Doug Glanville hit a line-drive single to left to make the score 9-3. Powell got a strikeout of Ron Gant to end the inning, and probably a stern talking-to from Expos manager Felipe Alou when he returned to the dugout. Whatever happened, Powell didn't give up any more runs and finished with three earned runs allowed over six innings in what turned out to be the last win of his major-league career. His success that night could be attributed, in part, to listening to his batterymate, Barrett.

"I wanted to throw more breaking balls, but he [Barrett] said to stay aggressive, stay with the fastball until I got ahead in the count, then use the breaking ball," said Powell. "It worked."[3]

The same can't be said for Philadelphia pitcher Amaury Telemaco. After a 1-2-3 inning when he took over in the fifth, he didn't quit while he was ahead, choosing instead to come out for the sixth. He started off well enough by striking out White, but gave up back-to-back singles to Bergeron and Barrett, which brought Guerrero up again. Maybe Guerrero had a train to catch because he swung on the first pitch again and launched it over the right-field fence for his 41st

Vladimir Guerrero

home run of the year and second three-run blast of the game. Take that, big brother.

Miguel Batista came on in the seventh and went the rest of the way to record his first major-league save, and was happy with the achievement. "Now I've got it all—a save, short relief, long relief, and a few starts," he said. "Now I can truly say I'm a complete right-handed utility pitcher."[4]

Montreal decided that 12 wasn't enough in the eighth and decided to go for a baker's dozen. With one out, Seguignol was safe on a fielder's choice, moved to second on Wilton Guerrero's single, and scored on a Coquillette base hit. That was Coquillette's third hit of the game, the only time he accomplished the feat in his 51-game major-league career. Final score: Montreal 13, Philadelphia 3.

Guerrero hit one more home run in his last game of the year to bring his total to 42, along with 131 RBIs and a .316 batting average. He set a career high in home runs with 44 in 2000, the only other time he hit more than 40 in a season.

SOURCES

In addition to the sources listed in the notes, the author consulted:

Baseball-reference.com.

Standard Speaker (Hazleton, Pennsylvania).

Ucs.mun.ca.

NOTES

1 Stephanie Myles, "Oh, what a night!," the *Montreal Gazette*, October 3, 1999.

2 Literally translated, "nos amours" means "our loves." The term was an affectionate nickname for the team.

3 Myles.

4 Ibid.

WILKERSON RIDES "LE CAROUSEL"[1]

June 24, 2003: Montreal Expos 6, Pittsburgh Pirates 4 At Olympic Stadium

By Norm King

THERE WAS ALMOST A POETIC IRONY WHEN the Montreal Expos moved to Washington in 2005 to become the Nats, because in the years prior to their departure, they were like gnats to the rest of the National League. They had this intangible way of irritating other teams, often being competitive when they shouldn't be and staying in division races despite having a payroll a fraction the size of their rivals. They finished second in the National League East in 2002 with an 83-79 record, albeit 19 games behind division champion Atlanta.

Major League Baseball decided to make things even more challenging for Montreal in 2003 by having them play 22 "home" games at Hiram Bithorn Stadium in San Juan, Puerto Rico. Despite the obstacles and ominous preseason predictions — *Sports Illustrated* had them finishing last in the National League East — the Expos nonetheless remained competitive early in the season. As of June 22, they held 42-34 record, a surmountable 7½ games behind division-leading Atlanta. Their success was due in part to the efforts of sparkplug players like Brad Wilkerson, who was entering his second full season after finishing second in Rookie of the Year voting in 2002 behind Colorado's Jason Jennings. Wilkerson showed no signs of a sophomore jinx — he was hitting .292 with 8 home runs and 37 RBIs in 64 games — as he prepared for a home game at Olympic Stadium on June 24 against Pittsburgh.

With June 24 being the St. Jean Baptiste holiday in Quebec, the 5,872 announced attendance at Olympic Stadium was disappointing. The few who were there saw Wilkerson become the fifth player in Expos history to hit for the cycle as Montreal defeated Pittsburgh 6-4.[2]

Pittsburgh went with Jeff D'Amico, 5-7 at the time, on his way to a 16-loss season, the most in the league.

He had gone six innings for the win in his previous start, on June 18, as Pittsburgh defeated the Expos, 7-3, at PNC Park. Tomo Ohka (also 5-7) started for Montreal. He had won his last start, also at PNC Park, on June 19, going six frames in the Expos' 5-2 win.

Each team failed to score early on, as they both missed golden opportunities. The Pirates almost blew it open in the first when they loaded the bases with two out. Brian Giles singled, then Ohka walked Aramis Ramirez and hit Matt Stairs with a pitch. Reggie Sanders struck out swinging to end that threat.

The Expos' first opportunity came in the bottom of the second when both sides played by-the-book fundamental baseball. Wilkerson got his first hit on a flawlessly executed one-out bunt single to third; Ramirez, who was playing several steps off the line, could only wait patiently while the ball gently rolled to him before he picked it up and tossed it back to D'Amico. Wil Cordero followed with a double to left, but the Pirates played it perfectly when left fielder Giles threw it to the cutoff man, shortstop Jack Wilson, who relayed it to catcher Jason Kendall in time to nab Wilkerson.

Expos third-base coach Manny Acta gave Wilkerson the idea for the bunt when he noticed that Ramirez always played well back. "I was thinking about it my last at-bat Monday night, but we had a three-run lead so I saved it, Wilkerson said. "I saw the opportunity and took advantage of it."[3]

The next few innings were scoreless as Ohka and D'Amico traded zeroes on the scoreboard. Wilkerson didn't bat again until the fifth, but continued his ride on *le carousel* by bouncing a double off the right-field wall. Pittsburgh opened the scoring in the top of the sixth, when Kenny Lofton doubled and scored on a Kendall single. Montreal got that run back and more in the bottom of the frame thanks to Wilkerson and some bad fielding. Leadoff hitter Endy Chavez was safe at first on a throwing error by shortstop Wilson, but was forced at second on a fielder's choice by Edwards Guzman. One out later, Jose Vidro walked, prompting Pirates manager Lloyd McClendon to replace D'Amico with Joe Beimel just as Wilkerson was coming to the plate. Wilkerson tripled, scoring Guzman and Vidro. Cordero was walked intentionally to bring up Ron Calloway, who drove Wilkerson in with a double, giving the Expos a 3-1 lead. Beimel then walked Brian Schneider intentionally, and was removed from the game without getting anybody out. His ERA didn't take any more of a hit when new pitcher Salomon Torres struck out Jose Macias, who was pinch-hitting for Ohka.

Montreal built on its lead in the seventh. Torres got the first two batters out easily, but became a victim of destiny when Cabrera singled and scored on a Vidro double, which brought Wilkerson to the plate. Swinging on a 1-and-2 pitch, he drove the ball to straightaway center field; Lofton chased after it only half-heartedly because he knew it was gone. After much high-fiving when he returned to the dugout, Wilkerson acknowledged the fans' cheers with a curtain call.

"I wasn't thinking about hitting a home run," Wilkerson said. "It was in the back of my mind, I guess—I would be lying to you if I said otherwise, but I was just trying to get the head (of the bat) out and hopefully get a pitch that I could drive in the gap and get up in the air."[4]

But Pittsburgh wasn't going to give up without a fight. Julio Manon, who had replaced Ohka in the seventh, started the top of the eighth by giving up a Kendall double and walking Giles. After he got Ramirez to pop out to first, Manon's night was over and Joey Eischen came on to face Craig Wilson. The echo of the public-address system's announcing of Eischen's name had barely ended when he was sent to the showers after Wilson singled on a 1-0 pitch to score Kendall and send Giles to third. Dan Smith came on to face pinch-hitter Adam Hyzdu, who drove Giles home with a groundball to third, cutting Montreal's lead to 6-3 after 7½. Pittsburgh got one more run in the ninth when Kendall singled off Expos closer Rocky Biddle to score Carlos Rivera, who had doubled. That ended the scoring, and Biddle got his 21st save of the season.

Expos manager Frank Robinson was effusive in his praise for Wilkerson. "To get four hits, No. 1, is a good day. But to hit for the cycle—*le carousel*—I like that better," Robinson said. "That's just a tremendous achievement."[5]

McClendon, who was famous for his temper tantrums, was furious with his team because he felt that D'Amico pitched well enough to win. The manager who once literally stole first base from the ground during an argument with an umpire, stormed out of his office session with reporters, but not before sweeping all the papers off his desk in one fell swoop.

As for Wilkerson, he decided that he liked hitting for the cycle so much that he did it again in the Nationals' second-ever game on April 6, 2005, a 7-3 win over Philadelphia.

SOURCES

In addition to the sources listed in the notes, the author consulted:

Sports Illustrated.

Ballparks.com.

Baseball-reference.com.

Mlb.com.

Network.suntimes.com.

NOTES

1   "Le carousel" is the French term for the cycle.

2   The other players who did it before him were Tim Foli (1976), Chris Speier (1978), Tim Raines (1987), and Rondell White (1995).

3   Stephanie Myles, "Wilkerson Cycles Past Pirates," the *Montreal Gazette*, June 25, 2003.

4   "Wilkerson First Expo to Hit for Cycle Since '95," *cbssports.com.*

5   Myles.

SMOLTZ BLOWS A RARE SAVE

July 25, 2003: Montreal Expos 9, Atlanta Braves 8 At Olympic Stadium

By Norm King

WAY BACK IN THE 1930S AND '40S, RADIO FANS listened to a horror program designed to scare the daylights out of people, called *Lights Out*. During the show's weekly introduction, the announcer advised people to turn off their radios if they couldn't handle the creepy happenings to come in the next 30 minutes.

While they were not creepy, the Atlanta Braves pitching staff of the 1990s and early 2000s was just as scary. It led the National League in ERA 10 times during the Braves' remarkable streak of 14 consecutive playoff appearances between 1991 and 2005. (A players' strike wiped out the postseason in 1994.) And as much as they would have liked to, opposition hitters unfortunately could not opt out of facing a conglomeration of arms that included three eventual Hall of Famers—Greg Maddux, Tom Glavine, and John Smoltz.

The 2003 Braves weren't as strong in the pitching department as their predecessors. They were ninth in team ERA (4.10) and earned runs allowed (663), 10th in walks (555), and 12th in shutouts (seven). Smoltz was one of the staff's bright spots; he was no longer a starter but had become the team's closer. (He returned to the rotation in 2005.) He led the NL with 55 saves in 2002, and when he came into a game, it was pretty much … well, you know.

Despite the poorer-than-usual pitching statistics, Atlanta was in its perennial perch on top of the National League East with a 67-34 record entering the game on July 25, 2003, against Montreal, 9½ games ahead of the Philadelphia Phillies. The Expos weren't in the race but they had a respectable 52-50 record.

Rookie Horacio Ramirez, the latest in a seemingly endless supply of Braves pitching talent, started for Atlanta. Ramirez had an 8-3 record, with a no-decision in his last start, an 11-8 Braves win over the Mets in which he gave up five runs (four earned) in 4⅔ innings.

Expos starter Claudio Vargas had a 6-6 record at game time, having lost his previous start 3-2 to the Phillies despite allowing only two earned runs in 6⅓ innings.

Atlanta opened the scoring in the second when consecutive two-out doubles by Javy Lopez and Vinny Castilla gave the Braves a 1-0 lead. Vladimir Guerrero's solo shot in the bottom of the inning got that run back quickly, then the Expos pulled ahead in the bottom of the third in a case of Ramirez gone wild. He started the frame by walking Jamey Carroll and Jose Vidro. Orlando Cabrera hit into a 4-6-3 double play that erased Vidro but moved Carroll to third. Guerrero, a free swinger who rarely walked, got a free pass on four pitches.[1] With two on, Wil Cordero doubled to right-center; Carroll scored easily, but Guerrero, who was moving gingerly at game time due to injury, was out at the plate. The Expos led 2-1 after three.

As a team, the 2003 Braves led the league in runs (907), hits (1,608), and home runs (235), and they used that power to build up a commanding lead. First, Chipper Jones tied the game in the sixth with a solo home run. They took the lead in the seventh on a one-out Castilla home run to left-center. After Ramirez grounded out, the Expos played hot-potato with the ball. Center fielder Brad Wilkerson bobbled Rafael Furcal's double, which allowed Furcal to reach third. Marcus Giles doubled Furcal home; he reached third on a Cabrera miscue, but he did not score.

Atlanta really poured it on in the eighth. Joey Eischen took the mound for the Expos, but he couldn't keep up with the Joneses, as Chipper and Andruw hit back-to-back singles to lead off the inning. With two on and nobody out, Expos manager Frank Robinson replaced Eischen with Julio Manon. Julio Franco, pinch-hitting for Robert Fick, greeted Manon with a base hit up the middle that scored Chipper and sent Andruw to second. A passed ball advanced the runners, but it didn't really matter because Lopez hit a liner over the fence for a three-run homer. Manon retired the next three batters but the damage was done and the Braves led 8-2 after 7½ innings.

The Braves pitching of previous seasons usually meant that an 8-2 lead in the eighth inning was a lock. Since the 2003 staff was weaker than others had been, opposition teams had a slightly better chance of coming back. But with only six outs to work with, the Expos still faced a monumental task, especially since Ramirez had given up only two runs on four hits to that point.

Nonetheless, Cox had Ramirez on a short leash, and removed him after he gave up a one-out double to Cabrera. Kevin Gryboski took the mound and walked Guerrero after a tough nine-pitch at-bat. In what proved to be an important move later on, Robinson sent rookie Ron Calloway in to pinch-run for the hurting Guerrero. Cordero singled to score Cabrera, with Calloway ending up on second. Ray King replaced Gryboski and got the first batter he faced, Brad Wilkerson, to fly to Chipper Jones in left. The baseball gods smiled on the Expos as Chipper dropped the fly for an error, which loaded the bases. When Jose Macias grounded to Furcal at short, Rafael went for the out at third, allowing Calloway to score what seemed an unimportant run.

Catcher Barrett was up next and he didn't waste any time atoning for his passed ball by driving King's first pitch over the fence for a three-run homer. The 10,069 fans in attendance roared their approval throughout the cavernous Olympic Stadium. Suddenly the score was 8-7.

The Braves were confident with their lead because they had Smoltz to save the game in the ninth. Smoltz was having a phenomenal season; he already had 37 saves and had blown only two save opportunities all year, the last one on June 19 at Philadelphia.

The ninth inning started easily enough for Smoltz when Carroll grounded out to third. Vidro grounded to short, but in what became the crucial play of the game, Furcal made an error, putting the tying run on base for Montreal. After Cabrera struck out, Calloway belted Smoltz's 1-and-1 pitch off the wall in center for a double that missed being a walk-off home run by inches. Vidro, who was off with the swing of the bat, scored easily from first; Blown Save number three was in the record books and the game was tied 8-8 after nine.

"The Big O was a loud environment to play in because you could bang those seats like crazy, said Mike Walker, a fan who was at the game. "The noise the fans made really rattled Smoltz."[2]

"Those of you who second-guessed me after I took Guerrero out, raise your hands," joked Robinson to reporters."[3]

The 10th inning was scoreless, as was the top of the 11th. Cox sent Jung Bong out to pitch in the bottom of the 11th. After Vidro grounded to short, Cabrera doubled to left, and Calloway walked. Bong made a big play by striking out pinch-hitter Brian Schneider. Two gone. Suddenly, the Atlanta bench started yelling at Furcal to watch Cabrera more closely. He didn't, so Cabrera daringly stole third.

Bong played only three seasons in the majors, due in part to his poor control. He walked almost five batters per nine innings in 2003 (4.9) and had six wild pitches for the season, both high numbers considering he threw only 57 innings.[4] One of those wild throws came on a 1-and-1 pitch to Macias that allowed Cabrera to scamper home with the winning run. The crowd, already hoarse from all the Expo heroics, reached down deep inside to cheer their team once more.

"The game was awesome," said Walker. "I don't think I had a voice at the end of [it]."[5]

"We've had the toughest breaks this year and something finally went our way," said Barrett.[6]

SOURCES

In addition to the sources listed in the notes, the author consulted:

oldtimeradiodownloads.com.

NOTES

1 Guerrero never placed in the top 10 in walks during his career. His career high for free passes was 84, set during the 2002 season.

2 Mike Walker, telephone interview, June 8, 2015.

3 Stephanie Myles, "Expos edge Braves on Bong's wild pitch," the *Montreal Gazette*, July 26, 2003.

4 The Expos' Zach Day led the league with 13 wild pitches in 131⅓ innings pitched.

5 Walker interview.

6 Myles.

A COMEBACK FOR THE AGES

August 26, 2003: Montreal Expos 14, Philadelphia Phillies 10 At Olympic Stadium

by Bob Webster

MAJOR LEAGUE BASEBALL INTRODUCED THE wild card with the hope of allowing more teams to compete for a playoff spot and therefore sustain fan interest.[1] That goal was succeeding in spades in 2003, during one of the wildest of wild-card races in baseball history; as eight National League teams were within three games of each other when the Expos and the Philadelphia Phillies met at Olympic Stadium on August 26 in the second game of a four-game series.

These were challenging times for the Expos. Jeffrey Loria sold the team in early 2002 to Major League Baseball. MLB named Frank Robinson manager and Omar Minaya vice president and general manager. The 2003 Expos played 22 home games at Hiram Bithorn Stadium in San Juan, Puerto Rico. It was a smaller ballpark, but the crowds in Puerto Rico outdrew the crowds in Montreal, helping the Expos draw over a million fans at home for the first time since 1998. Playing so many games in Puerto Rico also created a travel burden their competitors didn't have to face.

The roof of Olympic Stadium was closed the night of August 26 as Montreal tried to stay in the NL race. The 12,509 fans in attendance saw the Expos do just that, and in spectacular fashion, overcoming deficits of 8-0 and 10-3 to win 14-10. With the win, *Nos Amours* extended their winning streak to three games and moved to within two games of the Phillies and the Florida Marlins for the lead in the wild-card race.[2]

The Phillies' Ricky Ledee led off the game with a home run off the Expos' Zach Day. Jimmy Rollins then doubled to the left-center gap and Bobby Abreu singled him in to make the score 2-0 before the first out was recorded. The Expos got out of the inning without any more damage and the score held at 2-0 until the fourth inning, when Philadelphia's Mike Lieberthal led off with a single and moved to third on

a double by Chase Utley. Pat Burrell walked, and was forced at second on a fielder's choice by Tomas Perez that scored Lieberthal. Ledee drove in Utley and Perez and sent Zach Day to the showers with his second home run of the game. Eric Knott came in to pitch and quickly gave up back-to-back doubles to Rollins and Abreu, making the score 7-0. Lieberthal led off the fifth with a home run and the Phillies looked on their way to a blowout victory, leading 8-0.

The Phillies' starter, Vincente Padilla, gave up only one hit through four innings and that batter was erased on an inning-ending double play in the fourth. The Expos got to him in the fifth. Vladimir Guerrero led off with a single. Wil Cordero singled to right, sending Guerrero to second. Todd Zeile, just signed as a free agent on August 20, singled to load the bases. Brian Schneider grounded out to first, scoring Guerrero. Endy Chavez grounded out to short, scoring Cordero. Ron Calloway, pinch-hitting for Knott, stroked a base hit to right, scoring Zeile. Brad Wilkerson lined out to end the inning but not before the Expos got on the board and closed the gap to 8-3.

A two-out rally by the Phillies in their half of the sixth made the score 10-3. After Ledee flied out to center and Rollins struck out swinging, Abreu walked, and Jim Thome doubled to the left-center gap, sending him to third. Lieberthal hit a single that scored Abreu; Guerrero made an error on the play and Thome scored.

The Expos scored one in the bottom of the sixth when Orlando Cabrera doubled, reached third on an error by Abreu in right, and scored on a sacrifice fly by Jose Vidro to make it 10-4. Padilla finished the inning, but was lifted for a pinch-hitter in the top of the seventh.

In the bottom of the inning, Zeile and Schneider greeted Phillies reliever Terry Adams with singles to put runners on first and second. Zeile moved to third on Chavez's fielder's choice, and scored on a wild pitch. Jose Macias, pinch-hitting for pitcher Joey Eischen, singled to left, sending Chavez to third. Dan Plesac relieved Adams and gave up an RBI single to Wilkerson. Mike Williams replaced Plesac and struck out Cabrera. Vidro doubled in Macias and Wilkerson, Guerrero was intentionally walked, and Cordero doubled in Vidro and Guerrero to tie this wild game at 10-10. Zeile then singled for the second time in the inning to drive in Cordero. Schneider flied out to center for the third out, but the Expos had taken an 11-10 lead.

The Phillies almost retook the lead in the eighth when Jim Thome was hit by a pitch and Lieberthal singled to left. Chase Utley sent a drive to deep right field that had the distance, but Vladimir Guerrero jumped and made a great catch at the wall to retire the side and end a potential Phillies rally before it got started.

"I thought it was gone," said Vidro of Guerrero's catch. "When he hit it, it was like, 'Oh my God, no way!' But Vlady made a hell of a play and that was it right there."[3]

The Expos scored three more in the bottom of the eighth, highlighted by Cordero's two-run double, to make the score 14-10. Luis Ayala, who came in to pitch for the Expos in the eighth, retired the Phillies three up, three down in the ninth to give the Expos the come-from-behind victory.

Expos manager Frank Robinson, speaking of Cordero's two-run doubles in the seventh and eighth innings, said, "He's done a terrific job the last two weeks or so coming up with big, big, big hits."

"It's unreal," Robinson said. "You see it happening but you don't believe it. That was a great win for this ballclub, this organization, and for the fans and for this city. It's just a great win and it's what we really need to do."[4]

Robinson's excitement in this comeback was also conveyed by some of the players. "How exciting was that game?" Vidro said. "We came back—unbelievable, one of the most exciting games I've played since I've been in the big leagues."[5]

"The guys were energetic even when we were down 8-0, and then again 10-3," said Zeile. "This team always felt like we had a chance to win and I think that's why the result is what it is."[6]

Two days before this game, the Marlins and Phillies were four games ahead of the Expos in the NL wild-card race. At of the end of the day, the Marlins had lost six of seven, the Phillies had lost four in a row, and the Expos had won three in a row to cut their wild-card deficit from four games to two games. That said, they were one of eight teams in a mix that also included the Astros, Diamondbacks, Cubs, Cardinals, and Dodgers.

Table 1. 2003 National League Wild-Card Standings after games played on August 26:

Team	Record	GB
Phillies	70-61	-
Marlins	70-61	-
Astros[7]	69-62	-
Diamondbacks	69-63	1½
Cubs	68-62	1½
Cardinals	68-63	2
Expos	69-64	2
Dodgers	67-63	2½

The Expos inched a bit closer, as they won the next two games for a four-game sweep and a tie for the wild-card lead. They couldn't get any closer after that, as they lost 9 of their next 10 to fall out of the race. The Expos also suffered a huge blow on September 1 when MLB decided they could not afford to call up players from the minor leagues, as other teams could. They would have to make do with what they had. That decision took the heart out of the Expos. Fan attendance dropped off, and the Expos finished eight games out of the wild card.

"Baseball handed down a decree," Minaya said. "It was a message to the players; it was a momentum killer."[8]

SOURCES

In addition to the sources listed in the notes, the author consulted:

baseballchronology.com/baseball/Teams/Montreal/.

baseball-reference.com.

NOTES

1   The wild card was supposed to be implemented for the 1994 season, but due to the players strike that year, it was first used in 1995.

2   *Nos Amours* was a common nickname for the Expos. In French it means "our loves."

3   "Late offensive flurry boosts Montreal," ESPN.com, August 27, 2003.

4   Ibid.

5   Ibid.

6   Ibid.

7   Houston was leading the division, but was in a dogfight with Chicago and St. Louis for the top spot. Houston was in first place after this game and would have been in the playoffs had the season ended that night.

8   Les Carpenter, "Minaya Laid Foundation for Success," *Washington Post*, July 4, 2005.

GUERRERO HITS FOR THE CYCLE

September 14, 2003: Montreal Expos 7, New York Mets 3 At Olympic Stadium

By Adam J. Ulrey

BASEBALL IS A FUNNY GAME; YOU NEVER KNOW what might happen, even when two teams are playing for nothing coming down to the end of the season. On the afternoon of September 14, 2003, the Montreal Expos hosted the last-place New York Mets at Olympic Stadium. The Mets were just playing out the string at the end of a disappointing season; they were sitting at 63-84, 28 games out of first place coming into the game.

Tom Glavine, looking for career win number 252, was on the mound for the Mets. He was having a miserable season by his standards, with a 9-12 record and a 4.36 ERA. He faced the Expos' young rising-star Zach Day in front of a good late-season turnout of 21,417. The Expos were hovering above .500 at 75-74 but were 17 games behind the first-place Atlanta Braves. Hoping to just see the home team win, the crowd saw Vladimir Guerrero put on a show they would never forget.

Guerrero's 2003 campaign was his eighth, and last, as an Expo. There was very little chance that Major League Baseball—MLB ran the Expos that season as it tried sell the team and had hoped to trade Guerrero for some prospects—would sign him and saddle the team's new owner with a contract that promised to fall in the $50 million to $75 million range. So Guerrero was essentially on a season-long audition. But everyone tried to lowball the Expos, and MLB was not going to just give him away. He had been plagued by injuries and was on the disabled list with a herniated disk from June 5 to July 20. The injury ruined any chance of trading Guerrero, as teams didn't know how healthy he truly was. Despite all of this, Guerrero entered this game with 23 home runs and 74 RBIs, and was hitting .321 in just over 350 at-bats.

Guerrero doubled to right field to lead off the second inning with the Expos already in a 3-0 hole. He came home with the Expos' first run on Michael Barrett's triple to deep center field. Joe Vitiello's grounder to short brought Barrett home and made the score 3-2.

The Expos tied the game in the next inning and Guerrero got a single, but one had nothing to do with the other. Brad Wilkerson led off with a walk, moved to third on a single by Jose Vidro, and scored on Orlando Cabrera's sacrifice fly. Guerrero singled, moving Vidro to second, but the Expos couldn't score any more runs.

The Expos took the lead for good in the fifth. With two out, Cabrera reached first after being hit by a pitch and scored when Guerrero tripled off the right-field wall over Roger Cedeno. Guerrero scored on Todd Ziele's single to make the score 5-3 after five innings.

Guerrero knew he was close to the cycle when he stepped to the plate with one on to face Dan Wheeler in the seventh. All he needed now was the home run. "The first pitch was a breaking ball for a strike and then I was looking for the breaking ball and I got it," he said after the game. "There was just one at-bat to go and I just went up there and tried to swing as hard as I could and see what happens and it happened."[1] Guerrero crushed the ball to deep right field and knew it was gone right away as he just flipped his bat down and started his slow home-run trot. His two-run shot completed the scoring in the Expos' 7-3 win.

"He knew they were going to throw nothing he could pull, so he stayed back to hit that breaking-ball pitch and took it the other way. He's the only one who can do that. That's crazy," Cabrera said. "He was in the zone and he knew he had to take it the other way and he did. He's capable of doing all that stuff."[2]

Brad Wilkerson was also impressed by his teammate's abilities: "It was just amazing. I was sitting in the dugout and I said, 'He's going to do it. He didn't try to do too much. He took the ball the other way. He got the pitch he could hit hard. It's a special moment to do something like that.'"[3]

While the Expos were happy for their star outfielder, they wondered aloud what might have been if Guerrero had played the whole season. Despite his missing almost two months the Expos had a winning record coming into the game. "What's sad is I wonder where this team would have been if he hadn't been hurt. That's the only thing I think about," said general manager Omar Minaya. "I believe we had a team here that was as good as any team in the National League."[4]

Guererro became the sixth Expo to hit for the cycle, joining Wilkerson, Rondell White, Chris Speier, Tim Foli, and Tim Raines. He was the second Expo to do it during the 2003 season; Wilkerson had accomplished the feat on June 24 against the Pittsburgh Pirates. Oakland's Eric Byrnes and Cleveland's Travis Hafner were the only other players to hit for the cycle that year.

The Expos became the first team since the 1998 Colorado Rockies to have two players (Dante Bichette and Neifi Perez) hit for the cycle in the same season.

Before this game, the closest Guerrero had ever been to a cycle was in Double-A ball at Harrisburg in 1996. He was missing the double and hit a ball into the gap but stopped at first for a single.

Sadly for the Expos, Guerrero's cycle contributed to his passing the season-long audition; he signed a five-year, $70 million contract with the Anaheim Angels before the 2004 campaign. Yet another player exited through the Olympic Stadium's revolving door of magnificent talent.

SOURCES

In addition to the sources listed in the notes, the author consulted:

Baseballnews.com.

Baseball-reference.com.

Retrosheet.org.

SI.com.

NOTES

1   Bill Ladson, "Vladimir Guerrero Hits for Cycle Against Mets," MLB.com, September 15, 2003.

2   Associated Press, "Guerrero Stages One-Man Show," *Los Angeles Times*, September 15, 2003.

3   Ladson.

4   Ibid.

BLAST-OFF IN THE BIG O

June 19, 2004: Montreal Expos 17, Chicago White Sox 14 At Olympic Stadium

By Adam J. Ulrey

IT WAS JUAN WILD NIGHT IN AN OTHERWISE sad and dreary 2004 season at Olympic Stadium as the balls were flying out, even if the fans weren't filing in. And it's a game neither the Expos' Juan Rivera nor the White Sox' Juan Uribe was likely to forget.

This was a weird one in many ways: Rivera hit two home runs in one inning, including a grand slam; Uribe drove in seven runs; for White Sox starter Arnie Munoz, it was the first—and last—start of his major-league career; Expos reliever Jeremy Fikac made his final major-league appearance that night and won the seventh game of his career; and the Expos almost blew a 10-run lead.

At game time, the White Sox were in second place in the American League Central Division with a 35-28 record, a half-game behind the Minnesota Twins. The Expos, meanwhile, were going nowhere except to Washington with a 20-45 record and in last place in the National League East.

The game began innocently enough, with Expos starter Tony Armas setting the White Sox down 1-2-3 in the top of the first. In the bottom half of the inning, Munoz, making his first major-league appearance after being called up from the Birmingham Barons of the Double-A Southern Association, gave up a one-out double to third baseman Jamey Carroll. One out later, Carroll stole third with left fielder Carl Everett still waiting for the first pitch of his at-bat, then scored when Everett doubled to left to give the Expos a 1-0 lead. The White Sox tied it in the top of the second. Armas walked center fielder Aaron Rowand with two out, then gave up a run-scoring double to third baseman Jose Crede.

If Munoz had a case of the nerves in the first inning, he had an out-and-out anxiety attack in the second

as the Expos sent everyone but the batboy to the plate, scored nine runs, and had one of their players, Rivera, perform a feat that had previously been done only 27 times since the National League came into being in 1876.

The carnage began when shortstop Orlando Cabrera led off with a single and scored on Rivera's home run to left-center. Munoz then became his own worst enemy when he hit the number-eight hitter in the lineup, catcher Brian Schneider, with a pitch. That brought up Armas, who sacrificed Schneider to second. Center fielder Brad Wilkerson moved Schneider to third with a single, but then gave Munoz a break by getting caught trying to steal second. At this point there were two out and two runs in. With a little luck, Munoz could have gotten out of the inning without too much damage. But alas, it was not to be.

Munoz walked the next batter, Carroll, then moved him up to second with a wild pitch. Second baseman Jose Vidro doubled home Schneider and Carroll to make the score 5-1. Everett was walked intentionally to bring up first baseman Nick Johnson, the ninth batter of the inning. That move failed when Johnson singled to score Vidro and move Everett to third. Cabrera came up for the second time in the inning, so Munoz decided to prove that the wild pitch to Vidro was no fluke by uncorking another one that sent Johnson to second. Cabrera walked on four pitches, bringing Rivera up again with the bases loaded.

We'll pause at this juncture to give a brief history of players who have hit two home runs in one inning. The first to do it was Charley Jones of the Boston Red Stockings in 1880. Prior to this game, the feat had been achieved only 27 times in the National League and 18 times in the American League. Oddly enough, the Expos had already done it four times even though they had been around only since 1969, while the Mets, Padres, and White Sox hadn't.

It is unlikely any of these facts were on Rivera's mind when he strode to the plate and sent the fourth pitch of the at-bat over the wall for a grand slam; he not only made history, but he gave the Expos a seemingly insurmountable 10-1 lead.

For whatever reason, Munoz was still on the mound when Carroll came to the plate in the bottom of the third after Wilkerson singled. He tripled to center, his second extra-base hit of the game, driving in the Expos' 11th run. That was the extent of the damage and Munoz's night mercifully came to an end.

Many's the game where one team took a huge lead early only to fritter it away. Since the White Sox were proficient at both scoring runs (865, third in the American League in 2004) and home runs (242, tied for first in the AL in 2004 with the New York Yankees), it's no surprise that they didn't let an 11-1 deficit get to them. First baseman Paul Konerko led off the top of the fourth with a solo shot. Rowand followed that up with a double, and scored on a single by catcher Sandy Alomar. After Frank Thomas flied out pinch-hitting for the shell-shocked Munoz, leadoff hitter Timo Perez singled, and with runners on first and third, Uribe smacked a three-run shot to narrow the score to 11-6 Expos.

Cliff Politte came on in relief of Munoz and found out that *Nos Amours* really did have their hitting shoes on that night. He had a relatively easy fourth, giving up only a solo home run to first baseman Nick Johnson. The Expos then tacked on two more runs in the fifth. Wilkerson doubled, moved to third on a groundout by Carroll, and scored on a single by Vidro. Everett drove Vidro home with a double to right-center, giving the Expos a 14-6 lead.

Sun-Woo Kim had a scoreless fifth in relief of Armas, but his goose-egg streak ended at one. In the top of the sixth, singles by Alomar and Willie Harris (pinch-hitting for Politte) and a walk to Perez loaded the bases. Uribe then cleared the bases with a double to left. Expos manager Frank Robinson had seen enough and brought Rocky Biddle in to replace Kim. Biddle got the next three batters out to end the inning with the score now 14-9 Expos.

The Expos got one run back when the White Sox brought in reliever Michael Jackson to contribute to this thriller. Schneider singled with one out and was sacrificed to second by Biddle. Jackson walked Wilkerson intentionally, hit Carroll with a pitch to load the bases, then quite unintentionally gave Vidro a free pass and an RBI. After six, it was 15-9 Expos.

To the White Sox' credit, they didn't give up. In the top of the seventh, Biddle copied Jackson's style by loading the bases with one out. He hit Crede with a pitch, then walked Alomar. Harris singled to load the bases, and Biddle gave up a run-scoring single to Perez. Robinson, tired after all those walks to the mound, brought in Fikac. Uribe greeted him with a run-scoring single, and pinch-hitter Ross Gload drove home another two, also with a single. The Expos were still up, 15-13.

Something unusual happened in the bottom of the seventh. The Expos went down 1-2-3, thanks to the fourth White Sox pitcher of the game, Neal Cotts. It was the only inning in which they didn't score, and that gave the White Sox a fighting chance.

With all the runs, hits, and personnel changes, scorecards were starting to look like convoluted physics formulae. Chicago added to the mess in the top of the eighth. Rowand doubled and moved to third on a single by Kelly Dransfeldt (who had replaced Crede at third in the seventh), and scored when Alomar hit into a fielder's choice.

Now it was 15-14, but the Expos were determined not to let this one get away from them. Cotts did not duplicate his easy seventh. He gave up a single to Schneider and then a two-run homer to Terrmel Sledge, who came on as part of a double-switch in the top of the inning. Reliever Chad Cordero had a 1-2-3 ninth to end the game. After 31 runs, 35 players, and 33 hits, it was over. Final score: Expos 17, White Sox 14.

SOURCES

In addition to the sources listed in the notes, the author consulted:

Baseball-reference.com.

MLB.com.

Chicago Tribune.

CONTRIBUTORS

A lifelong Blue Jays fan who was born and raised in Toronto, **THOMAS AYERS** has earned degrees from the University of Toronto, the London School of Economics and Queen's University. Currently practicing labour and employment law, he has contributed several other biographies to the SABR Baseball Biography Project. He recently attended Game 5 of the 2015 ALDS between the Texas Rangers and Toronto Blue Jays, which was easily the most memorable game he's ever seen.

FREDERICK C. (RICK) BUSH, his wife Michelle, and their three sons Michael, Andrew, and Daniel live in northwest Houston. He has taught both English and German and is currently an English professor at Wharton County Junior College in Sugar Land. Though he is an avid fan of the hometown Astros, his youth has left him with an abiding affinity for the Texas Rangers and Pittsburgh Pirates as well. He has contributed articles to SABR's BioProject and Games Project sites and has written contributions for upcoming SABR books about the 1986 Boston Red Sox, 1979 Pittsburgh Pirates, 1972 Texas Rangers, Milwaukee's County Stadium, and baseball's winter meetings. Currently he is serving as an associate editor, photo editor, and contributing writer for a SABR book about the Houston Astrodome.

ALAN COHEN is a retired insurance underwriter who has been a member of SABR since 2011. He has written more than 25 biographies for SABR's BioProject, and has contributed to several SABR books. His first game story about Baseball's Longest Day—May 31, 1964 has been followed by several other game stories. His ongoing research into the Hearst Sandlot Classic (1946-1965), an annual youth All-Star game which launched the careers of 88 major-league players, first appeared in the Fall, 2013 edition of the *Baseball Research Journal*, and has been followed with a poster presentation at the SABR Convention in Chicago. He serves as the datacaster (stringer) for the New Britain Rock Cats of the Class-AA Eastern League. A native of Long Island, he now resides in West Hartford, Connecticut with his wife Frances, two cats and two dogs.

RORY COSTELLO has chronicled Expos history through the biographies of great figures such as Gary Carter and John McHale, as well as role players such as John Boccabella. He also wrote histories of Jarry Park (alas, he never saw a game there) and Olympic Stadium (which he visited many times with friends starting in the mid-1980s). The story of "The Big O" won a McFarland-SABR Baseball Research Award in 2014. Rory lives in Brooklyn, New York with his wife Noriko and son Kai.

DAVID DENOMME is an in-house lawyer working in Toronto and living in Mississauga, Ontario and has been a SABR member since 2008. He is a published author on legal issues but never before on baseball. He is enjoying the resurgence of baseball in Toronto, but remembers fondly his membership in the Bank of Montreal Young Expos Club in 1969, obtained by pestering his parents to open that first bank account.

GREG ERION and his wife Barbara live in South San Francisco. Retired from the transportation industry, he teaches history part time at the local community college. He is on the GamesProject Committee and is currently working on a book about the 1959 season.

DANNY GALLAGHER is a freelance writer and author, who has written six baseball books over the years, including four on the Expos, one of which appeared in French. He lives in Pickering, Ontario with his wife Sherry.

TOM HEINLEIN, a marketing manager for an environmental engineering firm in Boston, has also been a writer and editor for a range of business, engineering, and sports publications. For SABR, Tom serves as an editor for the Baseball Biography Project and for individual game articles, and he was associate editor of *Drama and Pride in the Gateway City: The 1964 St. Louis Cardinals* and a contributing writer to *Pitching to the Pennant: The 1954 Cleveland Indians*. He avidly follows the Montreal Baseball Project and hopes for a return of the Expos to the MLB.

SABR member **MICHAEL HUBER** is Dean of Academic Life and Professor of Mathematics at Muhlenberg College in Allentown, Pennsylvania, where he teaches an undergraduate course titled "Reasoning With Sabermetrics." He has published his sabermetrics research in several books and journals, including *The Baseball Research Journal, Chance, Base Ball, Annals of Applied Statistics,* and *The Journal of Statistics Education,* and he frequently contributes to SABR's Baseball Games Project.

NORM KING lives in Ottawa, Ontario, and has been a SABR member since 2010. He has contributed to a number of SABR books, including, *"That's Joy in Braveland." The 1957 Milwaukee Braves* (2014), *Winning on the North Side. The 1929 Chicago Cubs* (2015), and *A Pennant for the Twins Cities: The 1965 Minnesota Twins* (2015). He thought he was crazy to miss his beloved Expos after all these years until he met people from Brooklyn.

LEN LEVIN is a retired newspaper editor who has a part-time gig editing the decisions of the Rhode Island Supreme Court. He has been a copyeditor for most of SABR's recent publications.

A reporter for more than 40 years, **ROD MICKLEBURGH** has written about sports as often as his editors have allowed, including a piece on the last home game of the Montreal Expos (sniff). Final 23 years in the business were spent at the Globe and Mail, a time which included four years as the paper's China correspondent and co-winning the Michener Award for public service journalism. Now retired, concentrating on blogging and writing a book, he has been a die-hard fan of the Montreal Expos since watching their first game in 1969 on a small black and white television set at a friend's "hippie commune", the only baseball fan in the house.

BILL NOWLIN has been SABR's vice president since 2004. His favorite team, the Boston Red Sox, first played the Expos in Montreal in a June 1970 exhibition game but the first time Bill saw the Sox play at *Stade Olympique* was in September 1997, two months before Pedro Martinez was traded to the Red Sox.

He's since seen the Red Sox play in the Dominican Republic and Japan, and written or edited somewhere around 50 books.

BILL SCHNEIDER has been a baseball fan since being given his first pack of baseball cards in 1974, and a SABR member for several years. This is his first contribution to a SABR publication.

MARK SIMON is a digital publishing specialist for ESPN Stats & Information, for whom he has worked since 2002. He edits a blog, co-runs the @espnstatsinfo Twitter feed and writes for ESPN. com. He has previously been published in multiple editions of the *Baseball Research Journal,* and the SABR bioproject books for the 1964 Cardinals, 1969 Mets and 1986 Mets/Red Sox. You can follow him on Twitter at @msimonespn

MARK S. STERNMAN serves as Director of Marketing and Communications for MassDevelopment, the quasi-governmental economic-development authority of Massachusetts. A SABR member since 1990, he wrote about Chicago's three 1915 teams for the 2015 edition of *The National Pastime* and profiled former Montrealer Mike Stenhouse for the SABR book on the 1986 Mets and Red Sox. A fan of the Expos since 1978, Sternman continues to keep thoughts of the team alive by keeping an F.P. Santangelo baseball card in his office and an Expos cap on his head whenever he attends games or SABR conventions.

ADAM J. ULREY used to be the featured writer for "Inside Ducks Sports," and spent 10 years on the radio doing a sportstalk show in the beautiful Willamette Valley. He enjoys building his own Fly rods and being retired at the age of 54. He spends most of his free time in the outdoors doing everything from hiking to fishing in his own stream. But his favorite pastime is spending time with his wife Jhody and son Camran. He also has two beautiful dogs named Suzie and Bentley.

BOB WEBSTER grew up in Northwest Indiana and has been a Cubs fan since 1963. He has earned degrees from Linfield College and Marylhurst University. Now living in Portland, Oregon and recently retired, Bob is currently working on putting together the History of the Northwest League and researching the West Coast League along with the many other collegiate leagues. He is a member of the Northwest Chapter of SABR, on the Board of Executives of the Old-Timers Baseball Association of Portland, and a manager in the Great American Fantasy League.

A lifelong Pirates fan, **GREGORY H. WOLF** was born in Pittsburgh, but now resides in the Chicagoland area with his wife, Margaret, and daughter, Gabriela. A Professor of German Studies and holder of the Dennis and Jean Bauman Endowed Chair in the Humanities at North Central College in Naperville, Illinois, he edited the SABR books *"Thar's Joy in Braveland." The 1957 Milwaukee Braves* (2014), *Winning on the North Side. The 1929 Chicago Cubs* (2015), and *A Pennant for the Twins Cities: The 1965 Minnesota Twins* (2015). He is currently working on a project about the Houston Astrodome and co-editing a book with Bill Nowlin on the 1979 Pittsburgh Pirates.

BRIAN P. WOOD (Woodie) is a long time San Francisco Giants fan. He was born in Beeville, Texas, the son of a Navy pilot and resides in Pacific Grove, California with his wife Terrise and three sons, Daniel, Jack, and Nathan and dog Bochy. A retired U.S. Navy Commander and F-14 Naval Flight Officer, Woodie is a Research Associate on the faculty at the Naval Postgraduate School in Monterey, California specializing in Field Experimentation of new technologies before they are sent to military forces. He is active in youth sports, coaching 75 teams in baseball, soccer, and basketball. He has been a member of SABR since 1992

and has made a contribution to an upcoming book on the greatest games played at Milwaukee's County Stadium, assisted in editing an upcoming book on Ken Boyer, proofread part of the first issue of SABR's *The National Pastime* during its digitization process, and fact checked chapters for *100 — The 100 Year Journey of a Baseball Journeyman*, a book about the oldest living former major league baseball player Mike Sandlock.

BILL YOUNG, who lives in Hudson Quebec, is a retired academic administrator in the Quebec Community College system. For the past 15 years, he has directed his attention to baseball history, especially the baseball history of Quebec. In addition to numerous articles on the topic he has also co-authored (with colleague Danny Gallagher) two top-selling books on the Montreal Expos. These are: *Remembering the Montreal Expos* (2005) and *Ecstasy To Agony: The 1994 Montreal Expos — How The Best Team In Baseball Ended Up In Washington Ten Years Later.* (2013)

JACK ZERBY, a retired attorney and trusts/estates administrator, learned a lot about the glory days of the Expos while assisting with this book. He wishes Montreal all the best in its efforts to bring back major league baseball. Jack writes, edits, and does fact checks for the SABR Biography Project and the new Games Project. He lives in Brevard, North Carolina, with his wife Diana, a professional violinist. Jack joined SABR in 1994 and, before retirement, co-founded the Seymour-Mills Chapter in southwest Florida.

THE SABR DIGITAL LIBRARY

The Society for American Baseball Research, the top baseball research organization in the world, disseminates some of the best in baseball history, analysis, and biography through our publishing programs. The SABR Digital Library contains a mix of books old and new, and focuses on a tandem program of paperback and ebook publication, making these materials widely available for both on digital devices and as traditional printed books.

GREATEST GAMES BOOKS

BRAVES FIELD:
MEMORABLE MOMENTS AT BOSTON'S LOST DIAMOND
From its opening on August 18, 1915, to the sudden departure of the Boston Braves to Milwaukee before the 1953 baseball season, Braves Field was home to Boston's National League baseball club and also hosted many other events: from NFL football to championship boxing. The most memorable moments to occur in Braves Field history are portrayed here.
Edited by Bill Nowlin and Bob Brady
$19.95 paperback (ISBN 978-1-933599-93-9)
$9.99 ebook (ISBN 978-1-933599-92-2)
8.5"X11", 282 pages, 182 photos

INVENTING BASEBALL: THE 100 GREATEST GAMES OF THE NINETEENTH CENTURY
SABR's Nineteenth Century Committee brings to life the greatest games from the game's early years. From the "prisoner of war" game that took place among captive Union soldiers during the Civil War (immortalized in a famous lithograph), to the first intercollegiate game (Amherst versus Williams), to the first professional no-hitter, the games in this volume span 1833–1900 and detail the athletic exploits of such players as Cap Anson, Moses "Fleetwood" Walker, Charlie Comiskey, and Mike "King" Kelly.
Edited by Bill Felber
$19.95 paperback (ISBN 978-1-933599-42-7)
$9.99 ebook (ISBN 978-1-933599-43-4)
8"x10", 302 pages, 200 photos

BIOPROJECT BOOKS

WHO'S ON FIRST:
REPLACEMENT PLAYERS IN WORLD WAR II
During World War II, 533 players made the major league debuts. More than 60% of the players in the 1941 Opening Day lineups departed for the service and were replaced by first-times and oldsters. Hod Lisenbee was 46. POW Bert Shepard had an artificial leg, and Pete Gray had only one arm. The 1944 St. Louis Browns had 13 players classified 4-F. These are their stories.
Edited by Marc Z Aaron and Bill Nowlin
$19.95 paperback (ISBN 978-1-933599-91-5)
$9.99 ebook (ISBN 978-1-933599-90-8)
8.5"X11", 422 pages, 67 photos

VAN LINGLE MUNGO:
THE MAN, THE SONG, THE PLAYERS
Although the Red Sox spent most of the 1950s far out of contention, the team was filled with fascinating players who captured the heart of their fans. In *Red Sox Baseball*, members of SABR present 46 biographies on players such as Ted Williams and Pumpsie Green as well as season-by-season recaps.
Edited by Bill Nowlin
$19.95 paperback (ISBN 978-1-933599-76-2)
$9.99 ebook (ISBN 978-1-933599-77-9)
8.5"X11", 278 pages, 46 photos

ORIGINAL SABR RESEARCH

CALLING THE GAME:
BASEBALL BROADCASTING FROM 1920 TO THE PRESENT
An exhaustive, meticulously researched history of bringing the national pastime out of the ballparks and into living rooms via the airwaves. Every play-by-play announcer, color commentator, and ex-ballplayer, every broadcast deal, radio station, and TV network. Plus a foreword by "Voice of the Chicago Cubs" Pat Hughes, and an afterword by Jacques Doucet, the "Voice of the Montreal Expos" 1972-2004.
by Stuart Shea
$24.95 paperback (ISBN 978-1-933599-40-3)
$9.99 ebook (ISBN 978-1-933599-41-0)
7"X10", 712 pages, 40 photos

BASEBALL IN THE SPACE AGE:
HOUSTON SINCE 1961
Here we have a special issue of *The National Pastime* centered almost entirely on the Houston Astros (né Colt .45s) and their two influential and iconic homes, short-lived Colt Stadium and the Astrodome. If you weren't able to attend the SABR convention in Houston, please enjoy this virtual trip tour of baseball in "Space City" through 18 articles.
Edited by Cecilia M. Tan
$14.95 paperback (ISBN 978-1-933599-65-6)
$9.99 ebook (ISBN 978-1-933599-66-3)
8.5"x11", 96 pages, 49 photos

NORTH SIDE, SOUTH SIDE, ALL AROUND THE TOWN: BASEBALL IN CHICAGO
The National Pastime provides in-depth articles focused on the geographic region where the national SABR convention is taking place annually. The SABR 45 convention took place in Chicago, and here are 45 articles on baseball in and around the bat-and-ball crazed Windy City: 25 that appeared in the souvenir book of the convention plus another 20 articles available in ebook only.
Edited by Stuart Shea
$14.95 paperback (ISBN 978-1-933599-87-8)
$9.99 ebook (ISBN 978-1-933599-86-1)
8.5"X11", 282 pages, 47 photos

THE EMERALD GUIDE TO BASEBALL: 2015
The Emerald Guide to Baseball fills the gap in the historical record created by the demise of *The Sporting News Baseball Guide*. First published in 1942, *The Sporting News* Guide was truly the annual book of record for our National Pastime. The 2015 edition of the *Emerald Guide* runs more than 600 pages and covers the 2014 season; it also includes a 2015 directory of every franchise, rosters, minor league affiliates, and career leaders for all teams.
Edited by Gary Gillette and Pete Palmer
$24.95 paperback (ISBN 978-0-9817929-8-9)
8.5"X11", 610 pages

SABR Members can purchase each book at a significant discount (often 50% off) and receive the ebook edtions free as a member benefit. Each book is available in a trade paperback edition as well as ebooks suitable for reading on a home computer or Nook, Kindle, or iPad/tablet.
To learn more about becoming a member of SABR, visit the website: sabr.org/join

SABR BioProject Books

In 2002, the Society for American Baseball Research launched an effort to write and publish biographies of every player, manager, and individual who has made a contribution to baseball. Over the past decade, the BioProject Committee has produced over 3,400 biographical articles. Many have been part of efforts to create theme- or team-oriented books, spearheaded by chapters or other committees of SABR.

A PENNANT FOR THE TWIN CITIES:
THE 1965 MINNESOTA TWINS
This volume celebrates the 1965 Minnesota Twins, who captured the American League pennant in just their fifth season in the Twin Cities. Led by an All-Star cast, from Harmon Killebrew, Tony Oliva, Zoilo Versalles, and Mudcat Grant to Bob Allison, Jim Kaat, Earl Battey, and Jim Perry, the Twins won 102 games, but bowed to the Los Angeles Dodgers and Sandy Koufax in Game Seven
Edited by Gregory H. Wolf
$19.95 paperback (ISBN 978-1-943816-09-5)
$9.99 ebook (ISBN 978-1-943816-08-8)
8.5"X11", 405 pages, over 80 photos

MUSTACHES AND MAYHEM: CHARLIE O'S THREE TIME CHAMPIONS:
THE OAKLAND ATHLETICS: 1972-74
The Oakland Athletics captured major league baseball's crown each year from 1972 through 1974. Led by future Hall of Famers Reggie Jackson, Catfish Hunter and Rollie Fingers, the Athletics were a largely homegrown group who came of age together. Biographies of every player, coach, manager, and broadcaster (and mascot) from 1972 through 1974 are included, along with season recaps.
Edited by Chip Greene
$29.95 paperback (ISBN 978-1-943816-07-1)
$9.99 ebook (ISBN 978-1-943816-06-4)
8.5"X11", 600 pages, almost 100 photos

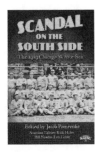

SCANDAL ON THE SOUTH SIDE:
THE 1919 CHICAGO WHITE SOX
The Black Sox Scandal isn't the only story worth telling about the 1919 Chicago White Sox. The team roster included three future Hall of Famers, a 20-year-old spitballer who would win 300 games in the minors, and even a batboy who later became a celebrity with the "Murderers' Row" New York Yankees. All of their stories are included in Scandal on the South Side with a timeline of the 1919 season.
Edited by Jacob Pomrenke
$19.95 paperback (ISBN 978-1-933599-95-3)
$9.99 ebook (ISBN 978-1-933599-94-6)
8.5"x11", 324 pages, 55 historic photos

WINNING ON THE NORTH SIDE
THE 1929 CHICAGO CUBS
Celebrate the 1929 Chicago Cubs, one of the most exciting teams in baseball history. Future Hall of Famers Hack Wilson, '29 NL MVP Rogers Hornsby, and Kiki Cuyler, along with Riggs Stephenson formed one of the most potent quartets in baseball history. The magical season came to an ignominious end in the World Series and helped craft the future "lovable loser" image of the team.
Edited by Gregory H. Wolf
$19.95 paperback (ISBN 978-1-933599-89-2)
$9.99 ebook (ISBN 978-1-933599-88-5)
8.5"x11", 314 pages, 59 photos

DETROIT THE UNCONQUERABLE:
THE 1935 WORLD CHAMPION TIGERS
Biographies of every player, coach, and broadcaster involved with the 1935 World Champion Detroit Tigers baseball team, written by members of the Society for American Baseball Research. Also includes a season in review and other articles about the 1935 team. Hank Greenberg, Mickey Cochrane, Charlie Gehringer, Schoolboy Rowe, and more.
Edited by Scott Ferkovich
$19.95 paperback (ISBN 9978-1-933599-78-6)
$9.99 ebook (ISBN 978-1-933599-79-3)
8.5"X11", 230 pages, 52 photos

THE 1934 ST. LOUIS CARDINALS:
THE WORLD CHAMPION GAS HOUSE GANG
The 1934 St. Louis Cardinals were one of the most colorful crews ever to play the National Pastime. Some of were aging stars, past their prime, and others were youngsters, on their way up, but together they comprised a championship ball club. Pepper Martin, Dizzy and Paul Dean, Joe Medwick, Frankie Frisch and more are all included here.
Edited by Charles F. Faber
$19.95 paperback (ISBN 978-1-933599-73-1)
$9.99 ebook (ISBN 978-1-933599-74-8)
8.5"X11", 282 pages, 47 photos

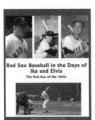

RED SOX BASEBALL IN THE DAYS OF IKE AND ELVIS: THE RED SOX OF THE 1950s
Although the Red Sox spent most of the 1950s far out of contention, the team was filled with fascinating players who captured the heart of their fans. In *Red Sox Baseball*, members of SABR present 46 biographies on players such as Ted Williams and Pumpsie Green as well as season-by-season recaps.
Edited by Mark Armour and Bill Nowlin
$19.95 paperback (ISBN 978-1-933599-24-3)
$9.99 ebook (ISBN 978-1-933599-34-2)
8.5"X11", 372 pages, over 100 photos

THE MIRACLE BRAVES OF 1914
BOSTON'S ORIGINAL WORST-TO-FIRST CHAMPIONS
Long before the Red Sox "Impossible Dream" season, Boston's now nearly forgotten "other" team, the 1914 Boston Braves, performed a baseball "miracle" that resounds to this very day. The "Miracle Braves" were Boston's first "worst-to-first" winners of the World Series. Includes biographies of every player, coach, and owner, a season recap, and other great stories from the 1914 season.
Edited by Bill Nowlin
$19.95 paperback (ISBN 978-1-933599-69-4)
$9.99 ebook (ISBN 978-1-933599-70-0)
8.5"X11", 392 pages, over 100 photos

SABR Members can purchase each book at a significant discount (often 50% off) and receive the ebook edtions free as a member benefit. Each book is available in a trade paperback edition as well as ebooks suitable for reading on a home computer or Nook, Kindle, or iPad/tablet.

To learn more about becoming a member of SABR, visit the website: sabr.org/join

Society for American Baseball Research

Cronkite School at ASU
555 N. Central Ave. #416, Phoenix, AZ 85004
602.496.1460 (phone)
SABR.org

Become a SABR member today!

If you're interested in baseball — writing about it, reading about it, talking about it — there's a place for you in the Society for American Baseball Research. Our members include everyone from academics to professional sportswriters to amateur historians and statisticians to students and casual fans who enjoy reading about baseball and occasionally gathering with other members to talk baseball. What unites all SABR members is an interest in the game and joy in learning more about it.

SABR membership is open to any baseball fan; we offer 1-year and 3-year memberships. Here's a list of some of the key benefits you'll receive as a SABR member:

- Receive two editions (spring and fall) of the *Baseball Research Journal*, our flagship publication
- Receive expanded e-book edition of *The National Pastime*, our annual convention journal
- 8-10 new e-books published by the SABR Digital Library, all FREE to members
- "This Week in SABR" e-newsletter, sent to members every Friday
- Join dozens of research committees, from Statistical Analysis to Women in Baseball.
- Join one of 70 regional chapters in the U.S., Canada, Latin America, and abroad
- Participate in online discussion groups
- Ask and answer baseball research questions on the SABR-L e-mail listserv
- Complete archives of *The Sporting News* dating back to 1886 and other research resources
- Promote your research in "This Week in SABR"
- Diamond Dollars Case Competition
- Yoseloff Scholarships

- Discounts on SABR national conferences, including the SABR National Convention, the SABR Analytics Conference, Jerry Malloy Negro League Conference, Frederick Ivor-Campbell 19th Century Conference
- Publish your research in peer-reviewed SABR journals
- Collaborate with SABR researchers and experts
- Contribute to Baseball Biography Project or the SABR Games Project
- List your new book in the SABR Bookshelf
- Lead a SABR research committee or chapter
- Networking opportunities at SABR Analytics Conference
- Meet baseball authors and historians at SABR events and chapter meetings
- 50% discounts on paperback versions of SABR e-books
- 20% discount on MLB.TV and MiLB.TV subscriptions
- Discounts with other partners in the baseball community
- SABR research awards

We hope you'll join the most passionate international community of baseball fans at SABR! Check us out online at SABR.org/join.

SABR MEMBERSHIP FORM

	Annual	3-year	Senior	3-yr Sr.	Under 30
U.S.:	❏ $65	❏ $175	❏ $45	❏ $129	❏ $45
Canada/Mexico:	❏ $75	❏ $205	❏ $55	❏ $159	❏ $55
Overseas:	❏ $84	❏ $232	❏ $64	❏ $186	❏ $55

Add a Family Member: $15 each family member at same address (list names on back)
Senior: 65 or older before 12/31 of the current year
All dues amounts in U.S. dollars or equivalent

Participate in Our Donor Program!

Support the preservation of baseball research. Designate your gift toward:
❏General Fund ❏Endowment Fund ❏Research Resources ❏_____
❏ I want to maximize the impact of my gift; do not send any donor premiums
❏ I would like this gift to remain anonymous.

Note: Any donation not designated will be placed in the General Fund.
SABR is a 501 (c) (3) not-for-profit organization & donations are tax-deductible to the extent allowed by law.

Name _____

E-mail* _____

Address _____

City _____ ST_____ ZIP_____

Phone _____ Birthday _____

* Your e-mail address on file ensures you will receive the most recent SABR news.

Dues $_____

Donation $_____

Amount Enclosed $_____

Do you work for a matching grant corporation? Call (602) 496-1460 for details.

If you wish to pay by credit card, please contact the SABR office at (602) 496-1460 or visit the SABR Store online at SABR.org/join. We accept Visa, Mastercard & Discover.

Do you wish to receive the *Baseball Research Journal* electronically?: ❏ Yes ❏ No
Our e-books are available in PDF, Kindle, or EPUB (iBooks, iPad, Nook) formats.

Mail to: SABR, Cronkite School at ASU, 555 N. Central Ave. #416, Phoenix, AZ 85004

Made in the USA
San Bernardino, CA
20 November 2019